Common Commission
By
Jesus is Lord

את־מי נועץ ויבינהו וילמדהו משפט
וילמדהו דעת ודרך תבונות יודיענו
(ישעיה מ: י"ד)

# דרך תבונות

# The Ways of Reason

# ספר דרך תבונות

כולל בו כל דרכי ההתבוננות
וההשכלה להבין בנקל דרכי התלמוד
ויסודות הפלפול בדרך קצרה חברו
וגם סדרו מעלת החכם הנעלה

## כמוהר"ר משה חיים לוצאטו זצ"ל

עם תרגום אנגלי ולוחות הסבר על ידי
הרב דוד סקטון והרב חיים צ'לקובסקי

הוצאת ישיבת התפוצות
_____
הוצאת ספרים פלדהיים

עיה"ק ירושלים תובב"א
שנת תשמ"ט

# The Ways of Reason

A guide to the Talmud and the foundations of dialectics
explaining all the principles of reason and logic
in a simple and concise way, conceived and written by
the exhalted and renowned

## Rabbenu Moshe Chaim Luzzatto zt'l

with English translation and explanatory charts prepared by
Rabbi David Sackton and Rabbi Chaim Tscholkowsky

Diaspora Yeshiva
Feldheim Publishers
Jerusalem, Israel

Book & Cover Design by
Esther Tscholkowsky

ISBN 0-87306-495-X

Published and Distributed by

PHILIPP FELDHEIM Inc.
200 Airport Executive Park
Spring Valley, NY 10977

FELDHEIM PUBLISHERS Ltd.
POB 6525
Jerusalem, Israel

Typeset by Ben-Ishai
Printed in Israel

This book is dedicated to:

Mr. & Mrs. Larry and Marsha Roth
and their children,
David, Hannah and Daniel

# Table of Contents

|  | Letters of Approbation | VIII |
|---|---|---|
|  | Preface by Rabbi Mordecai Goldstein, Shlita | XIII |
|  | Translators' Foreword | XVII |
|  | Author's Introduction | 2 |
| Chapter 1: | The Talmudic Method | 10 |
| Chapter 2: | Elements of Debate | 14 |
| Chapter 3: | Types of Statements | 22 |
| Chapter 4: | Juxtaposition of Statements | 48 |
| Chapter 5: | Inferences | 66 |
| Chapter 6: | Truth and Falsity of Statements | 76 |
| Chapter 7: | Creating Syllogisms | 92 |
| Chapter 8: | Acceptance and Rejection of Ideas | 112 |
| Chapter 9: | Elements of Debate in Detail | 162 |
| Chapter 10: | Order of Study | 190 |
| Chapter 11: | Logical Terminology | 222 |
|  | Appendix: | 248 |
|  | Chapter Outlines | 249 |
|  | General Index | 255 |
|  | Term Index | 259 |
|  | Source Index | 261 |

הרב שמחה זיסל ברוידא ראש ישיבת חברון עיה"ק ירושלים

**Rabbi S. Z. BROIDE** DEAN OF HEBRON YESHIVA JERUSALEM ISRAEL
P. O. B. 5162 Tel. 65933

ב"ה ירושלים _____ Jerusalem ו' אלול תשמ"ח

הנני להכיר ולהוקיר בזה את הישיבה המופלאה "ישיבת
התפוצות תורת ישראל" והמוסדות הנפלאים המסונפים לה. זכיתי
להכיר מקרוב מקום מיוחד זה ששם לו למטרה לקרב לאור התורה
והמצוה את נדחי ישראל. אחים יקרים שהיו רחוקים מעמם ותורתם
כרחוק מזרח ממערב, וישיבת התפוצות והעומדים בראשה מצאו
את הדרכים איך לחתור חתירה ולהגיע לנקודת היהודית החבויה
באחים אלו. אישית נוכחתי לראות איך גידלו פירות יקרים
ואחר כמה שנים של לימוד בהדרכת הרמיי"ם המסורים ובפרט ראש
הישיבה הדגול גדלו לאברכים מופלגים בתורה וזריזים וחרדים
על שמירת התורה והמצוות, ובפרט עלי לציין את האי גברא
יקירא מעלי וצנוע הנושא על שכמו את כל המעמסה האדירה
הלזו, הה"ה ידידי וחביבי הרה"ג המצויין רבי מרדכי גולדשטיין
שליט"א שבמסירות נפש ממש נושא בעול הגשמי והרוחני ונוסף
על הישיבה והכולל הקים מבוגרי הישיבה קהילה לתפארת עם
ת"ת לתשב"יר ובית-ספר לבנות מילדי הקהילה המנוהל בהפלא
על טהרת הקודש. ולפום צערא אגרא זכה וזוכה לראות ברכה
רבה בעמלו אשרי לו ואשרי חלקו.

ועתה הביאו לפני שני אברכים מצויינים מבוגרי הישיבה
הרב ר' דוד סקטון והרב ר' חיים צילקובסקי המשמשים עתה
בקודש כמגידי שיעור בישיבה ספר "דרך תבונות" לקדוש ה'
הרמח"ל ז"ל שערכו עם תרגום לאנגלית. נסיונם העשיר הראה
שעי"י ספר זה מצליחים הם לקרב את דעת הבאים מרחוק להסתופף
בחצרות ה' לדרכי לימוד הגמרא והבנתה. ואין צורך להסכים
על נחיצות עבודה זו, כי הרי נוכחתי בעצמי לראות בהצלחתם
המרשימה המעידה כי עי"י דרכים מיוחדות אלו מצליחים הם
להעמיד ת"ח מובהקים. והנסיון וההצלחה מעידים כי יש בזה
תועלת מרובה ושכר גדול.

לכן לפעלא טבא אמינא ואברכם כי יברך ה' פעלם ומעשה
ידיהם יכונן. ואוסיף בזה קריאה של חיבה לאחב"יי עם נדיבי
ה' כי יעמדו לימין הישיבה הקדושה הזו ובזה ישתתפו ויטלו
שכר בפעולותיה הברוכות.

הכו"ח לכבוד התורה אוהביה ומאהיביה

(translation)

## Rabbi S. Z. Broide, Dean of Hebron Yeshiva, Jerusalem, Israel

6 Elul 5748

I write this letter to recognize and express my esteem for an outstanding yeshiva, the Diaspora Yeshiva Toras Yisrael, and for the fine institutions which are under its auspices. I have been fortunate to know this special place of learning first-hand. The purpose which the Yeshiva has set for itself is to bring the dispersed of Israel, our dear brothers who have been as distant from their people and the Torah as east from west, close to the light of Torah and mitzvos. The Diaspora Yeshiva and those who guide it have found the ways to open a channel and penetrate that kernel of Yiddishkeit hidden within these students.

I have personally been present to witness how they have nurtured such precious fruits. After many years of study under the direction of dedicated "Ramim", and in particular the pre-eminent Rosh Ha-Yeshiva, they have produced students who are outstanding in Torah, zealous and exacting in the fulfillment of Torah and mitzvos. In particular, I wish to express my esteem for that precious, lofty and modest individual who carries on his shoulders all this enormous burden, my dear colleague and friend, Harav Hagaon, the distinguished Rabbi Mordecai Goldstein, Shlita, who bears with complete self-sacrifice this physical and spiritual yoke. In addition to the Yeshiva and the Kollel, he has established from the graduates of the Yeshiva an exemplary community with a Talmud Torah and a girls' elementary school for the children of the community, which are conducted entirely in pure holiness. According to the pain, so is the reward; he has merited and may he merit to see a great blessing in his toils; happy is he and happy is his lot!

IX

At this time, two distinguished gentlemen who are graduates of the Yeshiva, Harav David Sackton and Harav Chaim Tscholkowsky, have brought to me the sefer **Derech Tvunos** by the exalted Rabbi Moshe Chaim Luzzatto of blessed memory, which they have prepared to print together with an English translation. The authors are currently associated with the Yeshiva, where they give shiurim in Gemorah. Their rich experience has shown that it is possible to succeed by means of this book in bringing back those who are far away from the Torah to stand at the threshold of God's house and enter into the ways of studying and understanding the Gemorah. There is no need to give any approbation to the urgent need for their work, since I have been present myself to see that their impressive success bears witness to the fact that through this particular method of study they are able to raise up outstanding talmidei chachomim. Experience and proven success show us that there is in this book a great benefit and reward.

Therefore, I congratulate them and bless them; may Hashem bless their undertaking and may the work of their hands come to fruition. I may add to this my personal appeal to all our fellow Jews in caring generosity to stand at the right hand of this holy Yeshiva and in this way join with them and receive reward in this blessed work.

For the honor of Torah and those who love her and cause her to be loved,

Rabbi S. Z. Broide

ב"ה

**ישיבת התפוצות חורת ישראל**
DIASPORA YESHIVA TORAS YISRAEL
MOUNT ZION, P.O B. 6426, JERUSALEM, ISRAEL, CODE 91063 מיקוד
TEL. 02-716841 · TELEX: 26144 BXJM IL EXT. 7068

Rabbi Dr. Mordecai Goldstein
Dean · Rosh Yeshiva

25 Tamuz, 5748

    It is with great pleasure that I received the
completed manuscript of The Ways of Reason, Rabbi Moshe
Chaim Luzzatto's Derech T'vunos, in English translation.
I have read the work carefully and the translation is
exact and true to the original text. Countless hours of
work have been invested to produce a faithful and
authoritative expression of the author's intent. I am
sure that it will be a significant contribution to Torah
literature in English.

    The translators, Rabbi David Sackton and Rabbi Chaim
Tscholkowsky, are G-d fearing and have dedicated
themselves to the study of Torah and its dissemination.
Everyone should assist them in carrying out the important
task of bringing this work to the wider Jewish public.

                    For the honor of the Torah
                    and those who study it.

                    Rabbi Mordecai Goldstein,
                    Rosh HaYeshiva
                    Diaspora Yeshiva
                    Mount Zion, Jerusalem

**Rabbi CHAIM P. SCHEINBERG**

KIRYAT MATTERSDORF
PANIM MEIROT 2
JERUSALEM, ISRAEL

הרב חיים פנחס שיינברג
ראש ישיבת "תורה אור"
ומורה הוראה דקרית מטרסדורף
ירושלים טל.בנולנ5

BS'D

7 Menachem Av 5748

    Derech T'vunos is a classic guide to the study of
Talmud written by one of our great Sages, the Ramchal.
The nature of the work is defined by the author himself
as an analysis of Talmudic thought which will be a
great help to a student who has not reached proficiency
in Torah study as well as to the experienced student.
The translation is designed to present the Ramchal's
method in an organized fashion in order to facilitate
its study.

    The appearance of an English translation fulfills a
vital need in making this sefer accessible as an
educational tool for teachers and students alike.  The
translators are to be commended for undertaking this
exacting and laborious task and completing what will
surely be a great help to those who wish to embark upon
and pursue the study of Torah.  Although I do not give
Haskomos in any way,  I do give my blessing to this
project.  May Rabbi David Sackton and Rabbi Chaim
Tscholkowsky be blessed with the ability to continue in
their work to spread the teachings of our holy Torah.

*Chaim P. Scheinberg*

Rabbi Chaim P. Scheinberg

# Preface

## Rabbi Mordecai Goldstein, Shlita
Rosh HaYeshiva of the Diaspora Yeshiva

Of all our great Sages, Rabbi Akiva is most noted for his meteoric ascent from total ignorance of the Torah to the greatest heights of learning. What was the secret of his extraordinary accomplishment? The answer to this mystery is revealed by Rabbi Yehudah the Prince in Avos d'Rabbi Nossan (18:1).

Rabbi Yehudah the Prince said of Rabbi Akiva, "he is a storehouse bursting with knowledge". Rashi (Gittin 67a) describes this "storehouse" as analogous to "a large crate which is divided into compartmentalized boxes". The secret to Rabbi Akiva's success was his system of classifying and categorizing concepts and terms in a Torah thinking process with which he brought clarity to his vast knowledge.

Rabbi Yehudah expands his characterization of Rabbi Akiva with the following metaphor. "To what may Rabbi Akiva be compared? He is like a poor man who takes his basket out to the field. He finds some barley, reaps it and puts it in his basket; he finds some wheat, reaps it and puts it in his basket, and similarly with beans and lentils. When he returns to his house, he sorts them all according to kind. Such was the unique quality of Rabbi Akiva when he learned from his Rabbis. Having heard an explanation of the Written Law, followed by an explanation of Halachah, followed by one from the Midrash and another from Aggadah, he listened carefully, reviewed and absorbed all this knowledge until he gained complete mastery of it". Rashi explains the comparison to a poor man (Gittin 67a): Rabbi Akiva "learned everything in a jumbled manner and only then set himself the task of formulating and organizing what he had learned". Like a poor man seeking his sustenance, Rabbi Akiva gathered every morsel. In his tremendous desire for knowledge, he did not neglect any tidbit. A rich man whose task is to harvest barley does not turn aside from his appointed task to pick up a few peas or beans which he may happen to find in the field, nor does he have the task of sorting out each kind afterwards as a poor man must do. Thus, out of necessity, Rabbi Akiva came to profound insights into the learning process which enabled him to absorb vast Torah knowledge. By abstracting general rules and revealing the foundations of what he had learned, Rabbi Akiva found a process of dialectics and specialized terminology.

This innovative process was not only of great benefit to himself, but also enabled his students to learn everything which he handed down to them from his teachers, incorporating all the work which he had done himself.

The text in Avos d'Rabbi Nossan quoted above concludes, Rabbi Akiva "did not say, I shall first learn the Written Law alone, and only then the Midrash alone". Instead he learned everything together as it was taught to him. In the end, "when Rabbi Akiva had become a great scholar, he turned the whole Torah into rings upon rings linked together, comparable to handles with which large vessels may be held. He organized the Midrash, the Sifri, and the Sifra independently, and then taught his students each one separately. He did the same with Halachah and Aggadah, organizing and teaching each one separately." It is interesting that he "did not say, I shall first learn the Written Law alone, and only then the Midrash alone". And yet we see that his final goal was indeed just that – to teach his students the Midrash,

Sifri, Sifra and then the Halachah separately and independently. From this we see that the lack of systematic thinking is a common cause for a student's inability to grasp and absorb knowledge. And yet, Rabbi Akiva did not let the jumble of concepts and information which he received from his teachers become a factor which impeded his learning. On the contrary, he reviewed everything he learned until he became thoroughly familiar with it and "created" order and a clear "method" of Torah thinking out of disorder.

The significance of the classic **The Ways of Reason** by Rabbi Moshe Chaim Luzzatto, one of our greatest "later authorities", is that it provides the student with a Torah system of classification and categorization of conceptual ideas and terminology. These terms and methods are the "rings and handles" with which to acquire and handle Torah knowledge. **The Ways of Reason** gives us the tools which will allow anyone who studies this method to apply the formula of our Sages of blessed memory and follow in Rabbi Akiva's ways.

One of the unique ideas that is an innovation of the Diaspora Yeshiva is something I like to call "conscious learning", an awareness of the true nature of Torah learning. By recognizing the forms and structures which underlie the learning process, we have the tools for thinking and experiencing the Torah, which it is our privilege to learn. When the logical steps and abstractions of thinking are laid out in an open and honest way, there are endless insights and revelations which wait to be uncovered in every word of Torah, like messages sent to us by the Almighty Himself. Such a conscious awareness must, by definition, bring a dimension of excitement and vibrancy to our learning. For these insights are not part of a mystique guarded only for the privileged few. Everyone who devotes himself to the study of Torah must, by definition, produce his own novel insights. All

XV

# Translators' Foreword

The Creator of the universe revealed His will to us on Mount Sinai through the Torah. The Torah is expressed in words. Therefore, to understand His will, you must know how words work. There is a riddle here, for just as the Creator has no end, so His Torah has no end, and yet the infinite Torah is contained in a finite space. The Torah is expressed in a limited number of words, in the 304,840 letters of the Written Law and 2711 pages of the Oral Law. The answer to this riddle is that when you know how words work, the words come alive, and then the words of the Torah can be the medium through which you can understand the will of the Creator.

This is a book about how words work. It guarantees to every Jew his innate potential to receive the Torah from Mount Sinai. The Rambam writes in the **Laws of Talmud Torah** (Chap. 3, Halachah 1), "The Jewish people are crowned with three crowns: the crown of Torah, the crown of Priesthood, and the crown of Kingship. The crown of Priesthood belongs to Aharon and his children forever, and the crown of Kingship belongs to David and his children forever. But the crown of Torah remains unclaimed and available. Whoever so desires can come and claim it." The crown of Torah is not an exclusive inheritance; there are no barriers to its attainment. Anyone with the desire and aspiration can strive to be among the great Torah scholars of each generation.

In today's world, there is a proliferation of guides to Torah study and an increasing interest in Jewish education. However, only a Torah giant of the stature of Rabbi Moshe Chaim Luzzatto could write a guide which takes up the Rambam's challenge to make Talmudic learning accessible to every Jew. **The Ways of Reason** provides the reader with the tools of thinking, unlocking the doors which lead to the crown of Torah. This is not a book in which one can read more "about" Torah study and Judaism. Rather, it is an invitation to the reader to participate and experience the excitement of learning Gemorah. Rabbi Moshe Chaim Luzzatto writes that much of the knowledge of how words communicate ideas may be an inherent and natural part of our intelligence. Nonetheless, making a systematic and conscious study of words and ideas has many benefits. It adds clarity of understanding and increases one's ability to see and consider openly alternative possibilities. It enables one to create innovative understandings that bring words alive. Such a study also prevents error and makes critical thinking and evaluation possible. It increases speed and accuracy, allowing one to get the point quickly without aimless wandering. We decided to write an English translation of this classic work in light of all the tremendous benefit that may be derived from its study.

Rabbi Moshe Chaim Luzzatto is best known for his classic work on ethics, **Mesilas Yesharim**, which explains the practical steps to be followed towards the attainment of human perfection. As the Gaon of Vilna declared, such a practical guide could only have been composed by someone who had walked the path of righteousness to its very end. Had he been alive at the time of Rabbi Luzzatto, the Gaon added, he would have traveled on foot from Vilna to Italy to be his student even for a day. **The Ways of Reason** bears the stamp of the master in its exacting organization and systematic explanation of the subject, which never deviates from the realm of practical application. This is indeed a measure of his great wisdom that every aspect of learning is brought into reality to be fulfilled and applied. In this respect, **The Ways of Reason** is unsurpassed as a guide to Talmud

that is required is that we follow the formulas and instructions of our Sages.

I am very happy to see the completion of **The Ways of Reason** in English. It is my prayer that it will bring to the world at large some of the benefits which my students have already derived from this book.

Rabbi Mordecai Goldstein
Rosh HaYeshiva
Diaspora Yeshiva Toras Yisrael
Mount Zion, Jerusalem

study since it provides a practical bridge between logic and the Talmudic method. Rabbi Moshe Chaim Luzzatto is also not alone among our Sages in choosing to write a book on logic. The Rambam before him wrote on logic and the Vilna Gaon after him.

**The Ways of Reason** has been "required reading" in the Diaspora Yeshiva for many years and is used extensively by its students. It has been a tool which provides the student with a clear grasp of Talmudic thinking and erudition. Our rabbi and teacher Rabbi Mordecai Goldstein, while maintaining the highest standards of scholarship, has opened the doors of the Diaspora Yeshiva long before the "Baale T'shuvah" movement became popular. Thus, he has made the crown of Torah a lofty goal attainable to all who desire to study. The translators have taught classes in Talmud at the Diaspora Yeshiva for many years and have had considerable success in opening the field of Torah study to all students through the application of the Ramchal's system of Torah thinking. Indeed, Rabbi Moshe Chaim Luzzatto himself, in his introduction, states that the purpose of his work is to make the mastery of Talmud study quicker and easier for the beginner, as well as for the experienced student.

Rabbi Moshe Chaim Luzzatto's depth and precision in choosing each and every word cannot be overstated. This very conciseness of the original work has demanded more lengthy explanation in English in order to convey the intended meaning clearly. This is particularly true in the examples quoted from the Talmud. We must emphasize, as the author does in his introduction, that this is a book to be studied. It will be found that the Ramchal's system of categorizing ideas is not a mechanical process which can be a substitute for thinking. On the contrary, it facilitates deeper delving into a text by opening the range of possible interpretations. We have provided, as a study aid, an appendix containing outlines of each chapter together with a general index and an index of Hebrew terms. The charts in Hebrew and English show the overall structure of the book and the relationship between key concepts. It is important to progress through this guide step by step so that the number of distinctions and categories will not appear overwhelmingly complex. There are many terms used in the book in a specialized sense, and they are defined in the body of the text. At the point where the terms are defined, they appear in bold type. It is important to recognize the broad scope of the Ramchal's terminology. Thus, for example, the terms subject and predicate are not meant simply in a grammatical sense. Likewise, in the treatment of logical deductions, the Ramchal goes beyond the rules of validity to consider the basis on which statements should be accepted as true.

We wish to express our gratitude and acknowledgement to the Rosh HaYeshiva, Rabbi Mordecai Goldstein, who has guided us throughout our work. It is only through his teachings that we have come to understand the value of this book and put it to use. Whatever we have been able to do in helping others on the path of learning Torah is his doing. To the many people who have participated in this project, we express our heartfelt gratitude. In particular, we are indebted to our wives and our dear parents for their immeasurable support.

We offer thanks to the Almighty, who has brought us to the completion of this book and given us the merit to sit in the beis hamidrash. May it be His will that this book serves to return His people to His holy Torah.

Rabbi David Sackton
Rabbi Chaim Tscholkowsky
Diaspora Yeshiva
Mount Zion, Jerusalem

# The Ways of Reason

# דרך תבונות

# הקדמת הרב המחבר זצ"ל

חֶמְדַּת יְדִיעַת הָאֱמֶת הוּא עִנְיָן טִבְעִי אֶל הַנֶּפֶשׁ הַשִּׂכְלִית הַזֹּאת אֲשֶׁר בָּנוּ, עַד שֶׁלֹּא יִמָּצֵא אָדָם בָּרִיא בְּשִׂכְלוֹ שֶׁלֹּא יִתְאַמֵּץ וְיִשְׁתַּדֵּל כְּפִי כֹּחַ הַשֵּׂכֶל שֶׁבּוֹ לְגַלּוֹת אוֹתָהּ בָּעִנְיָנִים שֶׁיִּזְדַּמֵּן לוֹ לְהַשְׁקִיף עֲלֵיהֶם, וְלִדְחוֹת הַשֶּׁקֶר וּלְרַחֲקוֹ.

וְאִלּוּ הָיְתָה הָאֱמֶת נִגְלָה בְּכָל הָעִנְיָנִים, הִנֵּה לֹא הָיָה צָרִיךְ לָאָדָם לְשֶׁיִּתְחַכֵּם אֶלָּא הַהַשְׁקָפָה, שֶׁיִּהְיֶה מַרְבֶּה לְהַשְׁקִיף עַל עִנְיְנֵי הַמְּצִיאוּת, וְהָיָה מַרְבֶּה לְהִתְחַכֵּם. אָמְנָם, הִנֵּה אָנוּ רוֹאִים שֶׁאֵין הַדָּבָר כֵּן, לֹא מִצַּד הַמֻּשָּׂג וְלֹא מִצַּד הַמַּשִּׂיג. וְזֶה, כִּי הִנֵּה בֶּאֱמֶת אֵין לְךָ נִמְצָא שֶׁלֹּא תִהְיֶינָה בּוֹ בְּחִינוֹת רַבּוֹת כֻּלָּן אֲמִתִּיּוֹת, מֵהֶן בְּעַצְמוֹ וּמֵהֶן חוּץ מִמֶּנּוּ. דֶּרֶךְ מָשָׁל: צוּרַת הַשֻּׁלְחָן, מִדַּת אָרְכּוֹ וְרָחְבּוֹ וְכַיּוֹצֵא – הֵן בְּחִינוֹת בַּשֻּׁלְחָן עַצְמוֹ; תַּשְׁמִישׁוֹ, שָׁוְיוֹ וּזְמַן הֵעָשׂוֹתוֹ – הֵן בְּחִינוֹת חוּץ מִמֶּנּוּ.

וְאָמְנָם לֹא כָל הַבְּחִינוֹת מִתְגַּלּוֹת בְּשָׁוֶה, כִּי יֵשׁ בְּחִינוֹת נִגְלוֹת וּמֻשָּׂגוֹת מִיָּד עַל יְדֵי הַחוּשִׁים, וְיֵשׁ מִתְעַלְּמוֹת יוֹתֵר, שֶׁצְּרִיכָה הִשְׁתַּדְּלוּת לַעֲמוֹד עֲלֵיהֶן. וּבַנִּמְצָאִים עַצְמָם יֵשׁ חִלּוּק בֵּין נִמְצָא לְנִמְצָא. כִּי בְּחִינוֹת נִגְלוֹת בְּנִמְצָא אֶחָד, תִּהְיֶינָה נֶעֱלָמוֹת בְּאַחֵר. דֶּרֶךְ מָשָׁל: תַּשְׁמִישׁ הַשֻּׁלְחָן נִגְלֶה לַכֹּל – שֶׁהוּא לָשׂוּם עָלָיו אֳכָלִים אוֹ כֵלִים; תַּשְׁמִישׁ הַלֶּחֶם כְּמוֹ כֵן – שֶׁהוּא לַאֲכִילַת הָאָדָם; אַךְ תַּשְׁמִישׁ עֲשָׂבִים רַבִּים מֵעִשְׂבֵי הָאָרֶץ לֹא יֵדַע אֶלָּא אַחַר הִשְׁתַּדְּלוּת גְּדוֹלָה, אִם יִהְיֶה שֶׁיִּוָּדַע. נִמְצָא שֶׁאֵין כָּל הַנִּמְצָאִים מְגַלֵּי כָּל הַבְּחִינוֹת

# Author's Introduction

The pleasure in discovering truth is a natural trait of the intelligent soul that exists in every one of us. Any normal person, then, will make the utmost effort to reveal the true nature of anything he observes and banish falsehood.

If truth were self-evident, we could gain wisdom by simple observation. The more we observed the world around us, the wiser we would be. But, in fact, whether we consider the observer or what he observes, this is not true. For all objects must be considered in terms of many different logical aspects, both intrinsic and relational, all of which are equally true. For example, the *shape* of a table and its measurements, *length, width* and so forth, are intrinsic aspects of a table. The *use, worth,* and *age* of a table are relational aspects.

To complicate matters even further, not all aspects are equally apparent. Some are readily observable through our senses, others less so, requiring great effort to discern them. The problem is compounded in the objects themselves, because the same aspect that is apparent in one object may be hidden in another. For example, the *use* of a table is readily apparent, i.e., food and utensils are placed on it; similarly, the *use* of bread, i.e., it sustains mankind. However, the *use* of many wild plants can only be known, if at all, after long and intensive investigation. Thus we see that there is no object so apparent in all its aspects that its true nature can be understood solely through superficial observation.

שֶׁבְּהַשְׁקִיף עֲלֵיהֶן תַּשִּׂיג אֲמִתָּתָם.

וְזוּלַת כָּל זֶה הִנֵּה הַנִּסָּיוֹן עֵד נֶאֱמָן, שֶׁכַּמָּה וְכַמָּה מִן הַטָּעֻיוֹת מְצֻיָּרוֹת בְּלֵב רַבִּים מִבְּנֵי הָאָדָם לַאֲמִתִּיּוֹת, וְהֵם חֲזָקִים בְּאֱמוּנָתָם בָּהֶן, לֹא יִרְאוּ בָּהֶן שֶׁקֶר כְּלָל. וּכְבָר יִקְרֶה לְאָדָם אֶחָד עַצְמוֹ, שֶׁיַּחְשׁוֹב בַּתְּחִלָּה עִנְיָן מִן הָעִנְיָנִים אֲמִתִּי וּבָרוּר, וְאַחַר כָּךְ יִמְצָאֵהוּ כּוֹזֵב, וְיָשׁוּב מִמֶּנּוּ. אִם כֵּן וַדַּאי הוּא, שֶׁאֵין אֲמִתַּת הַנִּמְצָאִים נִגְלֵית וּמְבֹאֶרֶת, אֲבָל יֵשׁ לְטָעֻיוֹת מָקוֹם שֶׁאֶפְשָׁר לַשֶּׁקֶר שֶׁיֵּרָאֶה אֱמֶת, וְאֵין כֹּחַ הַשֵּׂכֶל חָזָק כָּל כָּךְ שֶׁיִּקָּלַע אֶל הָאֱמֶת וְלֹא יַחֲטִיא, אֲבָל אֶפְשָׁר לוֹ שֶׁיִּטֶּה מִן הַדֶּרֶךְ מִבְּלִי שֶׁיַּרְגִּישׁ.

וְכֵיוָן שֶׁהַדָּבָר כֵּן, וַדַּאי שֶׁרָאוּי הוּא שֶׁיִּמָּצֵא לוֹ הַדְרָכָה וְלִמּוּד, שֶׁבָּהֶם יִתְחַזֵּק בִּנְתִיב הַיָּשָׁר לְבִלְתִּי נְטוֹת מִמֶּנּוּ. וְאִם יֶאֱרַע לוֹ שֶׁיֵּצֵא כִּי לֹא נִשְׁמַר, כְּשֶׁיַּשְׁקִיף הֵיטֵב יַכִּיר אֶת טָעוּתוֹ וְיֵדַע לָשׁוּב אֶל הַמְּסִלָּה. וְאָמְנָם כְּלַל הַהַדְרָכָה הַזֹּאת – הוּא קִבּוּץ כָּל הַבְּחִינוֹת, אֲשֶׁר בַּנִּמְצָאִים לְמִינֵיהֶן, וּבֵאוּר דַּרְכֵיהֶן וְחֻקּוֹתֵיהֶן כְּפִי אֲמִתַּת הַמְּצִיאוּת, וְהָיוּ לַשֵּׂכֶל לְעֵינַיִם לָלֶכֶת בְּדֶרֶךְ הַהִתְבּוֹנְנוּת בְּלִי מִכְשׁוֹל; וַהֲרֵי זֶה כְּעִנְיָן מַה שֶּׁאָמְרוּ זִכְרוֹנָם לִבְרָכָה עַל שְׁלֹמֹה הַמֶּלֶךְ עָלָיו הַשָּׁלוֹם, שֶׁעָשָׂה אָזְנַיִם לַתּוֹרָה (עירובין כא ב), וְהַיְנוּ, כִּי עַל יְדֵי כְּלָלִים קְצָרִים וּמֻעָטִים, מְסֻדָּרִים כַּהֹגֶן, הִנֵּה יִלָּקַח שִׁעוּר גָּדוֹל מִן הַחָכְמָה עַל נְקֵלָה. וְלֹא תַחְשֹׁב, שֶׁיִּהְיוּ כְּלָלִים הָאֵלֶּה עִנְיָנִים עֲמֻקִּים מְאֹד וּרְחוֹקִים מִידִיעַת הֲמוֹן הָאֲנָשִׁים, כִּי אֵינָם אֶלָּא עִנְיָנִים קַלִּים וְנִגְלִים מְאֹד, וְלֹא נוֹסַף בָּהֶם אֶלָּא הַהֶעָרָה וְהַסִּדּוּר, כִּי כְבָר כֻּלָּם יִמָּצְאוּ בְּחֹק הַהַשְׂכָּלָה בַּטֶּבַע, אֶלָּא שֶׁעַד שֶׁלֹּא יִתְעוֹרֵר עֲלֵיהֶם הָאָדָם וְלֹא יִהְיוּ מְסֻדָּרִים וַעֲרוּכִים אֶצְלוֹ – לֹא יַעַזְרוּ לוֹ; וּכְשֶׁיִּסָּדְרוּ לְפָנָיו כָּרָאוּי

Aside from these difficulties, experience shows us that many people imagine false ideas to be absolutely true. They generally remain firm in their beliefs, refusing to see anything wrong with them. After initial study, a person may think that his ideas are clear and true, and only afterwards does he find them false and have to retract them. We can therefore say with certainty that the true nature of things is neither apparent nor readily understood, and there is, in fact, considerable room for mistakes, for what is false may appear true, and the human mind is not always discriminating enough to hit upon the truth. The mind, in fact, may even turn aside from the path of truth without being aware of doing so.

In light of this, it is beneficial for a person to find guidelines and a method to keep himself on the straight path without straying. For if he does carelessly go astray, he will, after thorough observation, be able to consciously recognize his error and return to the path. The basis of this method is the systematic compilation of all logical categories of things, explaining their functions and rules as they really are. This method is a guide, leading the mind unfalteringly in the search for wisdom. This is exactly what our rabbis of blessed memory meant when they praised King Solomon for making "handles for the Torah" (Eruvin 21b). He was able to acquire a large measure of knowledge with ease through the application of short, concise and properly ordered rules. Now do not think that these principles are so profound that they are beyond the understanding of ordinary people. On the contrary, they are extremely simple and obvious. My sole innovation in this book is the step of conscious awareness and organization. Even though all these rules are really natural laws of thinking, they cannot help anyone unless they are consciously used and organized as a tool. Once they are properly organized, a person has the "handles" with which to easily grasp the most profound and

– יִהְיוּ לָאָזְנַיִם לָקַחַת הַמִּשְׁקָלוֹת הַכְּבֵדָה שֶׁתִּתְנַשֵּׂא עַל יְדֵיהֶן בְּנָקֵל, וּכְמוֹ שֶׁכָּתַבְתִּי לְעֵיל.

וְהִנֵּה בִּרְאוֹתִי גֹּדֶל תּוֹעֶלֶת זֶה הָעִנְיָן וְרֹב הַצֹּרֶךְ בּוֹ, נִתְעוֹרַרְתִּי לְחַבֵּר חִבּוּר קָטָן זֶה, שֶׁיּוֹעִיל לְמִי שֶׁיִּרְצֶה לְהִשְׁתַּמֵּשׁ מִמֶּנּוּ לְהָקֵל עָלָיו הַהִתְלַמֵּד לְעַצְמוֹ וְהַלַּמֵּד לַאֲחֵרִים; וּבִתְנַאי שֶׁלֹּא יִהְיוּ בְּעֵינָיו הַדְּבָרִים קַלִּים, כְּמוֹ שֶׁהוּא הַכֹּל לְמִי שֶׁאֵינוֹ מֵבִין, אֶלָּא יְדַקְדֵּק בָּהֶם וְיִשְׁתַּדֵּל לַעֲמוֹד עַל בֻּרְיָם, כִּי לֹא הִנַּחְתִּי מִלְּדַקְדֵּק בְּדִבְרֵי לָשׁוּם הָעִנְיָנִים בְּבֵרוּר הָאֶפְשָׁרִי כְּפִי דַעְתִּי. וְהָיְתָה כַּוָּנָתִי בּוֹ לְסַדֵּר וּלְבָאֵר בְּאֹפֶן הַיּוֹתֵר קָצָר וּמַסְפִּיק דַּרְכֵי הַהִתְבּוֹנְנוּת וְהַהַשְׂכָּלָה, לְהַכִּיר אֶת הָאֱמֶת לְקָרְבָהּ וְאֶת הַשֶּׁקֶר לְהַרְחִיקוֹ.

וּבִהְיוֹת זֶה הַיָּם הַגָּדוֹל וּרְחַב יָדַיִם, יַם הַתַּלְמוּד, עָרוּךְ לְפָנֵינוּ, אַדִּירִים מִשְׁבְּרֵי פִלְפּוּלָיו, וְגַלֵּי הִלְכוֹתָיו יַעֲלוּ שָׁמַיִם יֵרְדוּ תְהוֹמוֹת, הֲלִיכוֹתָיו דֶּרֶךְ הֵנָּה, פְּנֵיהֶם לְבָרֵר וּלְלַבֵּן אֲמִתָּהּ שֶׁל תּוֹרָה – דֶּרֶךְ הַקֹּדֶשׁ יִקָּרֵא לָהּ, בָּחַרְתִּי לְיַסֵּד עָלָיו יְסוֹדוֹת בְּנִנְיֵי זֶה, לְמַעַן יַצְלִיחַ וְאֵדַע כִּי לֹא יִמּוֹט, וְיִהְיֶה זֶה בִּנְיַן-אָב לְכָל עִיּוּן וְהַשְׂכָּלָה.

וְהִנֵּה נִשְׁתַּדַּלְתִּי לְבָאֵר יְסוֹדוֹת הַפִּלְפּוּל הַיָּשָׁר וְשָׁרְשֵׁי הַמַּשָּׂא-וּמַתָּן שֶׁל הַשַּׁ"ס (שֵׁשֶׁת הַסְּדָרִים) בְּכָל חֲלָקָיו, שֶׁיּוֹעִיל לְמִי שֶׁלֹּא הִגִּיעַ עֲדַיִן לִידִיעַת לִמּוּד הַשַּׁ"ס וְרוֹצֶה לִכָּנֵס בּוֹ בְּיֹשֶׁר וּבְנָקֵל, שֶׁכְּשֶׁיַּקְדִּים לְהִתְלַמֵּד בְּחִבּוּר הַקָּטָן הַזֶּה, יִמְצָא אַחֲרֵי כֵן הֲלִיכוֹת הַהֲלָכוֹת מְרֻוָּחוֹת לְפָנָיו, וִיהַלֵּךְ בָּהֶן בְּיֹשֶׁר וְלֹא בַעֲקַלָּתוֹן; וּמַה שֶּׁהָיָה צָרִיךְ שֶׁיִּקְנֶה עַל יְדֵי זְמַן רַב וּשְׁקִידָה רַבָּה וְעָמָל גָּדוֹל, יִקְנֵהוּ עַל יְדֵי זֶה בִּזְמַן מְעַט וּבִמְעַט טֹרַח, בַּמֶּה שֶׁסִּדּוּר הַדְּרָכִים וְחִלּוּק הָעִנְיָנִים יַעַזְרוּהוּ עֵזֶר גָּדוֹל. וְגַם לְמִי שֶׁכְּבָר רָגִיל בַּשַּׁ"ס אֶפְשָׁר שֶׁיּוֹעִיל

intricate ideas, as I explained earlier.

When I became aware of the great benefit and necessity of this study, I was moved to compose this small work. Anyone who wants to approach it seriously will enhance his own learning, and his teaching of others. However, he must not minimize the task, for the way of the uneducated is to view everything simplistically. Read my words carefully and master every concept, for I have not been lax in choosing my words with exactness in order to express each point in the clearest possible way. My intention has been to arrange and explain the methods of understanding and knowledge in a style that is brief, yet sufficient. The goal of this method is to recognize truth and embrace it, and to uncover falsehood and reject it.

The Talmud is like a vast ocean set before us, whose arguments are mighty waves, whose laws roll forth rising to the heavens and plunging to the depths. Through the forward movement of these strong currents the Truth of Torah is clarified and distilled — this is called the Holy Way. It is in the Talmud that I have chosen to base my building, so that my method will be successful and immutable. This Torah method, then, is the paradigm for all understanding and wisdom.

I will explain in detail the foundations of analytical argument in the Talmud and principles of its dialectic thought. This will help anyone who is not already familiar with Talmud study and desires to embark upon it directly and easily. If he begins his study with the aid of this little book, he will find the avenues of Talmudic law open to him, and he will travel along them without needless detour. What might have taken long hours, great concentration, and hard work to acquire can be achieved with a minimum of time and effort, for he will be tremendously aided by an organized method and classification of ideas. Even someone who is already accustomed to Torah study may

לִפְעָמִים לְהַצִּילוֹ מִן הַטָּעֻיּוֹת.

וְהִנֵּה קָרָאתִי שְׁמוֹ כְּפִי עִנְיָנוֹ, **דֶּרֶךְ תְּבוּנוֹת.**

הָאֵל הַנּוֹתֵן דַּעַת וּתְבוּנָה, יְחָנֵּנוּ דֵעָה בִּינָה וְהַשְׂכֵּל, לְיִרְאָה אוֹתוֹ וְלַעֲשׂוֹת רְצוֹנוֹ וּלְעָבְדוֹ בְּלֵבָב שָׁלֵם, נֵצַח סֶלָה וָעֶד! אָמֵן, כֵּן יְהִי רָצוֹן!

occasionally be kept from falling into error.

For this reason I have named this book in accordance with its main idea, **The Ways of Reason.**

May the Almighty, who is the source of all knowledge and understanding, grant us knowledge, wisdom and understanding so that we may fear Him, do His will and serve Him with a complete heart for all eternity. Amen. May His will be so.

# פרק א

הַמַּשָּׂא־וּמַתָּן הָעִיּוּנִי הוּא הָעֵסֶק וְהַחֲקִירָה בְּמַאֲמָר מִן הַמַּאֲמָרִים אוֹ בְּדֵעָה מִן הַדֵּעוֹת, לְבָרֵר וּלְגַלּוֹת אִם הוּא אֲמִתִּי אִם לֹא. וְאָמְנָם, הַבֵּרוּר הַזֶּה יֵעָשֶׂה בְּעֵרֶךְ הַטְּעָנוֹת שֶׁיֵּשׁ לִטְעוֹן לְקַיְּמוֹ וּלְאַמְּתוֹ אוֹ לְבַטְּלוֹ וְלִסְתּוֹר אוֹתוֹ, בָּאֹפֶן שֶׁיִּבָּחֵן כֹּחַ הַטְּעָנוֹת הַמְאַמְּתוֹת אוֹתוֹ וְכֹחַ הַסּוֹתְרוֹת אוֹתוֹ וְיִכְרַע כְּפִי הַיּוֹתֵר נָאוֹתוֹת אֵצֶל הַשֵּׂכֶל.

וְהִנֵּה הָעֵסֶק הַזֶּה אֶפְשָׁר שֶׁיִּהְיֶה בֵּין רַבִּים, שֶׁאֶחָד מֵהֶם יַעֲמֹד לְצַד הָאֶחָד וְאֶחָד לְשֶׁכְּנֶגְדּוֹ. פֵּרוּשׁ: אֶחָד יַעֲמֹד לְצַד קִיּוּם הַמַּאֲמָר וְאֶחָד יַעֲמֹד לְצַד סְתִירָתוֹ וּבִטּוּלוֹ, וְיַעַרְכוּ טַעֲנוֹתֵיהֶם זֶה כְּנֶגֶד זֶה. וְאֶפְשָׁר שֶׁיִּהְיֶה עֵסֶק אִישׁ אֶחָד לְבַדּוֹ שֶׁיַּשְׁלִים לְכָל הַצְּדָדִים, פֵּרוּשׁ: שֶׁהוּא יַנִּיחַ אֶת הַמַּאֲמָר בַּתְּחִלָּה, וְהוּא עַצְמוֹ יַעֲרֹךְ נֶגֶד מַאֲמָרוֹ טַעֲנוֹת, מַה שֶּׁאֶפְשָׁר שֶׁיַּעֲרֹךְ נֶגְדּוֹ מִי שֶׁהוּא בַּעַל דֵּעָה הַהֲפָכִית לַמַּאֲמָר הַהוּא, וְהוּא עַצְמוֹ יַחֲזֹר וְיִסְתֹּר הַטְּעָנוֹת שֶׁהֵבִיא וִיקַיֵּם מַאֲמָרוֹ הָרִאשׁוֹן.

וּמִשְּׁנֵי הַדְּרָכִים הָאֵלּוּ נִמְצְאוּ בַּשַּׁ"ס וִכּוּחִים וּפִלְפּוּלִים, כִּי יֵשׁ שֶׁנָּשְׂאוּ וְנָתְנוּ רַבִּים בְּאֶחָד מִן הָעִנְיָנִים. זֶה הִקְשָׁה וְזֶה הֵשִׁיב; וְיֵשׁ שֶׁמְּסַדֵּר הַשַּׁ"ס עַצְמוֹ הִקְשָׁה וְהֵשִׁיב, כְּאִלּוּ הָיוּ רַבִּים הַמְדַבְּרִים בָּעִנְיָן הַהוּא; וְיֵשׁ שֶׁיֹּאמַר הַשַּׁ"ס בְּפֵרוּשׁ: "הוּא מוֹתִיב לַהּ וְהוּא מְפָרֵק לַהּ", וְהַיְנוּ שֶׁהַמַּקְשֶׁה עַצְמוֹ נָתַן תְּשׁוּבָה לְקֻשְׁיָתוֹ.

# Chapter One

Dialectic investigation is the process of analyzing a statement or idea in order to explain and clarify its truth or falsity. This process consists of setting forth all possible arguments which validate and establish the statement or nullify and disprove it. An arrangement must be chosen which will test the relative strengths of the arguments pro and con. Finally, the question must be resolved on the side that appears most pleasing to the mind.

This investigation can be conducted among many people, with one taking one side of the argument and the other opposing him; i.e., one endeavors to prove a statement and the other to disprove it, each opponent setting forth his argument to answer the other, point for point. It is also possible for one person to conduct the argument by himself, filling in each side. He proposes an initial statement, and then considers every possible rebuttal that might be made by a person holding the opposite point of view. He then disproves each of his own arguments, and returns to establish his original statement.

Both these styles are found in the arguments and disputes of the Talmud. For sometimes many rabbis debate one topic, some posing difficulties and the others answering, while at other times the Talmud itself questions and answers as if different rabbis were arguing an issue. At times the Talmud states explicitly, "The same one who asks has given the answer". That is, the one who presents a problem solves it himself.

וְאוּלָם כָּל הַדְּרָכִים לְמָקוֹם אֶחָד הֵם בָּאִים – שֶׁהוּא בֵּרוּר
אֲמִתַּת הַדְּבָרִים עַל יְדֵי עֲרִיכַת הַטְּעָנוֹת זוֹ לְעֻמַּת זוֹ. וּמִשְׁפַּט הַקֻּשְׁיָא
שֶׁיַּקְשֶׁה אֶחָד עַל מַאֲמַר זוּלָתוֹ, אוֹ הַקֻּשְׁיָא שֶׁיַּקְשֶׁה בַּעַל מַאֲמָר אֶחָד
עַל מַאֲמַר עַצְמוֹ – אֶחָד הוּא; וְכֵן מִשְׁפַּט הַתְּשׁוּבָה שֶׁתָּבוֹא עַל קֻשְׁיָא
מִן הַקֻּשְׁיוֹת, בֵּין שֶׁתִּהְיֶה דִּבְרֵי הַמַּקְשֶׁה עַצְמוֹ וּבֵין שֶׁתִּהְיֶה דִּבְרֵי
זוּלָתוֹ – אֶחָד הוּא; וְכֵן כָּל שְׁאָר חֶלְקֵי הַפִּלְפּוּל, כִּי אֲנַחְנוּ לֹא נַבִּיט
בְּכָל זֶה אֶל הַטּוֹעֲנִים, אֶלָּא אֶל הַטְּעָנוֹת.

However, all these forms of debate lead to the same end, i.e., the clarification of the truth by means of arranging every argument point for point. One judges a difficulty whether it is raised by someone else against a stated thought or the person raises a difficulty against himself in the same way. Similarly, with the resolution of any difficulty, there is no difference whether it is his own or someone else's. The same is true for every other element of dialectics, for we never judge a statement by its author, but only on its own merit.

# פרק ב

אָמְנָם חֶלְקֵי הַמַּשָּׂא-וּמַתָּן הָרָאשִׁיִּים, שֶׁמֵּהֶם נִבְנוֹת הַסֻּגְיוֹת כֻּלָּן בְּכָל הַתַּלְמוּד – שִׁבְעָה, וְהֵם: מֵימְרָא, שְׁאֵלָה, תְּשׁוּבָה, סְתִירָה, רְאָיָה, קֻשְׁיָא וְתֵרוּץ. וְזֶה פֵּרוּשָׁם:

**מֵימְרָא** – הוּא שֶׁיֹּאמַר אוֹמֵר מַאֲמָר אֶחָד.

**שְׁאֵלָה** – שֶׁיְּבַקֵּשׁ אֶחָד מֵאֶחָד יְדִיעַת עִנְיָן-מָה.

**תְּשׁוּבָה** – שֶׁיָּשִׁיב הַנִּשְׁאָל לַשּׁוֹאֵל עַל שְׁאֵלָתוֹ.

**סְתִירָה** – שֶׁיְּבַטֵּל מַאֲמָר שֶׁנֶּאֱמַר וִיכַחֵשׁ מִכֹּל וָכֹל.

**רְאָיָה** – שֶׁיּוּבָא מַה שֶּׁמִּמֶּנּוּ תִּתְבָּאֵר אֲמִתַּת אֶחָד מִן הַמַּאֲמָרִים שֶׁנֶּאֶמְרוּ אוֹ מִן הַדֵּעוֹת שֶׁנִּסְבְּרוּ.

**קֻשְׁיָא** – שֶׁיֵּרָאֶה הֱיוֹת בְּמַאֲמָר מִן הַמַּאֲמָרִים אוֹ בְּדֵעָה מִן הַדֵּעוֹת מַה שֶׁאֵינוֹ אֱמֶת אוֹ מַה שֶׁאֵינוֹ נָאוֹת.

**תֵּרוּץ** – שֶׁתּוּסַר הַקֻּשְׁיָא מִן הַמַּאֲמָר אֲשֶׁר הֻקְשָׁה עָלָיו אוֹ מִן הַדֵּעָה.

וְהִנֵּה כָּל אֶחָד מִן הַחֲלָקִים הָאֵלֶּה יִתְחַלֵּק עוֹד לַחֲלָקִים אֲחֵרִים, וְיִתְבָּאֲרוּ לְפָנֵינוּ בְּסִיַּעְתָּא דִשְׁמַיָּא.

# Chapter Two

Every Talmudic discussion is built from seven principal elements of dialectic reasoning. They are: Statement, Question, Answer, Contradiction, Proof, Difficulty and Resolution.

**Statement** – the speaker states a single idea.

**Question** – a person asks another a point of information.

**Answer** – the person asked responds to the question.

**Contradiction** – the speaker disproves a statement and totally refutes it.

**Proof** – the speaker presents evidence from which the truth of a statement or idea is made apparent.

**Difficulty** – a person points out something untrue or unpleasing in a statement or idea.

**Resolution** – a person turns aside the difficulty raised against a statement or idea.

Each of these elements has subcategories which will be explained later with the help of the Almighty.

It must be noted that dialectics are founded on first principles which are naturally found in our mind, and which lead us to an understanding of any statement, and to an acceptance or rejection of ideas. Every difficulty and resolution, every proof and disproof and all other parts of argumentation mentioned above are built on these foundations.

וּמַה שֶׁצָּרִיךְ שֶׁתֵּדַע הוּא, כִּי הִנֵּה כָּל הַמַּשָׂא־וּמַתָּן הַזֶּה נוֹסַד עַל
יְסוֹדוֹת רִאשׁוֹנִים, נִמְצָאִים בַּטֶּבַע בְּשִׂכְלֵנוּ, אֲשֶׁר עַל פִּיהֶם יִתְנַהֵג
לְהָבִין מַאֲמָר אֲשֶׁר יֵאָמֵר וּלְקַבֵּל דֵּעָה מִן הַדֵּעוֹת אוֹ לְהַכְחִישָׁם; כִּי
הִנֵּה עַל הַיְסוֹדוֹת הָאֵלֶּה יִבָּנוּ כָּל הַקֻּשְׁיוֹת וְהַתֵּרוּצִים, הָרְאָיוֹת
וְהַדְּחִיּוֹת, וְכֵן כָּל שְׁאָר הַחֲלָקִים הַנִּבְחָנִים בּוֹ.

דֶּרֶךְ מָשָׁל, כְּשֶׁאָמְרוּ (ברכות טו א): ״הַקּוֹרֵא,
דִּיעֲבַד – אִין, לְכַתְּחִלָּה – לָא״, הִנֵּה זֶה נוֹסַד
עַל מַה שֶׁמִּצְטַיֵּר בְּשִׂכְלֵנוּ מִלְּשׁוֹן זֶה, שֶׁכַּוָּנַת
אוֹמְרוֹ הָיְתָה לְדַבֵּר בְּמִי שֶׁכְּבָר קָרָא.

וְהֵפֶךְ זֶה (חולין ג א): ״הַכֹּל שׁוֹחֲטִין – לְכַתְּחִלָּה״,
כִּי טֶבַע הַלָּשׁוֹן מוֹרֶה לָנוּ כָּךְ.

וְכֵן, כְּשֶׁהִקְשׁוּ (פסחים ד ב): ״הַאי הַכֹּל נֶאֱמָנִים,
כָּל הַבָּתִּים בְּחֶזְקַת בְּדוּקִים מִבָּעֵי לֵהּ״ –

*For example, the Mishnah states (Berachos 15a), "One who read the Sh'ma without hearing his own words fulfills his obligation". The Gemorah infers, "One who read, that is, one who has already read, fulfills his obligation; however, in the first instance, he should read so as to hear what he says". This inference is based on the conceptual image which our minds construct from the words of the Mishnah, i.e., the intention is to refer to someone who has already read.*

*The opposite inference is made in the Gemorah (Chullin 2a). The Mishnah states, "Anyone may perform ritual slaughter and his slaughter is kosher". The Gemorah infers, "Anyone may perform ritual slaughter, that is, even in the first instance". Here, the nature of the language, "Anyone **may** slaughter", indicates that the Mishnah refers even to the first instance.*

*Another Gemorah (Pesachim 4a) presents a difficulty based on similar principles. Rav Nachman bar Yitzhak was asked: If one rents a house to his neighbor on the fourteenth of Nissan, does it have the legal status of having been checked for leaven? He answered by quot-*

נוֹסְדָה הַקֻּשְׁיָא הַזֹּאת עַל מַה שֶׁטֶּבַע הַלָּשׁוֹן זֶה
שֶׁל "הַכֹּל נֶאֱמָנִים" מוֹרֶה הֱיוֹת הַדִּין הַהוּא
הַמֻּזְכָּר שָׁם תָּלוּי בִּהְיוֹת הַכֹּל נֶאֱמָנִים עַל
הַבְּדִיקָה. וּלְפִי מַה שֶּׁרוֹצֶה לְהַעֲמִיד שָׁם
הַשַּׁ"ס, אֵינוֹ תָּלוּי בֶּאֱמֶת אֶלָּא בִּהְיוֹת חֶזְקָתָם
שֶׁל הַבָּתִּים שֶׁהֵם בְּדוּקִים. וְהַטֶּבַע מוֹרֶה לָנוּ,
שֶׁכְּשֶׁנִּרְצֶה לְהַגִּיד זֶה הָעִנְיָן לֹא נֹאמְרֵהוּ אֶלָּא
בְּלָשׁוֹן כָּזֶה: "כָּל הַבָּתִּים בְּחֶזְקַת בְּדוּקִים".

וְכֵן כָּל הַקֻּשְׁיוֹת כֻּלָּן וְכָל הַתֵּרוּצִים וְכָל שְׁאָר חֶלְקֵי הַפִּלְפּוּל,
כְּשֶׁתַּחְקֹר עֲלֵיהֶם בֶּאֱמֶת, תִּמְצָאֵם נוֹסָדִים עַל יְסוֹדוֹת כָּאֵלּוּ, עִנְיָנִים
חֲקוּקִים בְּטֶבַע הַהֲבָנָה הַשִּׂכְלִית, שֶׁשֵּׂכֶל הָאָדָם מְחַיְּבָם מֵעַצְמוֹ בְּלִי
שֶׁיִּצְטָרֵךְ לָזֶה לִמּוּד כְּלָל.

וְאָמְנָם, פְּעֻלּוֹת הַשֵּׂכֶל בְּהַשְׂכָּלָתוֹ – שָׁלֹשׁ:

*ing a text: All are believed concerning the re-*
*moval of leaven. The Gemorah presents a diffi-*
*culty, "The fact that all are believed does not*
*answer the question! It must be established*
*that all houses have the legal status of having*
*been checked for leaven". This difficulty is*
*based on a natural principle of language. The*
*phrase "All are believed" tells us that the desired*
*law is dependent upon the factor that **every-***
***one** is believed about checking for leaven.*
*However, on the other hand, the presumption of*
*the Talmud is that the desired law is dependent*
*upon another factor, that the **houses** have a le-*
*gal status of having been checked. To express*
*the latter factor properly, the nature of language*
*demands that we use the phrase "All the houses*
*have the legal status of having been checked".*

If the matter is investigated well, it will be apparent that every single difficulty and resolution and all the other elements of dialectics are founded on similar principles. These principles of language are inherent in the nature of intellectual understanding, for the human mind itself dictates their necessity even without study.

There are three processes that the mind uses in pursuit of understanding.

הָאַחַת – צִיּוּר הָעִנְיָנִים וַהֲבָנַת הַמַּאֲמָרִים וְהַסְּבָרוֹת כְּמוֹת שֶׁהֵם.

הַשֵּׁנִית – הֻלֶּדֶת תּוֹלְדוֹתֵיהֶם.

הַשְּׁלִישִׁית – קַבָּלָתָם אוֹ הַכְחָשָׁתָם.

וּבְכֻלָּן מִתְנַהֵג וְהוֹלֵךְ כְּפִי הַיְסוֹדוֹת הַחֲקוּקִים לוֹ בַּטֶּבַע, וּכְמוֹ שֶׁזָּכַרְנוּ, וְתֵרָאֶה עוֹד לְפָנִים בְּעֶזְרַת הַשֵּׁם. וְעַתָּה נְבָאֲרֵם בִּפְרָטֵיהֶם, כָּל אֶחָד וְאֶחָד בִּפְנֵי עַצְמוֹ.

The first is the building of a complete picture of the subject and an exact understanding of statements and ideas as they are intended (Chapters Three – Six).

The second is the derivation of new ideas from a stated premise (Chapter Seven).

The third is the acceptance or rejection of each premise and conclusion on the basis of proof (Chapter Eight).

In each of these processes the mind proceeds according to natural principles as we mentioned, and as we shall see further with the help of the Almighty. Now we will explain each process individually in detail.

# פרק ג

הִנֵּה כָּל מַאֲמָר שֶׁיֵּאָמֵר, סְבָרָא שֶׁתִּסְתַּבֵּר וְעִנְיָן שֶׁיְּצֻיָּר, אִי אֶפְשָׁר
שֶׁלֹּא יִהְיֶה נִבְנֶה מִשְּׁנֵי חֲלָקִים, דְּהַיְנוּ: מֵעִנְיָן שֶׁיְּקֻיַּם אוֹ יְשֻׁלַּל, וּמִדָּבָר
שֶׁבּוֹ יְקֻיַּם הָעִנְיָן הַהוּא אוֹ יְשֻׁלַּל מִמֶּנּוּ.

דֶּרֶךְ מָשָׁל (ברכות כ ג): אָמַר רַב אַדָּא בַּר אַהֲבָה:
"נָשִׁים חַיָּבוֹת בְּקִדּוּשׁ הַיּוֹם"; קִיֵּם עִנְיָן אֶחָד
שֶׁהוּא חוֹבַת קִדּוּשׁ הַיּוֹם, בְּדָבָר אֶחָד, דְּהַיְנוּ:
כְּלַל הַנָּשִׁים.

וְהִנֵּה הָעִנְיָן הַמְקֻיָּם אוֹ הַמְשֻׁלָּל, נִקְרָא "נָשׂוּא". וְהַדָּבָר שֶׁבּוֹ
קֻיַּם אוֹ שֻׁלַּל מִמֶּנּוּ, נִקְרָא "נוֹשֵׂא". נִמְצָא, נוֹשֵׂא הַמַּאֲמָר הַזֶּה –
נָשִׁים, וְהַנָּשׂוּא – הַחִיּוּב בְּקִדּוּשׁ הַיּוֹם.

וּמִצַּד זֶה וָזֶה, יֵחָלְקוּ הַמַּאֲמָרִים לְמִינִים שׁוֹנִים.

מִצַּד הַנּוֹשְׂאִים יִתְחַלְּקוּ הַמַּאֲמָרִים לִשְׁלֹשָׁה מִינִים: כּוֹלְלִים,
פְּרָטִיִּים, קְצָתִיִּים.

**כּוֹלְלִים** – הֵם הַמַּאֲמָרִים שֶׁנּוֹשְׂאָם כּוֹלֵל, דְּהַיְנוּ שֶׁיִּכְלֹל פְּרָטִים
רַבִּים, וּבְכֻלָּם יֵאָמֵר בָּהֶם הַנָּשׂוּא שֶׁבַּמַּאֲמָר הַהוּא.

# Chapter Three

Every conceivable statement, idea, or thought is necessarily constructed from two parts: a certain matter which is affirmed or denied, and a thing upon which it is affirmed or denied.

> *For example, (Berachos 20b) "Rav Ada bar Ahavah said, "Women are obliged to fulfill the mitzvah of kiddush". Here, a specific concept (the obligation to fulfill the mitzvah of kiddush) is affirmed in relation to a certain subject (that is, the category of women).*

We call that which is affirmed or denied the **Predicate**, and the thing upon which it is affirmed or denied we call the **Subject**. Accordingly, the subject of this statement is women, and the predicate is the obligation of kiddush.

With respect to subject or predicate all statements may be classified in different categories.

Statements are divided into three types according to their subjects: categorical, particular and partial.

**Categorical Statements** have as their subjects an entire class consisting of many particulars. The predicate of the statement must apply to all of them.

דֶּרֶךְ מָשָׁל (סנהדרין נ א): "כָּל יִשְׂרָאֵל יֵשׁ לָהֶם חֵלֶק
לָעוֹלָם הַבָּא", הִנֵּה זֶה כּוֹלֵל פְּרָטִים רַבִּים,
שֶׁהֵם אִישֵׁי הָאֻמָּה הַיִּשְׂרְאֵלִית, וּבְכֻלָּם יֵאָמֵר
הַנָּשׂוּא, שֶׁהוּא הַחֵלֶק בָּעוֹלָם הַבָּא.

**פְּרָטִיִּים** – הֵם שֶׁנּוֹשְׂאָם פְּרָט אֶחָד לְבַד.

דֶּרֶךְ מָשָׁל (נגעים פי"ב מ"ד): "יְרוּשָׁלַיִם אֵינָהּ
מְטַמְּאָה בַּנְּגָעִים".

**קְצָתִיִּים** – שֶׁיִּזָּכֵר בַּנּוֹשֵׂא קְצָת מִכְּלָל אֶחָד.

דֶּרֶךְ מָשָׁל (יבמות פד א): "יֵשׁ מֻתָּרוֹת לְבַעֲלֵיהֶן",
הַכַּוָּנָה בּוֹ: קְצָת מִכְּלַל הַנָּשִׁים יֵאָמֵר בָּהֶן
הַנָּשׂוּא, שֶׁהוּא – הַהֶתֵּר לְבַעֲלֵיהֶן.

וְאָמְנָם יֵשׁ הַמַּאֲמָר הַסְּתָמִי, שֶׁלֹּא נִזְכַּר בִּנְשׂוּאוֹ מִלַּת "כָּל", וְאַף
עַל פִּי כֵן כֹּחוֹ כְּכֹחַ הַמַּאֲמָר הַכּוֹלֵל.

> *For example, (Sanhedrin 90a) "All Jews have a*
> *portion in the world to come". This statement*
> *encompasses many particulars (every Jewish*
> *person) in a class, and predicates upon all of*
> *them that they have a portion in the world to*
> *come.*

**Particular Statements** have as their subjects one individual entity.

> *For example, (Nega'im Chapter 12 Mishnah 4)*
> *"Jerusalem does not become ritually impure*
> *through plagues".*

**Partial Statements** are those whose subjects contain only part of one class.

> *For example, (Yebamos 84a) "Some women are*
> *permitted to their husbands and forbidden to*
> *perform the leverite marriage". The meaning of*
> *this statement is that the predicate – that they*
> *are permitted to their husbands and forbidden*
> *to perform leverite marriage – is only applied to*
> *a part of the entire class of women.*

There are also unqualified statements that have the same force as a categorical statement even though their subjects are not qualified by the word *all.*

דֶּרֶךְ מָשָׁל (ברכות כ ג): "נָשִׁים חַיָּבוֹת בְּקִדּוּשׁ
הַיּוֹם", שֶׁזָּכַרְנוּ לְמַעְלָה, הִנֵּה הַכַּוָּנָה בּוֹ, שֶׁכָּל
הַנָּשִׁים חַיָּבוֹת בְּקִדּוּשׁ הַיּוֹם.

מִצַּד הַנְּשׂוּאִים יִתְחַלְּקוּ הַמַּאֲמָרִים לְאַחַד-עָשָׂר מִינִים, וְזֶה, כִּי
לֹא כָל נָשׂוּא שֶׁיִּהְיֶה יֵאָמֵר עַל כָּל נוֹשֵׂא שֶׁיִּהְיֶה בְּדֶרֶךְ אֶחָד, אֲבָל יֵשׁ
שֶׁיֵּאָמֵר בְּדֶרֶךְ אֶחָד וְיֵשׁ שֶׁיֵּאָמֵר בְּדֶרֶךְ אַחֵר, וּמִצַּד זֶה יִתְחַלְּפוּ
הַמַּאֲמָרִים לְמִינֵיהֶם.

הַמִּין הָאֶחָד – הוּא כְּלַל הַמַּאֲמָרִים שֶׁיֵּאָמֵר בָּהֶם נָשׂוּא בְּנוֹשֵׂא
בְּלִי שׁוּם תְּנַאי וּגְבוּל, כַּמַּאֲמָרִים שֶׁזָּכַרְנוּ לְמַעְלָה וַאֲחֵרִים זוּלָתָם.
וְנִקְרָא זֶה מַאֲמָר **סְתָם**.

הַמִּין הַשֵּׁנִי – אוֹתָם שֶׁיֵּאָמֵר בָּהֶם הַנָּשׂוּא בְּנוֹשֵׂא בְּדֶרֶךְ מְיֻחָד
וּמֻגְבָּל, כְּגוֹן שֶׁיֵּאָמֵר הַנָּשׂוּא בְּדֶרֶךְ וַדָּאוּת אוֹ הֶכְרֵחַ,

דֶּרֶךְ מָשָׁל (פסחים ט ג): "כֵּיוָן דְּחֻלְדָּה אוֹ בַּרְדְּלָס
מְצוּיִים שָׁם – וַדַּאי גְּרָרוּהוּ בְּהַהִיא שַׁעְתָּא";

אוֹ שֶׁיֹּאמְרוּהוּ בְּדֶרֶךְ אֶפְשָׁרוּת,

דֶּרֶךְ מָשָׁל (כתובות עה א): "אֶפְשָׁר לְעַבְּרָהּ בְּקִיּוּהָא
דְּחַמְרָא";

> *For example, (Berachos 20b) "Women are ob-*
> *liged to fulfill the mitzvah of kiddush". It is*
> *understood from this statement that **all** wom-*
> *en are obliged to fulfill the mitzvah of kiddush.*

Statements are divided into eleven types according to their predicates. Each of these types is distinct because all predicates are not applied to their subjects in the same way; rather, each different formula which is used implies a different type of predication.

1. **Simple Statement.** The category of statements whose predicates are applied to their subjects without any condition or limitation, as is seen in the previously mentioned examples and other similar statements.

2. **Qualified Statement.** In this category of statements the application of the predicate to the subject ranges from definitive to tentative. In one instance, the predicate may be stated as a certainty or a necessity. In the absence of certainty the predicate may be stated as a possibility.

> *For example, (Pesachim 9b) "Since weasels and*
> *martens are commonly found, they **certainly***
> *dragged away the fetus before the Cohen ar-*
> *rived".*
>
> *(Kesubos 75a) "It is **possible** for the Cohen to*
> *remove filth with wine vinegar before the Tem-*
> *ple service".*

אוֹ שֶׁיֹּאמְרוּהוּ בְּדֶרֶךְ סָפֵק,

דֶּרֶךְ מָשָׁל (פסחים קיג א): "כָּל אַשְׁרַאי – סָפֵק אָתֵי
סָפֵק לָא אָתֵי";

אוֹ שֶׁיֹּאמְרוּהוּ בְּדֶרֶךְ מְנִיעָה,

דֶּרֶךְ מָשָׁל (כתובות עה א): "גַּבֵּי אִשָּׁה לָא אֶפְשָׁר";

וְכֵן כֹּל כַּיּוֹצֵא בָזֶה.

הַמִּין הַשְּׁלִישִׁי – הוּא הַמַּאֲמָר שֶׁיֵּאָמֵר נָשׂוּא בַנוֹשֵׂא וְיִשָּׁלֵל מִכָּל
זוּלָתוֹ.

דֶּרֶךְ מָשָׁל מַאֲמָר הַכָּתוּב (שמות יב טז): "הוּא
לְבַדּוֹ יֵעָשֶׂה לָכֶם", אָמַר הֶתֵּר הָעֲשִׂיָּה בְּצֹרֶךְ
אֹכֶל נֶפֶשׁ, וְשָׁלַל אוֹתוֹ מִכָּל מַה שֶּׁזוּלַת זֶה.

וְנִקְרָא מַאֲמָר מְמַעֵט.

Alternatively, the predicate may be inconclusive or it may be stated as an impossibility.

> *For example, (Pesachim 113a) "In all sales involving credit, it is* **doubtful** *whether the money will be forthcoming or not".*

> *(Kesubos 75a) "The Cohen may alleviate foul breath by putting a peppercorn in his mouth and thus not be disqualified from Temple service. However, this option is* **impossible** *for a woman because she is in constant contact with her husband".*

This category of statements includes the entire range of variations from certainty to possibility and from doubt to impossibility.

**3. Statement of Exclusion.** In this type of statement the predicate is applied to the subject to the exclusion of any other subject.

> *For example, (Exodus 12:16) ". . . no manner of work shall be done on them, save that which every person must eat; that* **alone** *may be done by you". The permissibility of work is predicated on cases involving what a person needs in order to eat, and excluded from any other case.*

הַמִּין הָרְבִיעִי – שֶׁיּוֹצִיא הַנָּשׂוּא מִקְצָת מִמַּה שֶׁנִּכְלַל בְּנוֹשֵׂא הַמַּאֲמָר הַהוּא.

דֶּרֶךְ מָשָׁל (חולין ג א): "הַכֹּל שׁוֹחֲטִין וּשְׁחִיטָתָן כְּשֵׁרָה – חוּץ מֵחֵרֵשׁ שׁוֹטֶה וְקָטָן", שֶׁהֲרֵי חֵרֵשׁ שׁוֹטֶה וְקָטָן גַּם הֵם נִכְלָלִים בְּמַשְׁמָעוּת מִלַּת "הַכֹּל", וּמוֹצָא הַנָּשׂוּא מֵהֶם, דְּהַיְנוּ הֶתֵּר הַשְּׁחִיטָה, עִם מִלַּת "חוּץ".

וְנִקְרָא מַאֲמָר **מוֹצִיא**.

הַמִּין הַחֲמִישִׁי – שֶׁיֵּאָמֵר נָשׂוּא בַּנּוֹשֵׂא, אַךְ לֹא בְּהֶחְלֵט, אֶלָּא בִּבְחִינָה אַחַת אוֹ עִם תְּנַאי אֶחָד.

דֶּרֶךְ מָשָׁל (יבמות לח א): "כְּנָסָהּ, הֲרֵי הִיא כְּאִשְׁתּוֹ לְכָל דָּבָר – וּבִלְבַד שֶׁתְּהֵא כְּתֻבָּתָהּ עַל נִכְסֵי בַעְלָהּ הָרִאשׁוֹן";

וְכֵן (במא"י פ"א מ"ג): "וּמְחַלְּלִים אוֹתוֹ כֶּסֶף עַל כֶּסֶף, נְחֹשֶׁת עַל נְחֹשֶׁת, כֶּסֶף עַל נְחֹשֶׁת, וּנְחֹשֶׁת עַל הַפֵּרוֹת – וּבִלְבַד שֶׁיַּחֲזֹר וְיִפְדֶּה אֶת הַפֵּרוֹת".

וְנִקְרָא מַאֲמָר **מֻגְבָּל**.

**4. Statement of Exception.** In this statement the predicate is removed from some elements of the general class which constitutes the subject.

> *For example, (Chullin 2a) "All may slaughter and their slaughtering is valid **except** a deaf or insane person or a minor". Here, the deaf, the insane and the minor are included in the class of all Jews; however, they are excluded from the statement that all may slaughter because of the word **except**.*

**5. Conditional Statement.** In this kind of statement the predicate is not applicable in all cases; it is conditionally applied to the subject or it is only true in certain respects.

> *For example, (Yebamos 38a) "When one performs leverite marriage, the woman is his wife in every respect, **with the stipulation** that her ketubah shall be paid from the estate of her first husband".*

> *Similarly, (Demai Chapter 1 Mishnah 2) "Second tithe money of demai may be exchanged, silver for silver, copper for copper, silver for copper, and copper for fruit – **provided** that one has in mind to eventually return and redeem the fruit".*

הַמִּין הַשִּׁשִּׁי – שֶׁיִּתְלֶה מְצִיאוּת עִנְיָן אֶחָד בִּמְצִיאוּת עִנְיָן אַחֵר.

דֶּרֶךְ מָשָׁל (פסחים פ״ד מ״ד): "וְאִם הָיוּ כֹּהֵן אוֹ עָנִי
לְמוּדִים לֶאֱכֹל אֶצְלוֹ – יָבוֹאוּ וְיֹאכֵלוּ";

(סוכה נג א): "אִם אַתָּה תָּבוֹא אֶל בֵּיתִי – אֲנִי
אָבוֹא אֶל בֵּיתֶךָ".

וְנִקְרָא זֶה מַאֲמָר **תָּלוּי**. וְיִבָּחֲנוּ בּוֹ שְׁנֵי חֲלָקִים: הַקּוֹדֵם וְהַנִּמְשָׁךְ.
**הַקּוֹדֵם** – הוּא הַחֵלֶק שֶׁהֻזְכַּר בּוֹ הַתְּנַאי; דֶּרֶךְ מָשָׁל: "וְאִם הָיוּ כֹּהֵן
אוֹ עָנִי לְמוּדִים לֶאֱכֹל אֶצְלוֹ". **הַנִּמְשָׁךְ** – הוּא הַנִּתְלֶה בָּרִאשׁוֹן; דֶּרֶךְ
מָשָׁל: "יָבוֹאוּ וְיֹאכֵלוּ".

הַמִּין הַשְּׁבִיעִי – מַאֲמָר יֵאָמְרוּ בּוֹ שְׁנֵי נְשׂוּאִים אוֹ יוֹתֵר בְּנוֹשֵׂא
אֶחָד, אוֹ נָשׂוּא אֶחָד בִּשְׁנֵי נוֹשְׂאִים אוֹ יוֹתֵר. וְיִתְחַלֵּק לִשְׁנֵי חֲלָקִים:

הַחֵלֶק הָאֶחָד – שֶׁיֵּאָמְרוּ הַנְּשׂוּאִים בְּנוֹשֵׂא יַחַד, וְכֵן הַנָּשׂוּא
בְּנוֹשְׂאִים.

דֶּרֶךְ מָשָׁל (כלאים פ״ח מ״א): "כִּלְאֵי הַכֶּרֶם אֲסוּרִין

6. **Hypothetical Statement.** This statement establishes that the existence of one thing is dependent on the presence of another.

> *For example, (Demai Chapter 4 Mishnah 4) "A man may not deliver his tithes on the Sabbath, but **if** the Cohen and the poor man regularly eat at his table, **then** he may give them their tithes to eat on the Sabbath".*
>
> *(Sukkah 53a) "The Almighty says, **if** you come into My House, I will come into your house".*

In a hypothetical statement we must always differentiate between two distinct parts: the antecedent and the consequent. The **Antecedent** is the clause which states the condition (in the example above, "*if* the Cohen and the poor man regularly eat at his table"). The **Consequent** is the clause which is dependent on this antecedent ("*then* he may give them their tithes to eat on the Sabbath").

7. **Compound Statement.** These statements have two or more predicates with one subject, or one predicate with two or more subjects. This category has two types.

The first type is called a **Simple Compound.** This includes sentences with multiple predicates, all of which apply to their subject, and likewise sentences with one predicate applying to many subjects at once.

> *For example, (Kil'ayim Chapter 8 Mishnah 1) "Kil'ayim of the vineyard may not be planted or maintained, and it is forbidden to receive bene-*

מִלִּזְרוֹעַ וּמִלָּקַיֵּם וַאֲסוּרִין בַּהֲנָאָה", וְכֵן (תרומות פ"א מ"ז): "אֵין תּוֹרְמִין לֹא בְּמִדָּה וְלֹא בְּמִשְׁקָל וְלֹא בְּמִנְיָן". הִנֵּה כָּאן נֶאֶמְרוּ נְשׂוּאִים שׁוֹנִים, שֶׁהֵם: אִסּוּר הַקִּיּוּם, אִסּוּר הַזְּרִיעָה וְאִסּוּר הַהֲנָאָה בְּכִלְאֵי הַכֶּרֶם, וְכֵן אִסּוּר הַמְּדִידָה וְאִסּוּר הַמִּשְׁקָל וְאִסּוּר הַמִּנְיָן בְּהַפְרָשַׁת הַתְּרוּמָה.

וּכְשֶׁאָמְרוּ (דמאי פ"ו מ"א): "הַמְקַבֵּל שָׂדֶה מִיִּשְׂרָאֵל, מִן הַנָּכְרִי וּמִן הַכּוּתִי – יְחַלֵּק לִפְנֵיהֶם", נֶאֱמַר נָשׂוּא אֶחָד שֶׁהוּא הַחִלּוּק לִפְנֵיהֶם, בִּשְׁלשָׁה נוֹשְׂאִים שֶׁהֵם: הַמְקַבֵּל שָׂדֶה מִן הַכּוּתִי, הַמְקַבְּלוֹ מִיִּשְׂרָאֵל וְהַמְקַבְּלוֹ מִן הַנָּכְרִי.

וְהִנֵּה הַחֵלֶק הַזֶּה יִסְתָּעֵף עוֹד לִשְׁנֵי עֲנָפִים: הָאֶחָד – שֶׁיִּהְיוּ הַנְּשׂוּאִים נֶאֱמָרִים בְּהַשָּׁוָאָה אַחַת בְּנוֹשְׂאֵיהֶם; הַשֵּׁנִי – שֶׁאֶחָד מֵהֶם יֵאָמֵר בְּדֶרֶךְ חָדוּשׁ, וְהָאֶחָד כְּמוֹ עִנְיָן שֶׁכְּבָר נוֹדַע.

דֶּרֶךְ מָשָׁל (מעשר שני פ"א מ"ב): "הַבְּכוֹר מוֹכְרִין אוֹתוֹ: תָּמִים – חַי, וּבַעַל מוּם – חַי וְשָׁחוּט";

*fit from them". Similarly, (Terumos Chapter 1 Mishnah 7) "It is forbidden to give terumah according to any measure, weight or number". In these two examples the subjects have multiple predicates. The prohibitions of maintaining, planting and receiving benefit are predicated on intermingled plants in the vineyard, and the prohibitions of measuring, weighing and counting are predicated on the separation of terumah.*

*(Demai Chapter 6 Mishnah 1) "One who rents a field from a Jew, a non-Jew, and a Cuthean may give the landlord his portion untithed". In this example, one predicate (dividing the produce untithed) is applied to three subjects – one who rents from a Cuthean, one who rents from a Jew, and one who rents from a non-Jew.*

A simple compound statement has two subcategories: one where the predicates are applied to their subjects with equal significance, as in the above examples, and another in which one part of the compound statement is stated as a novel idea and the other as something obvious or previously self-evident.

*For example, (Ma'aser Sheni Chapter 1 Mishnah 2) "An unblemished first-born animal may be sold only when it is alive, but if it is blemished it may be sold alive and also after*

הִנֵּה מְכִירָתוֹ חַי כְּבָר נוֹדַע הֶתֵּרָה, שֶׁהֲרֵי אֲפִלּוּ
בְּתָמִים הִיא מֻתֶּרֶת, רַק מְכִירָתוֹ שָׁחוּט הוּא
הַחִדּוּשׁ שֶׁלֹּא הֻתְּרָה בְּתָמִים.

וְהִנֵּה בְּעִנְיָן זֶה יִמָּצְאוּ שְׁנֵי דְרָכִים: הָאֶחָד הוּא – שֶׁיְּקֻדַּם הַנּוֹדָע,
וְאַחַר כָּךְ יֻזְכַּר הַמְחֻדָּשׁ, וְנִקְרָא זֶה "לֹא זוֹ אַף זוֹ", וְהוּא כַּמָּשָׁל
שֶׁזָּכַרְנוּ "חַי וְשָׁחוּט"; הַשֵּׁנִי – שֶׁיֻּזְכַּר הַמְחֻדָּשׁ תְּחִלָּה וְאַחַר כָּךְ הַנּוֹדָע,
וְזֶה נִקְרָא "זוֹ וְאֵין צָרִיךְ לוֹמַר זוֹ",

דֶּרֶךְ מָשָׁל (כלאים פ"ח מ"א): "וּמֻתָּרִין בַּאֲכִילָה וְכָל
שֶׁכֵּן בַּהֲנָאָה".

הַחֵלֶק הַשֵּׁנִי מֵהַמִּין הַזֶּה – שֶׁיֵּאָמֵר בְּנוֹשֵׂא אֶחָד הֱיוֹתוֹ תָּלוּי בֵּין שְׁנֵי
נְשׂוּאִים אוֹ יוֹתֵר לְהִמָּצֵא בּוֹ אֶחָד מֵהֶם בִּלְבָד.

> *slaughtering". Here, the fact that a blemished animal may be sold when it is alive is obvious, for even an unblemished animal may be sold while alive. Only the fact that it may also be sold after it is slaughtered is a novel idea. For this is not allowed in the case of an unblemished animal, and so I might think that it is also not allowed in this case.*

In the latter subcategory there are two variations. The first is where the self-evident is mentioned before the novel part, and it follows the formula *"not only. . . but even. . .",* as in the above example (not only alive but even slaughtered). The second is where the novel is mentioned before the self-evident, and it follows the formula *"this. . . and needless to say. . . ".*

> *For example, (Kil'ayim Chapter 8 Mishnah 1) "Kil'ayim of grains and vegetables may not be planted or maintained; however, they may be eaten and all other benefit is surely permitted". Here, that they may be eaten is a novel idea and needless to say other benefit is permissible.*

The second type of compound statement is called a **Disjunction**. This type consists of those sentences whose subject is suspended between two or more predicates, and only one of them is actually applied to the subject.

דֶּרֶךְ מָשָׁל (יבמות קי"ג ב): "אוֹ חוֹלֵץ אוֹ מְיַבֵּם".

וְהִנֵּה כָּל הַמִּין הַזֶּה נִקְרָא מֵאֲמַר **מְרֻבֵּה־הָעִנְיָנִים**, שֶׁהוּא מְרֻבֵּה הַנּוֹשְׂאִים אוֹ הַנּוֹשָׂאִים.

הַמִּין הַשְּׁמִינִי – שֶׁיֵּאֲמֵר בְּנוֹשָׂא נָשׂוּא אֶחָד **בִּשְׁלִילַת** נָשׂוּא, אוֹ נוֹשֵׂא אַחֵר.

דֶּרֶךְ מָשָׁל (תרומות פי"א מ"ה): "לֹא יְאַבֵּד אֶת הַשְּׁאָר אֶלָּא יַנִּיחֶנּוּ בְּמָקוֹם מְצֻנָּע".

הַמִּין הַתְּשִׁיעִי – שֶׁיֵּאֲמֵר בְּנוֹשָׂא נָשׂוּא אֶחָד עִם הֱיוֹת בּוֹ נָשׂוּא אַחֵר **מַכְחִישׁ** אוֹתוֹ לִכְאוֹרָה.

דֶּרֶךְ מָשָׁל (מעשרות פ"ה מ"ח): "אַף עַל פִּי שֶׁאֲבִיהֶן תְּרוּמָה – הֲרֵי אֵלּוּ יֵאָכְלוּ", כִּי הִנֵּה הֱיוֹת אֲבִיהֶן תְּרוּמָה לִכְאוֹרָה הוּא מַכְחִישׁ הֶתֵּר אֲכִילַת הַגְּדוֹלִים, אַךְ בָּאֱמֶת אֵינוֹ כֵן.

> *For example, (Yebamos 112b) "He must perform*
> **either** *chalitzah* **or** *leverite marriage".*

Both simple compound statements and disjunctive statements are included in the category of compound statement since they have multiple predicates or subjects.

8. **Preclusive Statement.** Statements in which one predicate is applied to the subject and another predicate is excluded, or where the predicate is affirmed in one subject and some other subject is rejected.

> *For example, (Terumos Chapter 11 Mishnah 5)*
> *"In the case of terumah, one who sifts a kav or*
> *two of fine flour from a se'ah of wheat must*
> *not discard the remainder, but must rather put*
> *it in a hidden place".*

9. **Statement of Discrepancy.** There is one subject to which a certain predicate is applied together with another predicate that apparently contradicts the first.

> *For example, (Ma'aseros Chapter 5 Mishnah 8)*
> *"Seeds which are not normally considered food*
> *may be eaten by a non-Cohen,* **even though**
> *they came from plants which were terumah".*
> *The fact that these seeds come from a stock of*
> *terumah is an apparent contradiction to the*
> *ruling that they may be eaten by anyone.*
> *However, there is, in fact, no conflict.*

הַמִּין הָעֲשִׂירִי – שֶׁיֵּאָמֵר בּוֹ עִנְיָן בִּדְמִיּוֹן עִם עִנְיָן אַחֵר.

דֶּרֶךְ מָשָׁל (לחולין פ"ו מ"ה): "כְּשֵׁם שֶׁחוֹלְקִין בַּחֻלִּין –
כָּךְ חוֹלְקִין בַּתְּרוּמָה".

וְהִנֵּה בָּזֶה תִרְאֶה, שֶׁתָּמִיד יִקַּח עִנְיָן נוֹדָע וְיַשְׁוֶה לוֹ אַחֵר בִּלְתִּי נוֹדָע.

דֶּרֶךְ מָשָׁל בַּמַּאֲמָר שֶׁזָּכַרְנוּ, הִנֵּה חִלּוּקָם בַּחֻלִּין
הוּא נוֹדָע, וְהִשְׁוָה לוֹ הַחִלּוּק בַּתְּרוּמָה גַּם כֵּן,
וְגָזַר הֱיוֹתָם שָׁוִים בְּמִקַּבֵּל זֵיתִים לְשַׁמְּן.

וְנִקְרָא זֶה מַאֲמָר **מְדֻמֶּה**.

הַמִּין הָאַחַד-עָשָׂר – שֶׁיֵּאָמֵר בּוֹ נָשׂוּא **נִמְשָׁךְ** מִנָּשׂוּא אַחֵר.

דֶּרֶךְ מָשָׁל (מעשרות פ"ב מ"א): "הָיָה עוֹבֵר בַּשּׁוּק,
וְאָמַר: טְלוּ לָכֶם תְּאֵנִים – אוֹכְלִים וּפְטוּרִים,

10. **Comparative Statement.** In this statement an assertion is made on the basis of a comparison to some other topic. The rule in this type of sentence is that a known subject is always taken as the basis of comparison, and another unknown subject is equated to it.

> For example, *(Demai Chapter 6 Mishnah 5)* *"If a Jew rents olive trees from a Cohen or Levite for the olive oil, he and the landlord share the terumah just as they share the remaining produce"*. *Here, the method of apportioning ordinary produce is according to agreement, and this is known. The apportioning of terumah is equated to it, and the statement affirms their similarity in the case where one rents olive trees for their oil. (In the case where one rents* **land** *from a Cohen or Levite the ruling is that the terumah is given entirely to the landlord.)*

11. **Consequent Statement.** In this statement one predicate is stated as a consequence of another.

> For example, *(Ma'aseros Chapter 2 Mishnah 1)* *"When a man in the market passes by saying, 'Take some of my figs to eat', they may be eaten and they are exempt from tithes;* **therefore,** *upon bringing these figs into one's house the obligation to tithe is a certainty"*. *The undoubted obligation to tithe is a* **consequence** *of the*

לְפִיכָךְ אִם הִכְנִיסוּ לְבָתֵּיהֶם – מְתַקְּנִים וַדַּאי".

וּמַה שֶּׁצָּרִיךְ שֶׁתֵּדַע עוֹד, כִּי הִנֵּה דְּרָכִים רַבִּים יֵשׁ לִבְנֵי הָאָדָם לְפָרֵשׁ בִּלְשׁוֹנָם מַה שֶׁחָשְׁבוּ בְּמַחֲשַׁבְתָּם, כִּי הִנֵּה יֵשׁ שֶׁיַּאֲרִיכוּ בְּדִבְרֵיהֶם וְיֵשׁ שֶׁיְּקַצְּרוּ בָהֶם, יֵשׁ שֶׁיְּדַבְּרוּ בְּדֶרֶךְ הַגָּדָה, וְיֵשׁ שֶׁיְּדַבְּרוּ בְּדֶרֶךְ תְּמִיהָה, וְיֵשׁ שֶׁיְּדַבְּרוּ בְּדֶרֶךְ רֶמֶז; וּכְבָר נִתְבָּאֲרוּ כָּל הַחִלּוּקִים הָאֵלֶּה אֵצֶל בַּעֲלֵי הַדִּקְדּוּק וְהַמְּלִיצָה. אַךְ מַה שֶּׁצָּרִיךְ לָנוּ עַתָּה הוּא, כִּי כָל דִּבּוּר שֶׁיֵּאָמֵר, יִהְיֶה בְּאֵיזֶה סֵדֶר וְדֶרֶךְ שֶׁיִּהְיֶה, כְּשֶׁנֵּרֵד לְסוֹף כַּוָּנַת מְדַבְּרוֹ, נִמְצָא וַדַּאי שֶׁרָצָה בּוֹ אֲמִירַת נָשׂוּא בַּנּוֹשֵׂא, כִּי זוּלַת זֶה לֹא הָיָה בְּדִבּוּרוֹ מַמָּשׁ, וְלֹא הָיָה מִצְטַיֵּר מִמֶּנּוּ בְּשֵׂכֶל שׁוֹמְעוֹ שׁוּם צִיּוּר שָׁלֵם. וְלָכֵן אַל תָּשֶׁת לִבְּךָ אֶל דֶּרֶךְ הַדִּבּוּר אֶלָּא אֶל הַמַּאֲמָר הַמְכֻוָּן בּוֹ. וְאִם תִּרְאֶה הַדִּבּוּר קָצָר – תַּשְׁלִימֵהוּ בְּמַחֲשַׁבְתֶּךָ, וְאִם תִּרְאֵהוּ אָרֹךְ – תָּסִיר מִמֶּנּוּ אֶת הַמּוֹתָר, וְלֹא תְצַיֵּר בְּמַחֲשַׁבְתְּךָ אֶלָּא הַנּוֹשֵׂא שֶׁעָלָיו יְדַבֵּר וְהַנָּשׂוּא שֶׁיֵּאָמֵר בּוֹ וְהַדֶּרֶךְ שֶׁיֹּאמְרֵהוּ בּוֹ, וּכְמוֹ שֶׁאָמַרְתִּי לְעֵיל.

*fact that the figs were permissible before being brought into the house. For when an unlearned man carries produce through the market with no specific intent to sell, it is assumed that he never brought it into his own house from the field, and thus there is no obligation to tithe such produce in the marketplace. By the same token, the figs must certainly be tithed by the recipient in his own house since they were under no obligation to be tithed previously.*

In addition to being able to differentiate these eleven categories, it is essential to understand that people express their thoughts in words in various styles. Some use many words while others are exceedingly brief. Some people speak literally, while others speak rhetorically or metaphorically. These distinctions are well known in the disciplines of grammar and rhetoric. However, our current concern is simply this: no matter what order or manner of expression is used, when we penetrate the intention of a statement, we discover that the speaker desires to apply a particular predicate to a subject. Otherwise, his words have no substance, and no complete thought can be formed in the mind of the listener. Therefore, do not fix your attention on the manner of speech, but on the intended statement contained in the words. If the expression is condensed, you must supply what is missing in your mind, and if it is more lengthy, you must remove the extraneous parts, forming a conceptual image of the abstracted subject, predicate, and type of predication, as explained above.

דֶּרֶךְ מָשָׁל, כְּשֶׁתִּמְצָא (פסחים ז ג): "הָתָם הֵיכִי
נֵימָא? נֵימָא "לָמוּל" – לָא סַגִּיָא דְּלָאו אִיהוּ
מָהִיל". הִנֵּה זֶה לָשׁוֹן קְצָרָה – וּבְדֶרֶךְ תְּמִיהָה.
אַךְ הַכַּוָּנָה בָּזֶה הִיא, שֶׁשָּׁם אֵינוֹ יָכוֹל לְבָרֵךְ
אֶלָּא "עַל הַמִּילָה", לְפִי שֶׁאֵין שָׁם מָקוֹם לוֹמַר
"לָמוּל", מִפְּנֵי שֶׁאֵינוֹ מֻכְרָח שֶׁיִּהְיֶה הוּא הַמָּל.
וְנִמְצָא, שֶׁזֶּה מַה שֶּׁצָּרִיךְ שֶׁתְּצַיֵּר בְּמַחֲשַׁבְתְּךָ
מִתּוֹךְ כָּל הַמִּלּוֹת הָהֵן.

*For example, (Pesachim 7b) Rav Pappi said in Raba's name, one must bless "who has commanded us to remove leaven" and not "who has commanded us concerning the removal of leaven", because the latter implies an action which is already done. This would be invalid since a blessing must be said before the fulfillment of the commandment. An objection was raised from a text which states that on circumcision the blessing is "who has commanded us concerning circumcision". At this point, the Gemorah answers, "In that case how else could he say it?! Should he say 'to circumcise'? But is it only the Mohel who may circumcise?" In this answer, the Gemorah uses a concise expression and a rhetorical style. But the content of the statement is simply that the Mohel has no alternative but to bless "concerning circumcision". (This is an exclusive statement.) The reason for this is that, since he is not necessarily the one who must circumcise, it is impossible for him to bless "to circumcise". (This is a consequent statement.) These are the two statements that should be abstracted in your mind from all the words of the Gemorah.*

וְכֵן כְּשֶׁחָזַר וְאָמַר "אֲבִי הַבֵּן מַאי אִכָּא
לְמֵימַר", הַכַּוָּנָה שֶׁאֲבִי הַבֵּן צָרִיךְ שֶׁיֹּאמַר
"לָמוּל" לְפִי מַה שֶׁהִנִּיחַ שָׁם בַּתְּחִלָּה; וּכְשֶׁהֵשִׁיב
"אִין הָכִי נַמֵּי", הַכַּוָּנָה שֶׁכָּךְ הִיא הָאֱמֶת, פֵּרוּשׁ
שֶׁאֲבִי הַבֵּן צָרִיךְ שֶׁיֹּאמַר "לָמוּל". –

וְעַל דֶּרֶךְ זֶה תָּדוּן בְּכָל הַלְּשׁוֹנוֹת כֻּלָּן.

*The Gemorah continues, "What can you say in the case where the father circumcises his own son?" Here the abstracted statement is: according to your original understanding, the father should bless "to circumcise" and not "concerning circumcision". (This is a preclusive statement.) According to Rav Pappi, there should be a distinction between the Mohel and the father since it is only in the case of the Mohel that we say he cannot bless "to circumcise" because of the ensuing misconception that the obligation falls primarily on him and not on the father of the child.*

*The Gemorah answers: "Yes, this is indeed the case". That is to say, it is, in fact, true that the father should say "to circumcise". (This is a simple statement.)*

In every text this method of abstraction should be applied.

# פרק ד

הִנֵּה עַד הֵנָּה בֵּאַרְנוּ מַה שֶּׁנָּבִין מֵהַמַּאֲמָרִים, כָּל אֶחָד בִּפְנֵי עַצְמוֹ. עַתָּה נְבָאֵר מַה שֶּׁנָּבִין מֵהַעֲרִיךְ מַאֲמָר עִם מַאֲמָר אַחֵר. בִּבְחִינַת עֶרְכָּם וְיַחֲסָם, מִתְחַלְּקִים הַמַּאֲמָרִים לְשִׁשָּׁה מִינִים, וְהֵם: הַדּוֹמִים, הַמִּתְחַלְּפִים, הַהֲפָכִיִּים, הַחִלּוּפִיִּים, הַמִּתְהַפְּכִים וְהַנִּבְדָּלִים.

**הַדּוֹמִים** הֵם שְׁנֵי מַאֲמָרִים שֶׁיֹּאמְרוּ נָשׂוֹא אֶחָד בְּנוֹשֵׂא אֶחָד עַצְמוֹ, אֶלָּא שֶׁבְּאֹפֶן הָאֲמִירָה וְסֵדֶר הַדִּבּוּר יִהְיוּ מִתְחַלְּפִים; אוֹ שֶׁיֹּאמְרוּ נָשׂוֹא אֶחָד אוֹ שְׁנֵי נְשׂוֹאִים דּוֹמִים בִּשְׁנֵי נוֹשְׂאִים דּוֹמִים, אוֹ שֶׁיֹּאמְרוּ שְׁנֵי נְשׂוֹאִים דּוֹמִים בְּנוֹשֵׂא אֶחָד.

דֶּרֶךְ מָשָׁל, כְּשֶׁאָמְרוּ (כתובות לו ג): "רַבִּי יְהוּדָה וְרַבִּי דּוֹסָא אָמְרוּ דָּבָר אֶחָד, רַבִּי יְהוּדָה – הָא דְאָמְרָן, רַבִּי דּוֹסָא – דְּתַנְיָא: שְׁבוּיָה אוֹכֶלֶת בִּתְרוּמָה" וְכוּ', הִנֵּה אַף עַל פִּי שֶׁאֵין מִלּוֹתֵיהֶם שָׁווֹת, תִּמָּצֵא שֶׁכַּוָּנָתָם אַחַת.

# Chapter Four

Up to this point we have explained those things which may be understood in isolated statements. Now we shall concern ourselves with the juxtaposition of one statement with another. If we consider the arrangement and relationship between two statements we can discern six types, and they are: equivalent, variant, contradictory, converse, obverse and incongruent.

1. **Equivalent Statements** have identical subjects and predicates, but the manner of expression and the order of the sentence may be varied. Alternatively, they may have a single predicate or two similar predicates applied to two similar subjects, or they may have two similar predicates applied to the same identical subject.

> *For example, (Kesubos 36b) "Rabbi Yehudah and Rabbi Dosa have both said the same thing; Rabbi Yehudah – that which we have learned [in the Mishnah: If a female captive is ransomed, she is deemed a virgin even if she is of age], and Rabbi Dosa – as it is taught, a female captive [who is the daughter or wife of a Cohen] may eat terumah, etc.". In this case, even though their words differ, their statements are identical since the wife or daughter of a Cohen would be forbidden to eat terumah unless we presumed that she had not been violated by her captors.*

48

וְכֵן כְּשֶׁאָמְרוּ (פסחים פג ג): "רַבִּי יוֹחָנָן בֶּן בְּרוֹקָה
וְרַבִּי נְחֶמְיָה אָמְרוּ דָּבָר אֶחָד" וְכוּ', וּמְסַיֵּם
שָׁם "וְהָא אֲנִינוּת כִּלְאַחַר זְרִיקָה הַוְיָא" וְכוּ',
הִנֵּה אֵין שְׁנֵי הָעִנְיָנִים שֵׁם אֶחָד, אֶלָּא דּוֹמִים
זֶה לָזֶה.

*Similarly the Gemorah states, (Pesachim 82b) "Rabbi Yochanan said: Rabbi Yochanan ben Berokah and Rabbi Nechemiah said the same thing. Rabbi Yochanan ben Berokah said, If the owners of the Passover sacrifice were defiled even after the sprinkling of the blood, the animal must be burnt immediately'. Rabbi Nechemiah said, 'Aharon's sin offering was burnt immediately because of bereavement'". The Gemorah concludes by telling us that the cases are similar: "Behold, the defilement of a sin offering through bereavement [before the sprinkling of the blood] is like the defilement of a Passover sacrifice that occurs after the sprinkling of the blood". The Gemorah tells us that these two subjects are comparable even though they are not the same. For the defilement of a sin offering may be prior to the sprinkling of the blood while the defilement of a Passover sacrifice must not occur prior to the sprinkling of the blood. However, in both cases, the defilement which occurred does not invalidate the sprinkling of the blood, and the law which is predicated is the same, i.e., that the animal nonetheless may not be eaten and must be burnt immediately.*

**הַמִּתְחַלְּפִים** הֵם שְׁנֵי מַאֲמָרִים שֶׁיֵּאָמְרוּ בְּנוֹשֵׂא אֶחָד שְׁנֵי נְשׂוּאִים מִתְחַלְּפִים, אוֹ נָשׂוּא אֶחָד בִּשְׁנֵי נוֹשְׂאִים מִתְחַלְּפִים.

דֶּרֶךְ מָשָׁל (כתובות כז א): "רַבִּי טַרְפוֹן אוֹמֵר: נוֹתְנִין לָהּ הַכֹּל תְּרוּמָה; רַבִּי עֲקִיבָא אוֹמֵר: מֶחֱצָה חֻלִּין וּמֶחֱצָה תְּרוּמָה".

**הַהֲפָכִיִּים** הֵם שֶׁיֵּאָמְרוּ עַל נָשׂוּא אֶחָד בְּנוֹשֵׂא אֶחָד, אֶחָד – הֵן וְאֶחָד – לָאו.

דֶּרֶךְ מָשָׁל (יבמות נ א): "רַבָּן גַּמְלִיאֵל אוֹמֵר: אֵין גֵּט אַחַר גֵּט וְלֹא מַאֲמָר אַחַר מַאֲמָר; וַחֲכָמִים אוֹמְרִים: יֵשׁ גֵּט אַחַר גֵּט וְיֵשׁ מַאֲמָר אַחַר מַאֲמָר".

2. **Variant Statements** have the same subjects, but the predicates are changed in some way, or the predicates may be the same and the subjects are changed.

> *For example, (Kesubos 57a) "Rabbi Tarfon said, a Cohen may support his wife entirely with terumah. Rabbi Akiva said, half of her support must be profane and half may be terumah".*

3. **Opposite Statements** have identical subjects, but the same predicate that is affirmed in one satement is denied in the other.

> *For example, (Yebamos 50a) "Raban Gamliel said there is no validity for a Get after a Get or Ma'amar after Ma'amar. The rabbis said there is validity for a Get after a Get and for Ma'amar after Ma'amar". Raban Gamliel's view is that when a man gives bills of divorce to the two widows of his deceased brother, the first is valid to prevent the leverite marriage and the second is invalid and does not even render this man forbidden to the women's relatives. The ruling of the rabbis is that her relatives are forbidden to marry him. Similarly, Raban Gamliel states that when he gives a pledge of marriage to each of the two widows, the first is valid and the second is not. The rabbis argue that the second is equally valid, and, since he cannot be mar-*

וְאוּלָם לְשֶׁיִּקָּרְאוּ הַפְכִּיִּים, צָרִיךְ שֶׁיִּהְיוּ נְשׂוּאָם אֶחָד וְנוֹשְׂאָם אֶחָד , וְיוּבְנוּ בִּזְמַן אֶחָד, בְּמָקוֹם אֶחָד, בִּבְחִינָה אַחַת וּבַהֲבָנָה פְּשׁוּטָה בְּלִי שׁוּם שִׁתּוּף וְהַשְׁאָלָה.

פֵּרוּשׁ, כִּי הִנֵּה מַאֲמָר (שבת סב א): "לֹא תֵצֵא אִשָּׁה לֹא בְטוֹטֶפֶת וְלֹא בְסַנְבּוּטִין", וּמַאֲמָר: "יוֹצְאָה אִשָּׁה בְּטוֹטֶפֶת וּבְסַנְבּוּטִין" אֵינָם הַפְכִּיִּים, לְפִי שֶׁהָאֶחָד הוּא בִּזְמַן שֶׁאֵינָם תְּפוּרִים, וְהַשֵּׁנִי בִּזְמַן שֶׁהֵם תְּפוּרִים.

וְכֵן (שבת סב א): "וְלֹא בְכָבוּל" עִם "יוֹצֵאת בְּכָבוּל" אֵינָם הַפְכִּיִּים, כִּי אֵינָם בְּמָקוֹם אֶחָד, כִּי הָאֶחָד – לִרְשׁוּת הָרַבִּים, וְהַשֵּׁנִי – לֶחָצֵר.

וְכֵן בִּשְׁאָר הַתְּנָאִים שֶׁזָּכַרְנוּ.

*ried to both women, he consequently can marry*
*neither.*

Before we can say that satements are opposite they must have
the same predicates and the same subjects, and also they must be
understood in the same time, place and context. All the terms must
be used in their primary meanings, that is, none should be used as a
homonym or metaphor.

> *In this way, we understand that the following*
> *satements – (Shabbos 57a) "A woman **may***
> ***not** go out with frontlets and garlands" and "A*
> *woman **may** go out with frontlets and gar-*
> *lands" – are not actually contrary because the*
> *first is applicable when they are not sewn into*
> *her wig and the second when they are sewn in.*
>
> *Likewise, the statements (Shabbos 57a) "She*
> *should **not** go out with a hair net" and "She*
> ***may** go out with a hair net" are not contrary.*
> *These statements do not refer to the same place,*
> *since the first refers to the public domain and*
> *the second to a courtyard.*

Similarly, you must test opposite statements in every other aspect in order to be sure that their subjects and predicates are the
same.

וְכֵן מַאֲמָר (עירובין קג ב): "וְאִם תָּקַע – חַיָּב
חַטָּאת" אֵינוֹ הַפְכִּי לְמַאֲמָר (ראש השנה כט ב):
"תְּקִיעַת שׁוֹפָר וּרְדִיַּת הַפַּת חָכְמָה הִיא וְאֵינָהּ
מְלָאכָה", כִּי הֲבָנַת הָרִאשׁוֹן הִיא תְּקִיעַת הַצִּיר
בַּחוֹר שֶׁלּוֹ, וַהֲבָנַת הַשֵּׁנִי – הַתְּקִיעָה בַּשּׁוֹפָר.

וְצָרִיךְ שֶׁתֵּדַע, כִּי בַּהֲפָכִיִּים עַצְמָם יֵשׁ **הַפְכִּיִּים מַמָּשׁ** שֶׁהֵם מִן
הַקָּצֶה אֶל הַקָּצֶה, וְיֵשׁ שֶׁאֵינָם הַפְכִּיִּים כָּל כָּךְ, אַךְ עַל כָּל פָּנִים
מַכְחִישִׁים זֶה אֶת זֶה, וְנִקְרָאִים **מִתְנַגְּדִים.**

שְׁנֵי מַאֲמָרִים כְּלָלִיִּים אוֹ שְׁנֵי מַאֲמָרִים פְּרָטִיִּים, שֶׁאֶחָד יְחַיֵּב
וְאֶחָד יִשְׁלוֹל נָשׂוֹא אֶחָד בְּנוֹשֵׂא אֶחָד, הֵם הַהֲפָכִיִּים מִן הַקָּצֶה אֶל
הַקָּצֶה.

דֶּרֶךְ מָשָׁל (שבת קכד א): "כָּל הַכֵּלִים נִטָּלִין לְצֹרֶךְ
וְשֶׁלֹּא לְצֹרֶךְ; רַבִּי נְחֶמְיָה אוֹמֵר: אֵין נִטָּלִין
אֶלָּא לְצֹרֶךְ" – אֵלֶּה שְׁנֵי מַאֲמָרִים הֵם
הַהֲפָכִיִּים מַמָּשׁ, שֶׁשְּׁנֵיהֶם כְּלָלִיִּים.

*For example, the statement (Eruvin 102b) "If he gives a **blow** he is obligated for a sin offering [since this is a forbidden activity on the Sabbath]" is not in opposition to (Rosh Hashanah 29b) "**Blowing** the shofar and taking down bread from the oven are considered a skill and not a forbidden activity". The term "blow" is a homonym, for in the first satement it means a blow which is given to drive a peg into its socket, and in the second it refers to the blowing of the shofar.*

Take note that the category of opposite statements includes **Diametrically Opposed Statements,** and statements which are not altogether opposed although they still contradict. The latter group is called **Contradictory Statements.**

Two general or two particular statements, one of which affirms a particular predicate in a subject while the other negates it, are diametrically opposed.

*For example, (Shabbos 124a) "All utensils whose normal use is permitted **are not** mukzeh whether a person handles them to use them or not. Rabbi Nechemiah said all utensils whose normal use is permitted **are** mukzeh unless they are handled to use". These two statements are diametrically opposed since they are both general, and even though the first Tanna and*

(שבת כח ג): "רַבִּי אֱלִיעֶזֶר אוֹמֵר: טְמֵאָה הִיא
וְאֵין מַדְלִיקִין בָּהּ; רַבִּי עֲקִיבָא אוֹמֵר: טְהוֹרָה
הִיא וּמַדְלִיקִין בָּהּ" – הֲפָכִיים מַמָּשׁ, שֶׁשְּׁנֵיהֶם
פְּרָטִיִּים.

אַךְ מַאֲמָר (שבת עו ג): "וּמִצְטָרְפִין זֶה עִם זֶה,
מִפְּנֵי שֶׁשָּׁווּ בְּשִׁעוּרֵיהֶן, חוּץ מִקְּלִפֵּיהֶן" עִם
מַאֲמָר "רַבִּי יְהוּדָה אוֹמֵר: חוּץ מִקְּלִפֵּי
עֲדָשִׁים" – אֵינָם הֲפָכִיים, אֶלָּא מִתְנַגְּדִים, כִּי
תַּנָּא קַמָּא אָמַר עַל הַקְּלִפִּין שֶׁאֵינָם מִצְטָרְפִים
עִם הָאֹכֶל, וְרַבִּי יְהוּדָה אוֹמֵר עַל קְלִפֵּי
הָעֲדָשִׁים לְבַדָּם שֶׁמִּצְטָרְפִים עִם הָאֹכֶל,
וְנִמְצָא מַאֲמָר תַּנָּא קַמָּא – כְּלָלִי, וּמַאֲמָר רַבִּי
יְהוּדָה – פְּרָטִי, וּכְבָר יוֹדֶה רַבִּי יְהוּדָה לַתַּנָּא

*Rabbi Nechemiah appear to agree in the case where he handles the utensils to use them, they are actually diametrically opposed in their definition of mukzeh.*

*Another example: (Shabbos 28b) "Rabbi Eleazar said a piece of cloth rolled into a wick is ritually unclean, and it is forbidden to light it on the Sabbath. Rabbi Akiva said, it is ritually clean and one may light it on the Sabbath". These statements are also diametric opposites, and in this case, they are particular.*

*The following two statements in the Mishnah (Shabbos 76b) are not absolute opposites but contradictory statements: "One who carries out foodstuffs on the Sabbath is liable for anything as large as a fig and all kinds of food are added together to make up this measurement except for inedible husks. Rabbi Yehudah said, this excludes the husks of lentils". The ruling of the first Tanna is that all husks **are not** added to the food, while Rabbi Yehudah states that the husks of lentils alone **are** added to the food. Thus the statement of the first Tanna is general, and the statement of Rabbi Yehudah is particular. However, Rabbi Yehudah agrees with the first Tanna that all other husks are*

## קַמָּא בְּשֶׁאַר הַפְּרָטִים הַנִּכְלָלִים בִּכְלַל הַקְּלָפִין.

וְצָרִיךְ שֶׁתֵּדַע עוֹד, שֶׁכְּמוֹ שֶׁהֵם הַפְּכִיִּים הַשְּׁלִילָה וְהַקִּיּוּם, כָּךְ הֵם הַפְּכִיִּים שְׁנֵי עִנְיָנִים, שֶׁהַכַּוָּנָה בְּכָל אֶחָד מֵהֶם שְׁלִילַת חֲבֵרוֹ. דֶּרֶךְ מָשָׁל: "טָמֵא" וְ"טָהוֹר" הֵם הַפְּכִיִּים, כִּי כַּוָּנַת מִלַּת "טָמֵא" הִיא שְׁלִילַת הַטָּהֳרָה, וְכַוָּנַת "טָהוֹר" – שְׁלִילַת הַטֻּמְאָה. אָמְנָם צָרִיךְ שֶׁתֵּדַע, שֶׁיֵּשׁ הַפְּכִיִּים שֶׁבֵּינֵיהֶם אֶמְצָעִי, וְהַפְּכִיִּים שֶׁאֵין בֵּינֵיהֶם אֶמְצָעִי. דֶּרֶךְ מָשָׁל: "טָמֵא וְטָהוֹר" "אָסוּר וּמֻתָּר" – אֵין בֵּינֵיהֶם אֶמְצָעִי, אַךְ "רְשׁוּת וְחוֹבָה" – יֵשׁ בֵּינֵיהֶם אֶמְצָעִי שֶׁהוּא "מִצְוָה".

עוֹד יֵשׁ מַאֲמָרִים, שֶׁאֶחָד הוּא **חִלּוּפוֹ** מַמָּשׁ שֶׁל חֲבֵרוֹ; פֵּרוּשׁ שֶׁמַּה שֶׁהוּא הַנּוֹשֵׂא בָּאֶחָד יִהְיֶה הַנָּשׂוּא בַּשֵּׁנִי, וּמַה שֶׁהוּא נָשׂוּא בָּאֶחָד יִהְיֶה הַנּוֹשֵׂא בַּשֵּׁנִי.

דֶּרֶךְ מָשָׁל, כְּשֶׁתֹּאמַר (ירושלמי שבת פי"ג ה"ג): "רַבִּי יוֹנָה אָמַר: אֵין עֲבֵרָה מִצְוָה; רַבִּי יוֹסָה אָמַר: אֵין מִצְוָה עֲבֵרָה". הִנֵּה בָּאֶחָד, עֲבֵרָה הִיא נוֹשֵׂא, וּמִצְוָה – נָשׂוּא, וּבַשֵּׁנִי – לְהֵפֶךְ.

*added to the food in order to make up the
necessary measurement.*

Furthermore, just as statements may be opposite because one is affirmative and the other negative, so also they may be opposite through the affirmation of contradictory terms, i.e., when one term implies the exclusion of the other. For example, "clean" and "unclean" are contradictory terms since "clean" is the negation of "unclean" and vice versa. However, some contradictory terms have a mean term between them and others do not. For example, "clean" and "unclean", and "forbidden" and "permitted", have no mean term between them. But the terms "optional" and "obligatory" have a mean term, which is "praiseworthy".

4. There is another category of statements where one is the absolute **Converse** of the other. Whatever is the subject of the first becomes the predicate of the second, and what is the predicate of the first becomes the subject of the second.

*For example, one might say, "A sin is not a
mitzvah. A mitzvah is not a sin". In the first
statement the subject is a sin and the predicate
is a mitzvah. In the second statement it is reversed. The subject is a mitzvah and the predicate is a sin.*

וְאוּלָם הַחִלּוּף הַזֶּה יוּכַל לִהְיוֹת בִּשְׁלֹשָׁה דְּרָכִים:

הָאֶחָד – שֶׁיִּתְחַלֵּף **הַסֵּדֶר**, פֵּרוּשׁ, הַנּוֹשֵׂא וְהַנָּשׂוּא; וְתִשָּׁאֵר **הַכַּמּוּת**, פֵּרוּשׁ, שֶׁאִם הָיָה כְּלָלִי – יִשָּׁאֵר כְּלָלִי, וְאִם פְּרָטִי – יִשָּׁאֵר פְּרָטִי, וְכֵן **הַגְּזֵרָה**, פֵּרוּשׁ, שֶׁאִם הָיָה מְקַיֵּם יִשָּׁאֵר מְקַיֵּם, וְאִם שׁוֹלֵל – יִשָּׁאֵר שׁוֹלֵל. דֶּרֶךְ מָשָׁל, שְׁנֵי הַמַּאֲמָרִים שֶׁזָּכַרְנוּ: "אֵין עֲבֵרָה מִצְוָה" וְ"אֵין מִצְוָה עֲבֵרָה".

הַשֵּׁנִי – שֶׁיִּתְחַלֵּף הַסֵּדֶר וְגַם הַכַּמּוּת, אַךְ הַגְּזֵרָה תִּתְקַיֵּם;

דֶּרֶךְ מָשָׁל מַאֲמָר (יבמות סו א): "כֹּל שֶׁאֵינוֹ אוֹכֵל אֵינוּ מַאֲכִיל" עִם מַאֲמָר "יֵשׁ שֶׁאֵינוֹ מַאֲכִיל וְאֵינוֹ אוֹכֵל", שֶׁהָאֶחָד – כְּלָלִי, וְהַשֵּׁנִי – קְצָתִי.

הַשְּׁלִישִׁי – שֶׁיִּתְחַלְּפוּ הַסֵּדֶר וְהַגְּזֵרָה, וְתִשָּׁאֵר הַכַּמּוּת;

In the category of converse statements, three types are possible:

The first, which is a **Complete Converse**, changes the **order** of the statement, i.e., the subject and predicate are interchanged. However, the **distribution** of the statement remains unchanged, i.e., if it is general it remains general and if it is particular it remains particular. Also the **manner of predication** remains the same, i.e., the converse statements are both affirmative or both negative. An example of this type is the statements previously mentioned, "A sin is not a mitzvah. A mitzvah is not a sin".

The second type is a **Limited Converse**. The order of the statement is changed along with the distribution, but the manner of predication remains unchanged.

> *These statements are examples of limited converse: (Yebamos 66a) "All who may not eat terumah may not confer on others the right to eat terumah". "There are some who may not confer the right to eat terumah, and also they themselves cannot eat terumah". In this example, the first statement is general and the second is particular.*

The third type, which is a **Contrapositive Converse**, changes the manner of predication (i.e., if one statement is affirmative the other will be negative) and also subject and predicate are exchanged; however, the distribution remains the same.

דֶּרֶךְ מָשָׁל: "כָּל הָאוֹכֵל מַאֲכִיל" עִם מַאֲמָר "כֹּל שֶׁאֵינוֹ מַאֲכִיל אֵינוֹ אוֹכֵל".

**הַמִּתְהַפְּכִים** הֵם אוֹתָם שֶׁנּוֹשְׂאֵיהֶם וְנוֹשְׂאֵיהֶם שְׁנֵיהֶם הַפְּכִיִּים וְנִמְצָא עִנְיָנָם אֶחָד.

דֶּרֶךְ מָשָׁל "כָּל הָאוֹכֵל מַאֲכִיל, כֹּל שֶׁאֵינוֹ אוֹכֵל אֵינוֹ מַאֲכִיל".

אַךְ הַמַּאֲמָרִים שֶׁאֵין לָהֶם יַחַס מִשְׁתָּף כְּלָל, פֵּרוּשׁ, שֶׁאֵין נוֹשְׂאֵיהֶם וְלֹא נְשׂוּאֵיהֶם אֶחָד, וְגַם לֹא דוֹמִים כְּלָל, יִקָּרְאוּ **נִבְדָּלִים**.

> *For example, "All who may eat terumah may*
> *also confer the right on others to eat terumah.*
> *All who may not confer the right to eat*
> *terumah may not themselves eat terumah".*
> *These statements are contrapositive.*

5. **Obverse Statements** are those whose subjects and predicates are both opposites of one another, and thus their content is the same.

> *For example, "All who may eat terumah may*
> *confer the right on others to eat terumah. All*
> *who may not eat terumah may not confer on*
> *others the right to eat terumah".*

6. The last category is called **Incongruent Statements**. These have no common ground at all, that is, their subjects and predicates are not equivalent terms or even the least bit similar.

# פרק ה

הִנֵּה עַד הֵנָּה דִּבַּרְנוּ מִמַּה שֶּׁמִּצְטַיֵּר בְּשִׂכְלֵנוּ מִן הַמַּאֲמָרִים שֶׁנִּקְרָא אוֹ שֶׁנִּשְׁמַע, אָמְנָם עוֹד נֶחְקַק בְּטִבְעֵנוּ לְהִתְבּוֹנֵן מִתּוֹךְ הַנִּשְׁמָע מַה שֶּׁלֹּא נִשְׁמַע, מִפְּנֵי הֱיוֹתוֹ מִתְחַבֵּר בְּהֶכְרֵחַ עִם הַנִּשְׁמָע.

דֶּרֶךְ מָשָׁל, כְּשֶׁאָמְרָה הַתּוֹרָה (ויקרא יא ב): "זֹאת הַחַיָּה אֲשֶׁר תֹּאכֵלוּ", הִנֵּה מַאֲמָר זֶה נָבִין תְּחִלָּה כְּפִי הֲבָנַת מִלּוֹתָיו אֵלּוּ, שֶׁאֵלֶּה הַמִּינִים הַמֻּזְכָּרִים בַּפָּרָשָׁה, מֻתָּר לָנוּ לֶאֱכֹל אוֹתָם; אָמְנָם אִי אֶפְשָׁר לָנוּ שֶׁלֹּא נָבִין מִזֶּה גַּם כֵּן, שֶׁשְּׁאָר הַמִּינִים זוּלַת אֵלֶּה, אֵינָם מֻתָּרִים לָנוּ. וְכֵן כְּשֶׁאָמַר (שמואל ב כג א): "וְאֵלֶּה דִּבְרֵי דָוִד הָאַחֲרוֹנִים", נִתְבּוֹנֵן מִזֶּה "מִכְּלָל דְּאִיכָּא רִאשׁוֹנִים" (מועד קטן טז ב), כִּי אִי אֶפְשָׁר לְהָבִין אַחֲרוֹן מִבְּלִי רִאשׁוֹן.

וְאוּלָם כָּל מַה שֶּׁאָנוּ מְבִינִים מִתּוֹךְ מַאֲמָר אֶחָד וְלֹא פֵרַשׁ בּוֹ, נִקְרָאֵהוּ דִּיּוּק. וְעַתָּה נְבָאֵר מִשְׁפָּטָיו.

# Chapter Five

Up to this point we have been discussing the elements of written or oral statements from which the mind forms conceptions. However, in addition to this basic communication, the mind automatically understands other unstated meanings that are connected to the original statement by logical necessity.

> *For example, the Torah states, (Leviticus 11:2) "These are the animals that you may eat". The message derived from the precise meaning of this verse is: these types of animals mentioned in this chapter are permitted to be eaten. But in addition, it is impossible not to infer automatically that all **other** types of animals besides these are **not** permitted.*
>
> *Similarly from the verse (II Samuel 23:1) "These are the last words of David", we must infer, (Mo'ed Katan 16b) "by necessity, there were also first words". This inference is necessary because the word "last" makes no sense if there are no "first" words.*

However, everything which is not explicit in a statement does not carry the same weight as what *is* explicit even though it is logically necessary. These unstated meanings are called **Inferences**, and now we will explain their rules.

הִנֵּה כָּל מַאֲמָר שֶׁיֵּאָמֵר, רָאוּי שֶׁיִּשָּׁמְרוּ כָּל מְלוֹתָיו הָעֶרֶךְ
וְהַשִּׁעוּר הָרְאוּיִים לָהֶן. פֵּרוּשׁ, שֶׁלֹּא יְיֻחַד נָשׂוּא לְנוֹשֵׂא אֶחָד אִם הוּא
רָאוּי לָרַבִּים, וְלֹא יֵאָמֵר בְּנוֹשְׂאִים רַבִּים נָשׂוּא שֶׁאֵינוֹ רָאוּי אֶלָּא
לְאֶחָד מֵהֶם; וְכֵן עַל דֶּרֶךְ זֶה, לֹא יְיֻחַד לְנוֹשֵׂא נָשׂוּא אֶחָד אִם רָאוּי
לוֹ יוֹתֵר, וְלֹא יֵאָמְרוּ בְּנוֹשֵׂא נְשׂוּאִים רַבִּים אִם אֵין רָאוּי לוֹ אֶלָּא
אֶחָד מֵהֶם.

וְהִנֵּה עַל פִּי הַשֹּׁרֶשׁ הַזֶּה, כְּשֶׁיִּזְדַּמֵּן לְפָנֵינוּ מַאֲמָר מִן הַמַּאֲמָרִים,
יַבִּיט שִׂכְלֵנוּ אֶל חֲלָקָיו וְאֶל שִׁעוּרָם, וּכְפִי מַה שֶׁיִּרְאֵם, כָּךְ יִהְיֶה
הַצִּיּוּר שֶׁיְּקַבֵּל מֵהֶם, וְכָל מַה שֶׁהוּא חוּץ מִן הַגְּבוּל הַהוּא, יָדוֹן הֱיוֹתוֹ
נִדְחֶה.

דֶּרֶךְ מָשָׁל, שָׁנִינוּ (שבת קו א): "רַבִּי יְהוּדָה אוֹמֵר:
הַצָּד צִפּוֹר לַמִּגְדָּל וּצְבִי לַבַּיִת חַיָּב", וְדִיְּקוּ
בַּשַׁ"ס (ביצה כד א): "לַבַּיִת הוּא דְמִחַיַּב, אֲבָל
לַבִּיבָרִין – לָא". יְסוֹד הַדִּיּוּק הַזֶּה הוּא, כִּי
הִנֵּה יִחֵד רַבִּי יְהוּדָה הַחִיּוּב אֶל הַנָּשׂוּא הַמֻּגְבָּל
שֶׁל "צָד צְבִי לַבַּיִת", וּמִן הָרָאוּי שֶׁנָּדוֹן
מִדְּבָרָיו, שֶׁכָּל מִי שֶׁלֹּא יִהְיֶה מִכְּלַל הַנָּשׂוּא
הַזֶּה שֶׁהִגְבִּילוֹ, לֹא יִהְיֶה בּוֹ נָשׂוּא זֶה; פֵּרוּשׁ,

Anyone who makes a statement should choose his words so that his subject and predicate have the appropriate extent and distribution to convey his meaning. Thus, he should not apply a predicate to a particular member of a class when the proper distribution of the predicate is over a greater part of the class, neither should he state a predicate in reference to an entire class when it is only applicable to one member of that class. Similarly, he should not use a single predicate with his subject when the proper extent of his statement demands more than one predicate, nor should he state too many predicates in reference to his subject when only one is relevant.

With this as our starting point, we examine a statement, paying attention to its parts and the extent and distribution of its terms. Accordingly, a thought is conceived from the words, and anything which is outside the definition of this thought is considered to be excluded from the statement.

> *For example, we have learned, (Shabbos 106a)*
> *"Rabbi Yehudah said, one who traps a bird in a*
> *tower or a deer in a house has transgressed".*
> *The Talmud infers (Betzah 24a) "It is when he*
> *has trapped a deer in a **house** that he has*
> *transgressed, but not if he trapped the deer in a*
> *game preserve". The basis of this inference is*
> *that we take note that Rabbi Yehudah applied*
> *the predicate (of transgression) to the **limited***
> *subject of "one who traps a deer in a house".*
> *From his words it is proper to understand that*
> *anything which is not included in the subject,*
> *as he has defined it, will not have this predi-*

68

מִי שֶׁלֹּא יִהְיֶה צַד לַבַּיִת, אַף עַל פִּי שֶׁיִּהְיֶה צַד,
לֹא יִהְיֶה חַיָּב, כִּי אִלּוּ הָיְתָה דַעְתּוֹ שֶׁיִּהְיֶה
הַחִיּוּב עַל כָּל צַד בְּהֶחְלֵט, לֹא הָיָה מַזְכִּיר
בְּנוֹשְׂאוֹ הַצַּד בַּגְּבוּל, דְּהַיְנוּ הַצַּד לַבַּיִת. וְכֵן כָּל
כַּיּוֹצֵא בָזֶה.

וְאָמְנָם צָרִיךְ שֶׁתֵּדַע, שֶׁיֶּשְׁנָם בַּדִּיּוּקִים שְׁנֵי מִינִים: מֻכְרָח
וּבִלְתִּי-מֻכְרָח. הַ**בִּלְתִּי-מֻכְרָח** הוּא הַתָּלוּי בְּדִקְדּוּק סֵדֶר הַמִּלּוֹת
וְיַחֲסָן, שֶׁאַף עַל פִּי שֶׁתְּחִלַּת הַהִתְבּוֹנְנוּת נוֹתֶנֶת שֶׁנְּדַיְּקֵהוּ, כְּבָר יוּכַל
לִמְצֹא טַעַם שֶׁבַּעֲבוּרוֹ נוֹדֶה בַּמַּאֲמָר וְנַכְחִישׁ הַדִּיּוּק.

דֶּרֶךְ מָשָׁל, כְּשֶׁשָּׁנִינוּ (ברכות נג א): "אִם רַב יִשְׂרָאֵל
– מְבָרֵךְ", דִּיְּקוּ "הָא מֶחֱצָה עַל מֶחֱצָה אֵינוֹ
מְבָרֵךְ", וְאַחַר כֵּן אָמְרוּ: "בַּדִּין הוּא דַּאֲפִלּוּ
מֶחֱצָה עַל מֶחֱצָה נַמִּי מְבָרֵךְ, וְאַיְּדֵי דְתָנָא
רֵישָׁא רֹב כּוּתִים – תָּנָא סֵיפָא רֹב יִשְׂרָאֵל",

*cate. That is, someone who does not trap a deer in a house, even if we can say that he is trapping, has not transgressed. For if it was Rabbi Yehudah's intention that there is transgression in all cases of trapping categorically, he should not have qualified his subject (one who traps) with the limitation, "in a house".*

It is important to recognize that there are two types of inferences: those which are logically necessary and those which are not. **Inferences Which are Not Logically Necessary** are deduced from the order of the terms and their relationships. Even though our initial understanding of the statement leads us to make an inference, it is nonetheless possible to find a reason for accepting the statement while rejecting this inference.

*For example, we have been taught, (Berachos 53a) "If most of the people are Jewish, the blessing 'who creates the lights of the fire' may be recited upon seeing their lights". The Talmud infers, "Thus, if half of the population is Jewish and half non-Jewish, he should not recite the blessing". Afterwards, the Gemorah concludes, "In fact, the law is to recite the blessing even in this case. However, since the Tanna refers to a majority of non-Jews in the previous law, he continues in this case to speak in the same*

הִנֵּה נִדְחָה הַדִּיּוּק בַּמֶּה שֶׁאָמַר, שֶׁלֹּא נִתְכַּוֵּן
הַתַּנָּא לְהוֹצִיא מֶחֱצָה עַל מֶחֱצָה, אֶלָּא לְהַמְשֵׁךְ
אַחַר לְשׁוֹן הָרֵישָׁא.

אַךְ **הַמֻּכְרָח** הוּא הַתָּלוּי בְּעֶצֶם הַמַּאֲמָר, שֶׁאִי אֶפְשָׁר שֶׁנּוֹדֶה
בַּמַּאֲמָר וְנַכְחִישׁ הַדִּיּוּק הַהוּא, כִּי בֶאֱמֶת אֵינוֹ מִתְפָּרֵד מִמֶּנּוּ.

דֶּרֶךְ מָשָׁל, כֵּיוָן שֶׁיָּדַעְנוּ מַאֲמָר (חגיגה טו ג): "כָּל
מָאן דַּהֲוָה נְקִי אַגַּב אַמֵּהּ – סָלִיק", מֻכְרָח
שֶׁנֵּדַע גַּם כֵּן, שֶׁכָּל דְּלָא סָלִיק – לָא הֲוָה נְקִי
אַגַּב אַמֵּהּ.

אָמְנָם, כָּל הַדִּיּוּקִים הַמֻּכְרָחִים הֵם אֵלֶּה: כָּל מַאֲמָר כְּלָלִי
מְקַיֵּם יִדְיְקוּ מִמֶּנּוּ שְׁנֵי דִיּוּקִים. דֶּרֶךְ מָשָׁל: "כָּל דְּנְקִי אַגַּב אַמֵּהּ –
סָלִיק" יְדָיַּק מִמֶּנּוּ " כָּל דְּלָא סָלִיק – לָא הֲוָה נְקִי אַגַּב אַמֵּהּ",
וְנִקְרָא זֶה **חִלּוּף הַפְכִי כּוֹלֵל**; וְיִדְיַּק מִמֶּנּוּ שֶׁ"אֶחָד מִן הָעוֹלִים יָפֶה
הוּא הַנְּקִי אַגַּב אַמֵּהּ", וְנִקְרָא זֶה **חִלּוּף קְצָתִי**.

וְכָל מַאֲמָר כְּלָלִי שׁוֹלֵל, יְדָיַּק מִמֶּנּוּ דִיּוּק אֶחָד בִּלְבָד; דֶּרֶךְ
מָשָׁל (בראשית רבה נח ג): "אֵין דָּבָר רָע יוֹרֵד מִלְמַעְלָה" – "אֵין יוֹרֵד
מִלְמַעְלָה דָּבָר רָע", וְנִקְרָא זֶה **חִלּוּף כּוֹלֵל**.

*way about a majority of Jews". Here the infer-*
*ence was rejected because the Talmud tells us*
*that the intention of the Tanna was not to ex-*
*clude the case of half Jews and half non-Jews,*
*but simply to continue in the manner of the*
*previous law.*

In contrast, a **Logically Necessary Inference** is deduced from the essential content of the statement. It is impossible to accept the statement itself and reject the inference, for it is, in fact, inseparable from it.

*For example, when we posit the statement*
*(Chagigah 15b) "All the wool that was clean*
*when sheared comes out completely dyed", it is*
*necessary to infer: all the wool that does not*
*take the dye completely was not clean when*
*sheared.*

The entire set of necessary inferences is as follows: All categorical affirmative statements have two inferences. For example, from the above statement, "All clean wool dyes completely", it can be inferred, "All that does not dye completely was not clean wool in the first place." This inference is called a **Contrapositive** (categorically opposite converse). The second inference is, "One material that dyes completely is clean wool", and this is called a **Limited Converse.**

All categorical negative statements have only one inference. For example, (Bereshis Rabbah 51:3) "No evil comes from above" implies "Nothing that comes from above is evil"; this is called a

וְכָל מַאֲמָר קְצָתִי מְקַיֵּם, יְדַיְקוּ מִמֶּנּוּ שְׁלשָׁה דִיּוּקִים. דֶּרֶךְ מָשָׁל (פסחים נ ב): "יֵשׁ זָרִיז וְנִשְׁכָּר" יְדַיֵּק מִמֶּנּוּ "יֵשׁ זָרִיז וְאֵינוֹ נִשְׁכָּר", וְנִקְרָא זֶה **הֶפֶךְ**; וִידַיֵּק מִמֶּנּוּ "יֵשׁ שֶׁאֵינוֹ נִשְׁכָּר וְהוּא זָרִיז", וְנִקְרָא זֶה **חִלּוּף קְצָתִי הַפְכִי**; וִידַיֵּק מִמֶּנּוּ "אֶחָד מִן הַנִּשְׁכָּרִים הוּא הַזָּרִיז", וְנִקְרָא זֶה **חִלּוּף קְצָתִי**.

וְכֵן כָּל מַאֲמָר קְצָתִי שׁוֹלֵל, יְדַיְקוּ מִמֶּנּוּ שְׁלשָׁה הַדִּיּוּקִים הָאֵלֶּה. דֶּרֶךְ מָשָׁל: "יֵשׁ קָדָשִׁים שֶׁאֵין לָהֶם פִּדְיוֹן", תְּדַיֵּק מִזֶּה: "יֵשׁ קָדָשִׁים שֶׁיֵּשׁ לָהֶם פִּדְיוֹן", "יֵשׁ שֶׁיֵּשׁ לָהֶם פִּדְיוֹן וְהֵם קָדָשִׁים", "יֵשׁ שֶׁאֵין לָהֶם פִּדְיוֹן וְהֵם קָדָשִׁים".

### Complete Converse.

Every partial affirmative statement has three necessary inferences. For example, from the statement (Pesachim 50b) "Some industrious people receive reward", it can be inferred, "Some industrious people do not receive reward". This inference is called an **Absolute Opposite**. It can also be inferred, "Some who do not receive reward are industrious", and this is called a **Limited Contrapositive** (partial opposite converse). The third inference is, "One of those who is rewarded is industrious", and this is called a **Limited Converse**.

Every partial negative statement has these same three inferences. For example, from the statement "Some consecrated objects may not be redeemed", the first inference is, "Some consecrated objects may be redeemed". The second inference is, "Some objects that may be redeemed are consecrated objects". And the third is, "There is an object which may not be redeemed which is a consecrated object".

# פרק ו

כָּל הַמַּאֲמָרִים שֶׁיֵּאָמְרוּ, יִתְחַלְּקוּ לַאֲמִתִּיִּים וְכוֹזְבִים. הָאֲמִתִּיִּים הֵם שֶׁיֵּאָמְרוּ מַה שֶּׁהוּא, הַכּוֹזְבִים שֶׁיֵּאָמְרוּ מַה שֶׁאֵינוֹ.

וְהִנֵּה צָרִיךְ שֶׁתַּבְחִין בָּזֶה בֵּין הַמַּאֲמָרִים הַפְּשׁוּטִים וְהַמַּאֲמָרִים הַנֶּאֱמָרִים עַל דֶּרֶךְ הַשְׁאָלָה אוֹ הַהַפְלָגָה, כִּי הַפְּשׁוּטִים אֲמִתָּם וּכְזָבָם תְּלוּיִים בִּהְיוֹת צוֹדֵק אוֹ בִּלְתִּי־צוֹדֵק מַה שֶּׁנִּרְמַז בְּמִלּוֹתֵיהֶם לְפִי הַבֲנָתָן הַפְּשׁוּטָה. אַךְ בְּאוֹתָם שֶׁעַל דֶּרֶךְ הַשְׁאָלָה אוֹ הַהַפְלָגָה, אֵין הָאֱמֶת וְהַכָּזָב תְּלוּיִים בְּמַה שֶּׁמּוּבָן מִפְּשַׁט מִלּוֹתֵיהֶם, אֶלָּא בָּרֶמֶז הַמְכֻוָּן בָּהֶם.

דֶּרֶךְ מָשָׁל, כְּשֶׁאָמְרוּ לְרַבִּי יוֹחָנָן (בבא קמא קי"ז א'): "אֲרִי עָלָה מִבָּבֶל", אֵין אֲמִתַּת הַמַּאֲמָר הַהוּא בְּמוּבָן מִפְּשַׁט הַמִּלּוֹת, אֶלָּא בָּרֶמֶז הַנִּרְמָז, שֶׁהוּא – שֶׁאָדָם חָכָם גָּדוֹל בַּתּוֹרָה עָלָה מִבָּבֶל, וְהוּא רַב כַּהֲנָא.

עוֹד צָרִיךְ שֶׁתְּדַקְדֵּק בְּכָל מַאֲמָר שֶׁיִּהְיֶה, לָדַעַת סוֹף גְּזֵרָתוֹ, שֶׁבָּהּ תִּהְיֶה תְּלוּיָה אֲמִתַּת הַמַּאֲמָר אוֹ כְּזָבוֹ, וְזֶה יִתְחַלֵּף לְפִי הִתְחַלֵּף הַמִּינִים שֶׁזָּכַרְנוּ לְמַעְלָה.

75

# Chapter Six

All statements must be either true or false. Those which are true state what is, and those which are false state what is not.

In this respect, it is necessary to distinguish between literal sentences, and sentences which are figurative or hyperbolic. The truth and falsity of literal sentences depends on whether the simple intention of their words, as normally understood, is correct or incorrect. However, with figurative sentences and hyperbole, their truth and falsity does not depend on the simple understanding of the words, but on the intended allusion.

> *For example, the rabbis said to Rabbi Yochanan, (Babba Kamma 117a) "A lion has come from Babylon". The truth of this statement is not based on the literal meaning of the word "lion", but on the allusion expressed in the metaphor, which is, a man who is a great Torah sage has come from Babylon, and he was Rav Kahana.*

Further, every statement must be carefully examined to establish its ultimate intention, because the truth or falsity of the statement depends on this. The basic intention of each statement changes according to the eleven different types of predicates discussed in Chapter Three.

כִּי הִנֵּה הַמַּאֲמָר **הַסְּתָמִי** סוֹף גְּזֵרָתוֹ הוּא הִמָּצֵא הַנָּשׂוּא הַהוּא בַּנּוֹשֵׂא שֶׁיֹּאמְרֵהוּ בּוֹ אוֹ הֵעָדֵר מִמֶּנּוּ.

דֶּרֶךְ מָשָׁל (ברכות כ ג): "נָשִׁים חַיָּבוֹת בְּקִדּוּשׁ הַיּוֹם" סוֹף גְּזֵרָתוֹ, שֶׁיֵּשׁ לַנָּשִׁים חִיּוּב לְקִדּוּשׁ הַיּוֹם, וַאֲמִתָּתוֹ תְּלוּיָה בְּשֶׁתִּהְיֶה הָאֱמֶת כָּךְ, שֶׁתִּהְיֶינָה הַנָּשִׁים חַיָּבוֹת בְּקִדּוּשׁ הַיּוֹם.

אַךְ הַמַּאֲמָר **הַמְיֻחָד** שֶׁזָּכַרְנוּ, שֶׁהוּא הָאוֹמֵר הַנָּשׂוּא בַּנּוֹשֵׂא בְּדֶרֶךְ מְיֻחָד, הִנֵּה סוֹף גְּזֵרָתוֹ הוּא הִמָּצֵא הַנָּשׂוּא הַהוּא בְּאוֹתוֹ הַנּוֹשֵׂא בְּאוֹתוֹ הַדֶּרֶךְ, וְאִלּוּ יִמָּצֵא הַנָּשׂוּא בַּנּוֹשֵׂא אַךְ לֹא בְּאוֹתוֹ הַדֶּרֶךְ – לֹא יִהְיֶה הַמַּאֲמָר צוֹדֵק.

דֶּרֶךְ מָשָׁל מַאֲמָר (פסחים ט ג): "כֵּיוָן דְּחֻלְדָּה וּבַרְדְּלָס מְצוּיִּין שָׁם – וַדַּאי גְּרָרוּהוּ", אִלּוּ לֹא הָיָה וַדַּאי שֶׁיִּגְרְרוּהוּ, אֲפִלּוּ יֶאֱרַע כֵּן פְּעָמִים רַבּוֹת, לֹא הָיָה הַמַּאֲמָר צוֹדֵק.

הַמַּאֲמָר **הַמְמַעֵט**, שֶׁאוֹמֵר נָשׂוּא בְּנוֹשֵׂא וְשׁוֹלְלוֹ מִכָּל זוּלָתוֹ, סוֹף גְּזֵרָתוֹ הוּא, שֶׁבְּאוֹתוֹ הַדָּבָר לְבַדּוֹ נִמְצָא אוֹתוֹ הָעִנְיָן, וְאִלּוּ הָיָה נִמְצָא בְּזוּלָתוֹ – לֹא הָיָה צוֹדֵק.

In a **Simple Statement**, the ultimate intention is that the predicate is, in fact, found in (or absent from) the subject, as the statement asserts.

> *For example, (Berachos 20b) "Women are obliged to fulfill the mitzvah of kiddush". Here, the basic intention is that women have the obligation of kiddush, and the statement can only be true if this is indeed so, i.e., that they are required to fulfill this mitzvah.*

However, a **Qualified Statement**, as we said earlier, has a predicate applied to the subject as a certainty, a possibility, a doubt, or an impossibility. Therefore, its ultimate intent is that the predicate is, in fact, found in that subject *and* specifically in the manner stated. Even if the predicate is found in the subject, but not in the manner which the statement asserts, the statement is not correct.

> *For example, (Pesachim 9b) "Since weasels and martens are commonly found, they **certainly** dragged away the fetus before the Cohen arrived". If it is not a certainty that these animals dragged the fetus away, the statement cannot be correct even though, in fact, it may have often happened.*

In a **Statement of Exclusion**, whose predicate is applied to a certain subject to the exclusion of any other, the ultimate intention is that the predicate is applicable to that subject *alone*. If the predicate

דֶּרֶךְ מָשָׁל מַאֲמַר הַכָּתוּב (שמות יב טז): "הוּא לְבַדּוֹ יֵעָשֶׂה לָכֶם", אִלּוּ הָיְתָה מֻתֶּרֶת בְּיוֹם-טוֹב עֲשִׂיַת דְּבָרִים אֲחֵרִים זוּלָתִי צֹרֶךְ אֹכֶל נֶפֶשׁ, לֹא הָיָה הַכָּתוּב אוֹמֵר "לְבַדּוֹ", שֶׁהֲרֵי אֵינוֹ לְבַדּוֹ.

הַמַּאֲמָר **הַמּוֹצִיא**, שֶׁמּוֹצִיא קְצָת מִן הַנִּכְלָלִים בַּנּוֹשֵׂא מִן הַנָּשׂוּא, גְּזֵרוֹתָיו שְׁתַּיִם: אַחַת – שֶׁבַּנּוֹשֵׂא הַהוּא נִמְצָא הַנָּשׂוּא הַהוּא. שְׁנִיָּה – שֶׁאוֹתָם הַמּוֹצָאִים, אַף עַל פִּי שֶׁהֵם מִן הַנּוֹשֵׂא הַהוּא, אֵין בָּהֶם הַנָּשׂוּא הַהוּא. וְאִם יִמָּצֵא גַּם בַּמּוֹצָאִים, הִנֵּה לֹא יִהְיֶה כָּל הַמַּאֲמָר כּוֹזֵב, אֶלָּא הַגְּזֵרָה הַשְּׁנִיָּה תִּהְיֶה כּוֹזֶבֶת, וְהָרִאשׁוֹנָה – צוֹדֶקֶת.

דֶּרֶךְ מָשָׁל (חולין ב א): "הַכֹּל שׁוֹחֲטִין וּשְׁחִיטָתָן כְּשֵׁרָה, חוּץ מֵחֵרֵשׁ שׁוֹטֶה וְקָטָן", אִלּוּ הָיָה הַדִּין שֶׁהַכֹּל שׁוֹחֲטִין וְגַם חֵרֵשׁ שׁוֹטֶה וְקָטָן שׁוֹחֲטִין, לֹא נֶאֱמַר שֶׁכָּל הַמַּאֲמָר כּוֹזֵב, אֶלָּא

is also found in reference to another subject, the statement is not correct.

> *For example, the Torah states, (Exodus 12:16) ". . . no manner of work shall be done on them, save that which [is needed for] every person to eat; that **alone** may be done by you". If, on holidays, any other work were permissible besides that which is needed to prepare food, then the Torah would not have said "alone", for the permissibility of work would not be limited exclusively to that case.*

In a **Statement of Exception**, which removes the predicate from some elements of the class which comprises the subject, there are *two* basic intents. One is that the predicate is, in general, found to be true in reference to the subject. The other is that those particulars on which an exception is made do *not* have this same predicate even though they *are* included in the general class of the subject. Now, if the predicate is also found in these exceptional cases, the entire sentence is not false. Only the second fundamental intention (to make an exception) is false, but the first (to affirm the predicate in general) is nonetheless correct.

> *For example, (Chullin 2a) "All may slaughter and their slaughtering is valid **except** a deaf or insane person or a minor". Even if the law were that all could slaughter, including a deaf or insane person and a minor, we would not say*

הַגְּזֵרָה הָרִאשׁוֹנָה "הַכֹּל שׁוֹחֲטִין" – צוֹדֶקֶת,
וְהַשְּׁנִיָּה "חוּץ מֵחֵרֵשׁ שׁוֹטֶה וְקָטָן" – אֵינֶנָּה
צוֹדֶקֶת.

וְכֵן הַמַּאֲמָר הַמֻּגְבָּל, אִם יִהְיֶה הַגְּבוּל בִּלְתִּי צוֹדֵק, לֹא מִפְּנֵי זֶה
יִהְיֶה בִּלְתִּי צוֹדֵק כָּל הַמַּאֲמָר, אֶלָּא הַגְּזֵרָה הָרִאשׁוֹנָה – צוֹדֶקֶת,
וְהַשְּׁנִיָּה – בִּלְתִּי צוֹדֶקֶת.

דֶּרֶךְ מָשָׁל (דמאי פ״א מ״ג): "וּמְחַלְּלִים אוֹתוֹ כֶּסֶף
עַל כֶּסֶף – וּבִלְבַד שֶׁיַּחֲזֹר וְיִפְדֶּה אֶת הַפֵּרוֹת",
אִלּוּ לֹא הָיָה זֶה הַתְּנַאי אֲמִתִּי וְלֹא הָיָה זֶה
הַחִיּוּב, אַף עַל פִּי כֵן הָיְתָה אֲמִתִּית הַגְּזֵרָה
הָרִאשׁוֹנָה "מְחַלְּלִים אוֹתוֹ כֶּסֶף עַל כֶּסֶף".

וְהַמַּאֲמָר הַתָּלוּי, שֶׁתּוֹלֶה מְצִיאוּת עִנְיָן אֶחָד בִּמְצִיאוּת עִנְיָן
אַחֵר, הִנֵּה אֵין סוֹף גְּזֵרָתוֹ שׁוּם אֶחָד מִן הָעִנְיָנִים בִּפְנֵי עַצְמוֹ, אַךְ סוֹף
גְּזֵרָתוֹ הוּא הֱיוֹתָם נִתְלִים זֶה בָּזֶה, וְאִלּוּ הָיוּ שְׁנֵי הָעִנְיָנִים אֱמֶת כָּל

*that this statement is entirely false. Rather, the*
*first intent (all may slaughter) would be correct*
*and the second intent (**except** a deaf or in-*
*sane person or a minor) would be incorrect.*

Similarly, in the case of a **Conditional Statement**, even if the condition or stipulation is incorrect, the entire statement is not neces-sarily incorrect. The first basic intention of the statement (i.e., the affirmation of the predicate) may be correct, while only the second intention (i.e., that this predication is contingent on some stipulation) is incorrect.

*For example, (Demai Chapter 1 Mishnah 2)*
*"Second-tithe money of demai may be ex-*
*changed, silver for silver, copper for copper,*
*silver for copper, and copper for fruit – **provid-***
***ed** [that he intended] to eventually return and*
*redeem the fruit". Even if this condition does*
*not obtain, and he is not, in fact, obligated to*
*fulfill it, the first intent of the statement can*
*still be true, i.e., "the money may be exchanged*
*silver for silver, etc.".*

A **Hypothetical Statement** establishes that the existence of one thing is dependent on the presence of another. Here, the ultimate intention of the statement is not the predication contained in the an-tecedent, nor is it the predication in the consequent; rather it is only the assertion that one is dependent on the other. For even if both the antecedent and the consequent are true in themselves, and

אֶחָד בִּפְנֵי עַצְמוֹ, אַךְ תְּלִיָּתָם זֶה בָּזֶה בִּלְתִּי צוֹדֶקֶת – יִהְיֶה הַמַּאֲמָר כּוֹזֵב. וְאִלּוּ הָיוּ הָעִנְיָנִים בִּפְנֵי עַצְמָם כּוֹזְבִים וּתְלִיָּתָם זֶה בָּזֶה אֱמֶת – יִהְיֶה הַמַּאֲמָר אֲמִתִּי.

דֶּרֶךְ מָשָׁל, כְּשֶׁאָמַר הֶחָכָם לְאוֹתוֹ הַמִּין (סנהדרין סו א) : "אִם אַתָּה עוֹשֶׂה כֵן – רוֹפֵא אֻמָּן תִּקָּרֵא", לֹא הָיְתָה כַּוָּנָתוֹ שֶׁיַּעֲשֶׂה כֵן, וְלֹא שֶׁיִּקָּרֵא רוֹפֵא אֻמָּן, אֶלָּא שֶׁאִם הָיָה יָכוֹל לַעֲשׂוֹת כֵּן, הָיָה נִקְרָא רוֹפֵא אֻמָּן; וּבֶאֱמֶת לֹא הָיָה יָכוֹל לַעֲשׂוֹת כֵּן, וְלֹא הָיָה נִקְרָא רוֹפֵא אֻמָּן.

וְכֵן כְּשֶׁאָמַר אֵלִיָּהוּ (מלכים א יח כא): "וְאִם הַבַּעַל – לְכוּ אַחֲרָיו", לֹא הָיָה מוֹדֶה אֵלִיָּהוּ חַס וְחָלִילָה שֶׁהַבַּעַל הוּא אֱלֹהִים, וְלֹא הָיָה אוֹמֵר לִבְנֵי יִשְׂרָאֵל שֶׁרָאוּי שֶׁיֵּלְכוּ אַחֲרָיו, אֶלָּא שֶׁאִם הוּא אֱלֹהִים – רָאוּי שֶׁיֵּלְכוּ אַחֲרָיו, וְזֶה הַמַּאֲמָר אֲמִתִּי בְּעַצְמוֹ, כִּי שְׁנֵי הַדְּבָרִים תְּלוּיִים זֶה בָּזֶה בֶּאֱמֶת, אַךְ שֶׁקֶר הוּא שֶׁיִּהְיֶה הַבַּעַל אֱלֹהִים, וְשֶׁקֶר שֶׁיִּהְיֶה רָאוּי שֶׁיֵּלְכוּ אַחֲרָיו.

only their dependence is incorrect, the statement will be false. Similarly, if both parts are false in themselves and yet it is true that one should depend on the other – then the statement will be true.

> *For example, (Sanhedrin 91a) a certain heretic was angered by Gebiha ben Pesisa, who was a hunchback, and said to him, "If I stood up and kicked you, I could straighten out your hump!" The Sage replied, "If you could do that, you would be called a great doctor and command large fees!" He did not mean that the heretic could cure his hunchback or that he should be called doctor, but only if he could do so then he should be called doctor. But, in fact, the heretic could not cure him and did not deserve to be called a great doctor.*

> *Likewise, when Eliyahu said, (I Kings 18: 21) "If the Almighty be God, follow Him, but if it is the Ba'al, then follow him", Eliyahu was not agreeing, heaven forbid, that the Ba'al is God, nor was he saying to the Jewish people that they should follow the Ba'al. He was only stating a condition, that if he were, then it would be proper to follow him. This statement is true in itself since in truth one part is dependent on the other, but it is false to say, heaven forbid, that the Ba'al is God, or that it is right to*

וְהֵפֶךְ זֶה, אִם יִהְיוּ הָעִנְיָנִים אֱמֶת וּתְלִיָּתָם זֶה בָּזֶה שֶׁקֶר – יִהְיֶה הַמַּאֲמָר כּוֹזֵב. דֶּרֶךְ מָשָׁל, אִם תֹּאמַר: אִם מֹשֶׁה קִבֵּל אֶת הַתּוֹרָה – שָׁאוּל הוּא הַמֶּלֶךְ הָרִאשׁוֹן שֶׁמָּלַךְ עַל יִשְׂרָאֵל! הִנֵּה שְׁנֵי הָעִנְיָנִים אֲמִתִּיִּים כָּל אֶחָד בִּפְנֵי עַצְמוֹ, אַךְ אֵינָם תְּלוּיִים זֶה בָּזֶה כְּלָל, וְהַמַּאֲמָר הַזֶּה שֶׁתּוֹלֶה אוֹתָם זֶה בָּזֶה הוּא בִּלְתִּי צוֹדֵק.

אַךְ הַמַּאֲמָר הַ**מְרֻבֶּה**, שֶׁמְּקַבֵּץ נְשׂוּאִים רַבִּים בְּנוֹשֵׂא אֶחָד אוֹ נוֹשְׂאִים רַבִּים לְנָשׂוּא אֶחָד, הִנֵּה סוֹף גְּזֵרָתוֹ, שֶׁכָּל אוֹתָם הַנְּשׂוּאִים הֵם בְּאוֹתוֹ הַנּוֹשֵׂא, אוֹ בְּכָל אוֹתָם הַנּוֹשְׂאִים יִהְיֶה אוֹתוֹ הַנָּשׂוּא, וְעַל כֵּן לְשֶׁיִּהְיֶה צוֹדֵק, צָרִיךְ שֶׁכֻּלָּם יִהְיוּ אֱמֶת.

דֶּרֶךְ מָשָׁל, כְּשֶׁאָמַר (יבמות קי"ב ג'): "אוֹ חֹלֵץ אוֹ מְיַבֵּם", אִם הָאֱמֶת הָיָה שֶׁחוֹלֵץ וְלֹא מְיַבֵּם, הִנֵּה הַמַּאֲמָר הָיָה בִּלְתִּי צוֹדֵק, אַף עַל פִּי שֶׁחֵלֶק מִמֶּנּוּ שֶׁהוּא חוֹלֵץ הָיָה צוֹדֵק.

וְכֵן כָּל כַּיּוֹצֵא בָזֶה.

*follow him.*

Conversely, if both the antecedent and the consequent are true, but their dependence is false, the statement will be false. For example, one might say, if Moshe received the Torah, then Shaul would have been the first king to rule over Israel! Here, both of these statements are true in themselves, but one does not depend on the other whatsoever. Thus, the statement is incorrect because it makes one part conditional on the other.

On the other hand, with a **Compound Statement** in which multiple predicates are applied to one subject, or one predicate is applied to multiple subjects, the ultimate intention is that *all* those predicates must, in fact, be found in their subject, or in *all* the subjects the particular predication must be applicable. Consequently, for the statement to be true, all its particular predications must be correct.

> *For example, the Talmud states, (Yebamos 112b) "He must perform either chalitzah or leverite marriage". If he can only perform chalitzah, and he has no option of leverite marriage, the entire statement is incorrect, even though one part was, in fact, correct, i.e., that he had an option to perform chalitzah.*

All the different categories of compound statements follow this rule.

וְעַל דֶּרֶךְ זֶה שְׁלשָׁה הַמִּינִים, הַשְּׁמִינִי, הַתְּשִׁיעִי וְהָעֲשִׂירִי, שֶׁכֻּלָּם
מְקַבְּצִים עִנְיָנִים הַרְבֵּה כְּאֶחָד לִהְיוֹת הַמַּאֲמָר צוֹדֵק, צָרִיךְ שֶׁכָּל
אוֹתָם הָעִנְיָנִים יִהְיוּ כְּמוֹ שֶׁנֶּאֶמְרִים בַּמַּאֲמָר.

אַךְ הַמִּין הָאֶחָד-עָשָׂר, שֶׁהוּא שֶׁיֵּאָמֵר בּוֹ עִנְיָן נִמְשָׁךְ מֵעִנְיָן אַחֵר,
הִנֵּה גִּזְרוֹתָיו שָׁלשׁ: הַמָּצֵא הַקּוֹדֵם, וְהַמָּצֵא הַנִּמְשָׁךְ, וֶהֱיוֹת מְצִיאוּת
הַנִּמְשָׁךְ הֶמְשֵׁךְ מִמְּצִיאוּת הַקּוֹדֵם. וְתִרְאֶה, שֶׁבָּזֶה יִבָּדֵל הַמִּין הַזֶּה מִן
הַמַּאֲמָר הַתָּלוּי, כִּי בַּתָּלוּי אֵין הַגְּזֵרָה עַל מְצִיאוּת שׁוּם אֶחָד מִן
הָעִנְיָנִים אֶלָּא עַל הִתָּלוּתָם לְבָד, אַךְ זֶה גּוֹזֵר מְצִיאוּת שְׁנֵי הָעִנְיָנִים
וְגוֹזֵר הִתָּלוּתָם זֶה בָּזֶה.

דֶּרֶךְ מָשָׁל הַמַּאֲמָר שֶׁהֲבֵאנוּ לְמַעְלָה (מעשרות פ"ג
מ"א): "הָיָה עוֹבֵר בַּשּׁוּק, וְאָמַר: טְלוּ לָכֶם
תְּאֵנִים – אוֹכְלִים וּפְטוּרִים, לְפִיכָךְ אִם
הִכְנִיסוּ לְבָתֵּיהֶם –מְתֻקָּנִים וַדַּאי", הִנֵּה שְׁלשָׁה
עִנְיָנִים נִגְזָרִים בַּמַּאֲמָר הַזֶּה:
אֶחָד – שֶׁיְּכוֹלִים הַפּוֹעֲלִים לֶאֱכֹל בַּמָּקוֹם
שֶׁהֵם בְּלִי הַפְרָשַׁת מַעֲשֵׂר, וְזֶה הַקּוֹדֵם;

The next three types of statements follow this same pattern. **Preclusive Statements, Statements of Discrepancy**, and **Comparative Statements** all contain two or more ideas in a single sentence. In order for the statement to be correct, *all* these parts must be exactly as the statement asserts.

In the eleventh type of statement, a **Consequent Statement**, in which one predicate is stated as a consequence of another, there are *three* intentions. They are: that the antecedent exists in reality, that the consequent exists in reality, and that the consequent in reality follows from the antecedent. This, then, is the point of distinction between a consequent statement and a hypothetical statement, for in a hypothetical statement, the ultimate intent is not based on the reality of either the antecedent or the consequent, but only on their dependence. But here, the presumption is that the antecedent, the consequent *and* their dependence are all true.

> *This is exemplified in the text quoted earlier: (Ma'aseros Chapter 2 Mishnah 1) "When a man in the market passes by saying, 'Take some of my figs to eat', they may be eaten and they are exempt from tithes; **therefore**, upon bringing these figs into one's house, the obligation to tithe them is a certainty". There are three separate intentions in this statement:*
>
> *First – the workers who bring produce from the field may eat it where they are without separating any tithe – this is the antecedent.*

שֵׁנִי – שֶׁאִם הִכְנִיסוּ לְבָתֵּיהֶם, חַיָּבִים לְתַקֵּן
וַדַּאי, וְזֶה הַנִּמְשָׁךְ;
שְׁלִישִׁי – שֶׁחִיּוּבָם וַדַּאי בְּהִכָּנְסָם לַבַּיִת, תָּלוּי
בַּהֶתֵּר שֶׁהֵם מֻתָּרִים לֶאֱכֹל בְּלִי הַפְרָשָׁה
בַּמָּקוֹם שֶׁהֵם.

וְהִנֵּה, כְּדֵי שֶׁיִּהְיֶה מַאֲמָר כָּזֶה אֱמֶת, צָרִיךְ שֶׁכָּל שְׁלֹשֶׁת הַחֲלָקִים
יִהְיוּ אֱמֶת, וְאִם אֶחָד מֵהֶם לֹא יִהְיֶה אֱמֶת – הַמַּאֲמָר בִּלְתִּי צוֹדֵק.

*Second – when they take this produce into their house there is a definite obligation to tithe – this is the consequent.*

*Third – the fact that the obligation is a certainty when they enter the house is **dependent** on the fact that they were permitted to eat without separating the tithe in the market. (Why does it follow that the obligation is a certainty? Since the produce was permitted in the marketplace, it must be that it was **never** brought into a house, and thus we are certain that no separation of tithes has yet been performed.)*

Now in order for a statement like this to be true, all three parts must be true; if even one of them is not true, the entire statement is false.

# פרק ז

הִנֵּה עַד הֵנָּה בֵּאַרְנוּ הַיְסוֹד הָרִאשׁוֹן שֶׁהוּא בַּהֲבָנַת הַמַּאֲמָרִים. עַתָּה נְבָאֵר הַיְסוֹד הַשֵּׁנִי שֶׁהוּא בְּהֻלֶּדֶת הַתּוֹלָדוֹת.

טֶבַע הַהִתְבּוֹנְנוּת נוֹתֵן, שֶׁכַּאֲשֶׁר יֵאָמֵר נָשׂוּא אֶחָד בְּנוֹשֵׂא אֶחָד, כָּל מַה שֶׁיִּהְיֶה נִכְלָל אוֹ מִתְחַבֵּר בֶּאֱמֶת בַּנָּשׂוּא הַהוּא, יֵאָמֵר בְּאוֹתוֹ הַנּוֹשֵׂא, וְכֵן כָּל מַה שֶׁנִּכְלָל בְּאוֹתוֹ הַנּוֹשֵׂא יֵאָמֵר בְּאוֹתוֹ הַנָּשׂוּא. וְעַל פִּי הַשֹּׁרֶשׁ הַזֶּה, כְּשֶׁנִּשְׁמַע מַאֲמָר מִן הַמַּאֲמָרִים, יִוָּלְדוּ לָנוּ מִמֶּנּוּ מַאֲמָרִים הַרְבֵּה, כֻּלָּם נִמְשָׁכִים בֶּאֱמֶת מִן הַמַּאֲמָר הַהוּא שֶׁשָּׁמַעְנוּ וְנִכְלָלִים בּוֹ כְּדֶרֶךְ שֶׁנִּכְלָלִים הַפְּרָטִים בִּכְלָלֵיהֶם.

דֶּרֶךְ מָשָׁל, שָׁמַעְנוּ שֶׁהָעוֹשֶׂה אַב מְלָאכָה בַּשַּׁבָּת חַיָּב סְקִילָה (שבת ע״א, סנהדרין ס״ו א). הִנֵּה נֵדַע, שֶׁכָּל מַה שֶׁהוּא אַב מְלָאכָה יֵשׁ בּוֹ עִנְיָן זֶה שֶׁל חִיּוּב סְקִילָה, מֵעַתָּה כָּל מַעֲשֶׂה שֶׁנֵּדַע הֱיוֹתוֹ אַב מְלָאכָה, נֵדַע וַדַּאי שֶׁיֵּשׁ בּוֹ חִיּוּב סְקִילָה, וְנוֹלִיד מִזֶּה, שֶׁהַכּוֹתֵב בַּשַּׁבָּת חַיָּב סְקִילָה, שֶׁהַחוֹרֵשׁ חַיָּב סְקִילָה, וְכֵן כֻּלָּם, כִּי כָל אֵלֶּה

# Chapter Seven

In the previous chapters we have described the first basic thought process, which is how to arrive at a complete understanding of statements. Now we will consider a second thought process, which is the derivation of new ideas from a given premise.

Logical investigation into any statement dictates that if a predicate is applied to a subject, then whatever is a subcategory or attribute of the predicate must also be applicable to the same subject. In addition, whatever is a subcategory of the subject must have the same predicate applied to it. On this basis, we find that any statement gives rise to many derivatives, all of which are consequences of the original statement. They are, so to speak, part of the original statement just as particulars are part of a general category.

> *For example, (Shabbos 70a and Sanhedrin 53a) we have been taught that anyone who does a primary work on the Sabbath incurs the penalty of stoning. Thus we know that every primary work on the Sabbath carries a penalty of stoning. We can apply the rule that every particular act which we know to be a primary work must also carry this penalty. Hence, we derive that one who writes on the Sabbath is liable to stoning, and one who kneads dough on the Sabbath is liable to stoning, and so forth, since all of these are included in the subject of the*

נִכְלָלִים בְּנוֹשֵׂא הַמַּאֲמָר הָאֶחָד, דְּהַיְנוּ "הָעוֹשֶׂה
אַב מְלָאכָה".

וְכֵן אִלּוּ שָׁמַעְתָּ מַאֲמָר, שֶׁהָאִזְמֵל שֶׁל מִילָה
הוּא מֻקְצֶה, הִנֵּה כָּל מַה שֶּׁיִּוָּדַע לָנוּ הֱיוֹתוֹ
מִתְחַבֵּר לְנִשׂוֹא זֶה שֶׁל מֻקְצֶה, תָּדִין בְּלִי סָפֵק
הִמָּצְאוֹ בָּאִזְמֵל שֶׁל מִילָה, וְעַל כֵּן כְּשֶׁתֵּדַע
שֶׁהַמֻּקְצֶה אָסוּר בְּטִלְטוּל, תֵּדַע שֶׁהָאִזְמֵל שֶׁל
מִילָה אָסוּר בְּטִלְטוּל.

וְהִנֵּה הַמַּאֲמָר הָרִאשׁוֹן שֶׁמִּמֶּנּוּ יִמָּשֵׁךְ הַשֵּׁנִי נִקְרָא **הַקְדָּמָה,**
וְהַנִּמְשָׁךְ נִקְרָא **תּוֹלָדָה**, וְהוֹלָדַת הַתּוֹלָדָה מֵהַקְדָּמָתָהּ, נִקְרֵאת **הֶקֵּשׁ**
וּכְשֶׁיִּהְיֶה עַל דֶּרֶךְ זֶה, נִקְרָא **הֶקֵּשׁ מוֹפְתִי.**

וְאוּלָם הִנְּךָ רוֹאֶה, שֶׁהֶמְשֵׁךְ תּוֹלָדָה זוֹ בָּא מִהְיוֹת נְשׂוֹא הַתּוֹלָדָה
מִתְחַבֵּר בֶּאֱמֶת אֶל נְשׂוֹא הַהַקְדָּמָה, אוֹ נוֹשֵׂא הַתּוֹלָדָה נִכְלָל תַּחַת
נוֹשֵׂא הַהַקְדָּמָה. וְאִלּוּ תִמָּצֵא, שֶׁאֵין נְשׂוֹא הַתּוֹלָדָה נִכְלָל אוֹ מִתְחַבֵּר
בְּהֶכְרֵחַ וְתָמִיד בְּנִשׂוֹא הַהַקְדָּמָה, הִנֵּה הַתּוֹלָדָה לֹא תִוָּלֵד.

דֶּרֶךְ מָשָׁל מִשַּׁבָּת, שֶׁהַהַבְעָרָה אַב מְלָאכָה,
וְשָׁמַעְתָּ שֶׁכָּל הָעוֹשֶׂה אַב מְלָאכָה בַּשַּׁבָּת חַיָּב
מִיתָה (שבת ע א) וְאַחַר כָּךְ שָׁמַעְתָּ: רַבִּי יוֹסֵי

> *original statement, which is "anyone who does a primary work".*
>
> *Likewise, if we posit the statement that the knife of circumcision is mukzeh, then anything which is included in the predicate, mukzeh, must, without a doubt, be applicable to the circumcision knife. Therefore, since mukzeh is forbidden to handle, it follows that the knife of circumcision may not be handled on the Sabbath.*

In this context, the first statement, from which another is derived, is called the **Premise**. The second, which is derived from it, is called the **Conclusion**, and the process of deduction is called a **Syllogism**. A **Classical Syllogism** is one which follows the pattern of the above examples.

However, we must take note that the entire force of the deduction rests on an understanding that the predicate of the conclusion is, in fact, a part of the predicate of the premise, or that the subject of the conclusion is a subcategory of the subject of the premise. Thus, if the predicate of the conclusion is not absolutely and consistently an attribute or subcategory of the predicate of the premise, then it is impossible to make the desired deduction.

> *To continue the example from Shabbos: It may be presumed that lighting a fire is included in the category of primary works of the Sabbath. We have also stated the premise (Shabbos 70a)*

אוֹמֵר, שֶׁאֵינָהּ אַב מְלָאכָה, הִנֵּה לֹא תוֹלִיד
עוֹד שֶׁהַמַּבְעִיר יִהְיֶה חַיָּב מִיתָה.

וְכֵן כְּשֶׁיָּדַעְתָּ שֶׁהַמֻּקְצֶה אָסוּר בְּטִלְטוּל, וְחָשַׁבְתָּ
שֶׁלְּטַלְטְלוֹ מִן הַצַּד יִהְיֶה גַּם כֵּן אָסוּר (שבת מג ב),
וְאַחַר כָּךְ שָׁמַעְתָּ שֶׁטִּלְטוּל מִן הַצַּד אֵין שְׁמוֹ
טִלְטוּל, הִנֵּה לֹא תָדִין עוֹד שֶׁיִּהְיֶה הַמֻּקְצֶה
אָסוּר לְטַלְטְלוֹ מִן הַצַּד.

וְאָמְנָם בַּדָּבָר הַזֶּה תִּפֹּל הַטָּעוּת בְּשִׂכְלוֹ שֶׁל הָאָדָם, שֶׁיַּחְשֹׁב
מִתְּחִלָּה הֱיוֹת הַדָּבָר בְּדֶרֶךְ אֶחָד וְיִמְצָאֵהוּ אַחַר כָּךְ בְּדֶרֶךְ אַחֵר, וְגַם
יִפְּלוּ הַמַּחֲלֹקֶת וְהַהֶפְרֵשׁ בֵּין הַסְּבָרוֹת, וְעַל כֵּן יִקְרֶה שֶׁאֶחָד יוֹלִיד
תוֹלָדָה אַחַת וְאַחֵר יַכְחִישָׁהּ.

עוֹד מִטֶּבַע הַהִתְבּוֹנְנוּת הוּא, שֶׁהַדּוֹמִים יִלְמְדוּ זֶה מִזֶּה; פֵּרוּשׁ –
שֶׁאִם מָצָאנוּ שְׁנֵי נוֹשְׂאִים דּוֹמִים, וּמָצָאנוּ בְּאֶחָד מֵהֶם מִפֹּרָשׁ נָשׂוּא
אֶחָד, בְּדִין הַמָּצֵא הַנָּשׂוּא הַהוּא גַּם בַּשֵּׁנִי, אַף עַל פִּי שֶׁלֹּא פֹרַשׁ בּוֹ,
וְנִקְרָא **בִּנְיַן־אָב** אוֹ **מַה־מָּצִינוּ**. וְכֵן עַל דֶּרֶךְ זֶה נָדוֹן מֵהַפָּחוֹת עַל

> *that anyone who does a primary work on the*
> *Sabbath incurs the death penalty. However, the*
> *Talmud states that Rabbi Yosi declared that*
> *lighting a fire is not a primary work. Thus,*
> *according to him, it is no longer legitimate to*
> *deduce that one who lights a fire on the Sab-*
> *bath will incur the death penalty.*
>
> *Likewise, since we know that it is forbidden to*
> *carry mukzeh, we might deduce that carrying*
> *it in an unusual way is also forbidden. But*
> *later, we learn (Shabbos 43b) that carrying in*
> *an unusual way is not the same as carrying,*
> *and therefore we no longer draw the conclusion*
> *that it is forbidden to carry mukzeh in an*
> *unusual way.*

It is here that many errors arise in our thinking, for we may at first define something one way, and only afterwards find that it is better to define it differently. In addition, there may be arguments and differences of opinion about the definition of certain terms, and thus it is possible for one person to come to a certain conclusion while someone else may come to a contrary one.

In addition to this kind of deduction called a classical syllogism, we may reason by analogy to draw conclusions from any subject about any other similar subject. That is, when we have two subjects which are similar, and a certain predicate is explicit in one of them, then logically it must be found also in the second, even though it is not mentioned. This is called an **Analogism**. Likewise, if there is a basis

הַיָּתֵר אוֹ לְהֵפֶךְ, וְהַיְנוּ שֶׁאִם נִמְצָא נָשׂוּא בַּנּוֹשֵׂא שֶׁהוּא פָּחוֹת מֵחֲבֵרוֹ, וְרָאוּי אוֹתוֹ נָשׂוּא לְהִמָּצֵא בַּנּוֹשֵׂא שֶׁהוּא יוֹתֵר מִמֶּנּוּ, נָדוּן הֱיוֹתוֹ בּוֹ. וְכֵן מֵהַיָּתֵר לַפָּחוֹת. וְזֶה נִקְרָא **כָּל־שֶׁכֵּן וְקַל־וָחֹמֶר.**

דֶּרֶךְ מָשָׁל, אָמְרוּ (תורת כהנים דיבורא דחטאת פרשה ה):
"יָחִיד מוּצָא מִכְּלַל צִבּוּר וְנָשִׂיא מוּצָא מִכְּלַל
צִבּוּר, מַה יָחִיד מֵבִיא אָשָׁם תָּלוּי – אַף נָשִׂיא
מֵבִיא אָשָׁם תָּלוּי" – זֶה לִמּוּד מִכֹּחַ דִּמְיוֹן.

וּכְשֶׁאָמְרוּ (תורת כהנים שם): "וּמָה אִם הַיָּחִיד שֶׁאֵין
מֵבִיא עַל הַוָּדְעוֹ זָכָר – מֵבִיא אָשָׁם תָּלוּי,
נָשִׂיא שֶׁמֵּבִיא עַל הַוָּדְעוֹ זָכָר – אֵינוֹ דִין
שֶׁיָּבִיא אָשָׁם תָּלוּי" – זֶה נִקְרָא קַל־וָחֹמֶר.

of comparison between two subjects, and we can view them on a scale from lesser to greater, then we may draw conclusions by projecting from the lesser to the greater, or the reverse. Thus, if a certain predicate is applied explicitly to the lesser of two subjects, and it is reasonable that it should also apply to the greater subject, then we make the deduction that the same predicate is applied to the greater subject, even though it is not stated. The same kind of deduction can also be made from the greater to the lesser. This is called **A Fortiori**.

> *For example, (Toras Cohanim, Sin Offerings, Section 5) "The sacrifice of an individual is unlike the public sacrifices and also that of a prince is unlike the public sacrifices. What is the law for an individual? He can bring a doubtful guilt offering! Therefore, also a prince can bring a doubtful guilt offering". This deduction is an analogism.*

> *The same conclusion can also be drawn a fortiori: (Toras Cohanim, ibid.) "What shall we say? If an individual, who does **not** bring a male sacrifice for a sin that becomes known to him only afterwards, nonetheless **can** bring a doubtful guilt offering, therefore a prince, who **does** bring a male sacrifice for such a sin, **surely** should be able to bring a doubtful guilt offering".*

וְהִנֵּה אִם תִּמְצָא, שֶׁהַנּוֹשְׂאִים שֶׁחָשַׁבְתָּ הֱיוֹתָם דּוֹמִים שֶׁאֵינָם
דּוֹמִים בֶּאֱמֶת – תְּבַטֵּל הַתּוֹלָדָה; וְכֵן אִם תִּמְצָא, שֶׁאוֹתוֹ שֶׁחָשַׁבְתָּ
פָּחוֹת אוֹ יָתֵר, אֵינוֹ פָּחוֹת אוֹ יָתֵר – תְּבַטֵּל הַתּוֹלָדָה; אוֹ אִם תִּמְצָא
נוֹשֵׂא אַחֵר דּוֹמֶה לְנוֹשֵׂא הַנִּדּוֹן שֶׁאֵין בּוֹ הַנָּשׂוּא הַהוּא – תְּבַטֵּל
תּוֹלַדְתֶּךָ.

דֶּרֶךְ מָשָׁל, כְּשֶׁהָיִינוּ חוֹשְׁבִים שֶׁיְּלַמֵּד צִבּוּר
מִנָּשִׂיא, הֵשִׁיב הַשַׁ"ס (כריתות כו א): "צִבּוּר מִנָּשִׂיא
לָא אָתֵי, דְּאִיכָּא לְמִפְרָךְ: מַה לַנָּשִׂיא שֶׁכֵּן יֵשׁ
בְּקָרְבָּנוֹ נְקֵבָה", וְנִמְצָא, שֶׁאֵין הַצִּבּוּר וְהַנָּשִׂיא
דּוֹמִים בֶּאֱמֶת.

וְכֵן כְּשֶׁלָּמְדוּ בְּקַל־וָחֹמֶר נָשִׂיא מִמָּשִׁיחַ (הוריות י
א): "וּמָה, מָשִׁיחַ שֶׁמֵּבִיא חַטָּאתוֹ מִשֶּׁעָבַר –
אֵין מֵבִיא עַל הַקּוֹדְמוֹת, נָשִׂיא שֶׁאֵין מֵבִיא

Now, if it is proven that the two subjects which were supposed to be similar are not really similar, then the conclusion will be invalid. Also, if it is proven that what you thought was lesser or greater is not lesser or greater, then the conclusion will be invalid. Thirdly, if you find another subject similar to the subject in question, and it does not have the desired predicate, this will also prove that the conclusion is invalid.

*Here is an example of the first type of fallacy, where the terms which were supposed to be similar are shown to be dissimilar. (Kerisos 26a) It was thought at first that a law of public doubtful sin offerings could be derived from the doubtful sin offering of a prince, but the Talmud responded, "That of the public cannot be derived from that of the prince because there is an objection: a prince may sometimes bring a female offering [while the public sacrifices are always males]". Thus, the public sacrifices cannot really be compared with those of the prince.*

*An example of the second type of fallacy mentioned above can be found where the Talmud derives the law of a prince from that of a Cohen Gadol, a fortiori. (Horayos 10a) "What shall we say? A Cohen Gadol must bring the sin offering designated for his rank even for a sin committed after he is no longer Cohen Gadol. However, he does not bring this same sin*

חַטָּאתוֹ מִשֶּׁעָבַר – אֵינוֹ דִין שֶׁלֹּא יָבִיא עַל
הַקּוֹדְמוֹת", סָתְרוּ הַקַּל־וָחֹמֶר בְּאָמְרָם: "מַה
לַמָּשִׁיחַ שֶׁכֵּן אֵינוֹ מֵבִיא בְּשִׁגְגַת מַעֲשֶׂה, תֹּאמַר
בַּנָּשִׂיא שֶׁמֵּבִיא בְּשִׁגְגַת מַעֲשֶׂה"; וְזֶה מִפְּנֵי
שֶׁבַּתְּחִלָּה חָשַׁבְנוּ הֱיוֹת מָשִׁיחַ יוֹתֵר מִנָּשִׂיא, וְעַל
כֵּן לָמַדְנוּ, שֶׁאִם הוּא אֵינוֹ מֵבִיא קָרְבָּן עַל
הַקּוֹדְמוֹת, כָּל שֶׁכֵּן הַנָּשִׂיא שֶׁהוּא פָּחוּת מִמֶּנּוּ;
וְאַחַר כָּךְ מְצָאֲנוּ, שֶׁאֵין הַנָּשִׂיא פָּחוּת, שֶׁהֲרֵי
בִּבְחִינָה אַחֶרֶת הוּא יוֹתֵר מִמֶּנּוּ, וְאִם כֵּן אִי
אֶפְשָׁר לָדוּן מִזֶּה עַל זֶה.

*offering for a sin committed before his appointment to office. Now, a prince does **not** bring the sin offering designated for his rank for a sin committed when he is no longer a prince. Does it not follow that he **surely** would not bring the sin offering of a prince for a sin committed before his appointment"? Later, the Talmud refutes this deduction by saying, "A Cohen Gadol does not bring a sin offering for an error in action alone [i.e., unaccompanied by ignorance of the law]. How then can the law of a prince be derived, since the prince **does** bring a sin offering for an error in action alone"? In this case, it was first assumed that a Cohen Gadol is greater than a prince. Therefore, we came to the conclusion that if the Cohen Gadol is not obligated to bring the sacrifice appropriate to his office for a sin committed before his appointment, then, a fortiori, this law also should not apply in the case of a prince, who is less than the Cohen Gadol. Afterwards, we find that a prince is not the more lenient of the two cases because in some other respect a stricter ruling is applied to him. Consequently, it is impossible to make any deduction at all from one to the other since it is not clearly established which is the stricter case and which is the more lenient.*

וּכְשֶׁרָצוּ לִלְמֹד נָשִׂיא מִיָּחִיד, בְּאָמְרָם (תורת
כהנים דיבורא דחטאת פרשה ה): "וּמָה, אִם הַיָּחִיד שֶׁאֵין
מֵבִיא עַל הוֹדְעוֹ זָכָר – מֵבִיא אָשָׁם תָּלוּי,
נָשִׂיא שֶׁמֵּבִיא עַל הוֹדְעוֹ זָכָר – אֵינוֹ דִין
שֶׁיָּבִיא אָשָׁם תָּלוּי", סָתְרוּ הַדִּין בְּאָמְרָם:
"מָשִׁיחַ יוֹכִיחַ, שֶׁמֵּבִיא עַל הוֹדְעוֹ זָכָר וְאֵין
מֵבִיא אָשָׁם תָּלוּי"; וְזֶה, מִפְּנֵי שֶׁכְּבָר מָצָאנוּ
נוֹשֵׂא דוֹמֶה לְנוֹשֵׂא הַנִּדוֹן, שֶׁאֵין בּוֹ אוֹתוֹ
הַנָּשׂוּא.

*The last type of fallacy mentioned above involves a third case, which carries a different law than what would be expected. For example, (Toras Cohanim, Sin Offerings, Section 5) the rabbis sought to derive the law of a prince from that of an individual. "What shall we say? If an individual, who does **not** bring a male sacrifice for a sin that becomes known to him only afterwards, nonetheless brings a doubtful guilt offering, then all the more so, a prince, who **does** bring a male sacrifice for such a sin, **surely** should also bring a doubtful guilt offering". Then they rejected this argument in the following way: "The case of a Cohen Gadol proves otherwise, for he **does** bring a male sacrifice for a sin that becomes known to him only afterwards, and yet he does **not** bring a doubtful guilt offering". The force of this rebuttal is that there exists another subject (Cohen Gadol) similar to the subject in question (a prince) which does not have the desired predicate (the law of a doubtful guilt offering), and therefore the similarity of the first two cases (an individual and a prince) cannot be the basis for a valid deduction.*

עוֹד מִטֶּבַע הַהִתְבּוֹנְנוּת, שֶׁשְּׁנֵי עִנְיָנִים, שֶׁהֵם אֶחָד קוֹדֶם וְאֶחָד נִמְשָׁךְ, יַכְרִיחוּ זֶה אֶת זֶה; פֵּרוּשׁ, שֶׁבְּהִמָּצֵא הַקּוֹדֵם – יִמָּצֵא הַנִּמְשָׁךְ, וּבְהֵעָדֵר הַנִּמְשָׁךְ – יֵעָדֵר הַקּוֹדֵם.

דֶּרֶךְ מָשָׁל (פסחים יט א): "וְאִי סָלְקָא דַעְתָּךְ סָבַר כְּרַבִּי עֲקִיבָא, נִתְנֵי נַמִּי רְבִיעִי בַּתְּרוּמָה וַחֲמִישִׁי בַּקֹּדֶשׁ", הִנֵּה זֶה הַהֶכְרֵחַ נוֹסַד עַל יְסוֹד זֶה שֶׁאָמַרְנוּ, וְהַיְנוּ כִּי זֶה וַדַּאי, שֶׁאִם הָיָה סוֹבֵר כְּרַבִּי עֲקִיבָא – הָיָה נִמְשָׁךְ מִזֶּה שֶׁהָיָה שׁוֹנֶה רְבִיעִי וַחֲמִישִׁי; כֵּיוָן שֶׁאָנוּ רוֹאִים שֶׁאֵינוֹ שׁוֹנֶה רְבִיעִי וַחֲמִישִׁי – אִם כֵּן וַדַּאי שֶׁאֵינוֹ סוֹבֵר כְּרַבִּי עֲקִיבָא.

הִנֵּה הַדִּין הַזֶּה נִקְרָא הֶקֵּשׁ **תָּלוּי**, לְפִי שֶׁהַקְדָּמָתוֹ מַאֲמָר תָּלוּי.

עוֹד מִטֶּבַע הַהִתְבּוֹנְנוּת, שֶׁנּוֹשְׂאִים שׁוֹנִים, שֶׁמִּכָּרַח הַמָּצֵא אֶחָד מֵהֶם לְבַדּוֹ בַּנּוֹשֵׂא, כְּשֶׁיִּתְבָּרֵר לָנוּ מְצִיאוּת הָאֶחָד – יִכָּרַח הֵעָדֵר כָּל

Thus far we have discussed conclusions deduced from a Classical Syllogism and from an Analogism. Now, we will discuss the third type of deduction, which is a **Hypothetical Syllogism**. Logic dictates that each part of a hypothetical statement necessitates the other. That is, when the antecedent is established it can be logically deduced that the consequent is true, and when the consequent is proven false, the antecedent must also be false.

> *For example, (Pesachim 19a) "If you suppose that Rabbi Yosi agrees with Rabbi Akiva, then he should also have taught that there is impurity in terumah even four degrees removed, and there is impurity in sanctified objects even five degrees removed [and this is not the case]". The following deduction can be constructed according to the principle we have just stated: If Rabbi Yosi agreed with Rabbi Akiva, he would have taught us that there is a fourth or fifth degree of impurity. Since we know that he did not teach us that there is impurity even to the fourth or fifth degree, therefore it is certain that he disagrees with Rabbi Akiva.*

This is a hypothetical syllogism since its premise is a hypothetical statement.

The fourth type of logical deduction is a **Disjunctive Syllogism**. It is based on the principle that disjunctive predicates negate one another. Since it is necessarily true that only one of the predicates is

הָאֲחֵרִים, וּכְשֶׁיִּתְבָּרֵר לָנוּ הֶעְדֵּר כֻּלָּם חוּץ מֵאֶחָד– תֻּכְרַח מְצִיאוּת הָאֶחָד הַנִּשְׁאָר.

דֶּרֶךְ מָשָׁל, אָמְרוּ (פסחים ה ג): "שָׁמַע מִנַּהּ: הַבְּעֵרָה לְחַלֵּק יָצָאת", נוֹסַד זֶה הַלִּמוּד עַל הַיְסוֹד הַזֶּה שֶׁזְּכַרְנוּ, כִּי הִנֵּה הַבְּעֵרָה לֹא יָצְתָה אֶלָּא לְחַלֵּק אוֹ לְלָאו; כֵּיוָן שֶׁרָאִינוּ שֶׁלֹּא יָצְתָה לְלָאו – אִם כֵּן מֻכְרָח שֶׁיָּצְתָה לְחַלֵּק.

attributed to the subject, it follows that whenever we determine the truth of one, all the others are denied. Alternatively, when all but one of the disjunctive predicates have been disproven we may conclude that the remaining one is true.

> For example, (Pesachim 5b) the Talmud con-
> cludes, "We can establish that Rabbi Akiva
> follows the interpretation that every primary
> work on the Sabbath is punished separately
> [when several are violated on the same day]". A
> disjunctive syllogism is employed to reach this
> conclusion according to the rule we have
> described. On the verse (Exodus 35:3) "You
> shall kindle no fire . . . on the Sabbath day", the
> Talmud asks: **either** this act is singled out in
> the verse to teach us that lighting a fire and
> every other primary work is punishable
> separately; **or** it is singled out to teach us that
> lighting a fire is a mere prohibition and not a
> primary work at all. Now, Rabbi Akiva specifi-
> cally stated that lighting a fire is **not** a mere
> prohibition but rather a primary work.
> Therefore, we must conclude, according to him,
> that this act was singled out in the verse to
> teach us the law of separate punishments.

וְכֵן כְּשֶׁאָמְרוּ (בבא קמא קד א): "הֵיכִי דָּמֵי? אִי דְּלָא
עֲשָׂאוֹ בְּעֵדִים – מְנָא יָדְעִינָן? אֶלָּא לָאו –
דַּעֲשָׂאוֹ בְּעֵדִים". יְסוֹד זֶה הוּא, כִּי אַחַת
מֵאֵלֶּה לֹא יִמָּנַע, אוֹ עָשָׂה בְּעֵדִים אוֹ שֶׁלֹּא
בְּעֵדִים; כֵּיוָן שֶׁנִּתְבָּרֵר לָנוּ שֶׁאִי אֶפְשָׁר שֶׁלֹּא
בְּעֵדִים, שֶׁאִם כֵּן מְנָא יָדְעִינָן – מֻכְרָח שֶׁעָשָׂה
בְּעֵדִים.

וְהִנֵּה דִּין זֶה נִקְרָא **הֶקֵּשׁ מְחַלֵּק**, לְפִי שֶׁהַקְדָּמָתוֹ מַאֲמָר מְחַלֵּק;
אוֹ נָשׂוּא זֶה אוֹ נָשׂוּא זֶה יֵשׁ בְּנוֹשֵׂא זֶה, אוֹ לְהֶפֶךְ, אוֹ לְנוֹשֵׂא זֶה אוֹ
לְנוֹשֵׂא זֶה יִיָחֵס זֶה הַנָּשׂוּא, וּכְמוֹ שֶׁאָמַרְנוּ לְמַעְלָה.

*In another example, a lender sends a cow to a borrower by an agent, and the rabbis ruled that this agent must be appointed in front of witnesses. (Babba Kamma 104a) "How shall we imagine this case? If the agent was not appointed in the presence of witnesses, how can we be sure that he is an agent at all? In fact, it must be that he was appointed in the presence of witnesses!" The principle on which this deduction is based is that one of two predicates must be applied to the case: either there were witnesses or there were none. Since it is impossible in this case for the agent to be appointed without witnesses, for we would then not be sure that he is an agent at all, it follows that there must have been witnesses.*

This deduction is called a disjunctive syllogism since its premise is a disjunctive statement. That is, either this predicate or that predicate is found in a subject; or alternatively, either this subject or that subject has some predicate applied to it. This was explained in Chapter Three.

# פרק ח

כְּבָר בֵּאַרְנוּ הֲבָנַת הַמַּאֲמָרִים וְהֻלֶּדֶת הַתּוֹלָדוֹת. עַתָּה נְבָאֵר
קַבָּלַת הַדֵּעוֹת אוֹ הַכְחָשָׁתָן.

כָּל מַאֲמָר שֶׁנִּשְׁמַע – אֶפְשָׁר שֶׁנְּקַבֵּל אוֹתוֹ, וְאֶפְשָׁר שֶׁנַּכְחִישֵׁהוּ,
וְאֶפְשָׁר שֶׁנִּסְתַּפֵּק בּוֹ. מַאֲמָר שֶׁתָּבוֹא לָנוּ רְאָיָה עַל אֲמִתּוֹ – נְקַבְּלֵהוּ,
מַאֲמָר שֶׁתִּהְיֶה לָנוּ רְאָיָה עַל כִּזְבּוֹ – נַכְחִישֵׁהוּ, וְשֶׁלֹּא תִהְיֶה לָנוּ רְאָיָה
לֹא עַל אֲמִתּוֹ וְלֹא עַל כִּזְבּוֹ – נִסְתַּפֵּק בּוֹ.

הָרְאָיָה עַל אֲמִתַּת הַמַּאֲמָר, מִתְחַלֶּקֶת לִשְׁלֹשָׁה מִינִים: רְאָיָה
מִצַּד הַטֶּבַע, רְאָיָה מִצַּד הַהַסְכָּמָה וּרְאָיָה מִצַּד הַהֶקֵּשׁ.

**רְאָיָה מִצַּד הַטֶּבַע** הִיא – שֶׁיִּהְיֶה הַמַּאֲמָר מִן הַדְּבָרִים
הַמְאֻמָּתִים אֵצֶל הַכֹּל בַּטֶּבַע, אוֹ נוֹסָד עַל אֶחָד מִן הַדְּבָרִים הָאֵלֶּה.
פֵּרוּשׁ – הִנֵּה שְׁנֵי מִינֵי עִנְיָנִים יֵשׁ שֶׁהֵם מְאֻמָּתִים מִצַּד עַצְמָם וְאֵינָם
צְרִיכִים רְאָיָה אַחֶרֶת, וְהֵם הַמֻּשְׂכָּלוֹת הָרִאשׁוֹנִים וְהַמּוּחָשׁוֹת.
**הַמֻּשְׂכָּלוֹת הָרִאשׁוֹנִים** הֵם הָעִנְיָנִים, שֶׁשֵּׂכֶל הָאָדָם מוֹרֶה אוֹתָם
מֵעַצְמוֹ, וְלֹא יִצְטָרֵךְ עַל זֶה לִמּוּד, וְלֹא יִסְתַּפֵּק בָּהֶם מִי שֶׁהוּא בָּרִיא
בְּשִׂכְלוֹ. דֶּרֶךְ מָשָׁל, שֶׁשְּׁנַיִם יוֹתֵר מֵאֶחָד, שֶׁהַחֵצִי פָּחוֹת מֵהַכֹּל, וְכֵן כָּל
כַּיּוֹצֵא בָזֶה. **הַמּוּחָשׁוֹת** – מַה שֶׁהַחוּשׁ מֵעִיד עָלָיו, כְּגוֹן שֶׁהָאֶבֶן קָשָׁה,
שֶׁהַמַּיִם לַחִים.

# Chapter Eight

We have now completed our discussion on how to understand statements and deduce new ideas, and at this point we will consider how opinions should be accepted or rejected.

With absolutely any statement there is a possibility to accept it or to reject it or to remain in doubt about it. Only when we are presented with a proof of a statement should we accept that statement as being true. If a proof is brought that a statement is false, then we must reject that statement; and if no proof exists for either the truth or the falsity of the statement – we will remain in doubt.

## Proofs of Statements

The truth of any statement can be established in three ways: postulated proof, proof through convention, and logical proof.

**Postulated Proof** – when the statement in question is one of those truths which is naturally manifest to all or that it is based upon such a truth. There are two types of things whose truth is self-evident; they are axiomatic principles and direct sense perceptions. **Axiomatic Principles** are concepts dictated by the intellect itself without any training and about which no normal person can have any doubt, for example, that two is greater than one, and that the half is less than the whole, and so forth. **Sense Perceptions** are things to which our senses testify, such as that stones are hard or that water is wet.

דֶּרֶךְ מָשָׁל, כְּשֶׁאָמְרוּ (סוכה מ א): "יָצְאוּ עֵצִים, שֶׁהֲנָאָתָן אַחַר בִּעוּרָן", הִנֵּה אֲמִתַּת זֶה הַמַּאֲמָר מִתְבָּרֶרֶת לָנוּ מִן הַחוּשׁ, שֶׁהֲרֵי בְּעֵינֵינוּ אָנוּ רוֹאִים וּמַרְגִּישִׁים אָנוּ זֶה, שֶׁאֵין הֲנָאַת הָעֵצִים אֶלָּא אַחַר שֶׁנִּבְעָרוּ; וְכֵן כָּל כַּיּוֹצֵא בָּזֶה.

רְאָיָה מִצַּד הַהַסְכָּמָה הִיא – שֶׁיִּהְיֶה הַמַּאֲמָר מַה שֶּׁדַּעַת כָּל הָאֲנָשִׁים מַסְכִּימָה עָלָיו, אוֹ נוֹסָד עַל זֶה, שֶׁאָז יִהְיֶה אוֹתוֹ הַמַּאֲמָר מֻאֲמָת לְכָל מִי שֶׁיִּהְיֶה מִן הַכְּלָל הַהוּא. וְיֵחָלֵק זֶה לִשְׁנֵי מִינִים: הָאֶחָד – הַמְפֻרְסָמוֹת, וְהַשֵּׁנִי – הַמְקֻבָּלוֹת. הַמְפֻרְסָמוֹת – הֵם שֶׁדַּעַת רֹב הָאֲנָשִׁים מַסְכִּימָה עֲלֵיהֶם מִצַּד הֱיוֹתָם אֱנוֹשִׁיִּים. דֶּרֶךְ מָשָׁל, שֶׁהַגַּאֲוָה מְגֻנָּה וְשֶׁהָעֲנָוָה מְשֻׁבַּחַת, וְכֵן כָּל כַּיּוֹצֵא בָּזֶה. הַמְקֻבָּלוֹת – מַה שֶּׁנִּמְסַר בַּמָּסֹרֶת מֵהָאָבוֹת וְהַמְלַמְּדִים, וְנִכְלְלוּ בָּזֶה לָנוּ כָּל כִּתְבֵי הַקֹּדֶשׁ וְכָל הֲלָכָה לְמֹשֶׁה מִסִּינַי וְכָל שְׁלֹשׁ-עֶשְׂרֵה הַמִּדּוֹת שֶׁהַתּוֹרָה נִדְרֶשֶׁת בָּהֶן עִם כָּל מִשְׁפְּטֵיהֶן. וְנִמְצָא, שֶׁיֶּאֱמַת לָנוּ מַאֲמָר, כְּשֶׁיִּמָּצֵא אֶחָד מִן הַכְּתוּבִים, אוֹ מִן הַהֲלָכוֹת שֶׁבְּעַל-פֶּה, אוֹ מִמַּאַמְרֵי מִי שֶׁאִי אֶפְשָׁר לָנוּ לַחֲלֹק עָלָיו, שֶׁיְּאַמֵּת מַאֲמָרֵנוּ.

*For example, (Sukkah 40a) the Gemorah interprets the following verse: "The Torah states, 'it shall be for you for food'. Those products whose benefit is simultaneous with their consumption, like food, shall have the holiness of the Seventh Year, excluding wood used to make charcoal, whose benefit is derived only after the wood has been destroyed". The truth of this statement is demonstrated to us clearly by our senses since we see with our eyes and feel that no benefit is derived from wood which has been made into charcoal until after it has been destroyed.*

A **Proof Through Convention** is adduced when a particular statement is, or is based on, some view which is held in common by many people. This statement will then be true according to all those people. This kind of proof has two subcategories: common sense and accepted tradition. **Common Sense** is a basis for proof whenever an opinion is held by a majority of people by virtue of their human nature. For example, it is deemed common sense that pride is reprehensible and humility is praiseworthy, and so forth. **Accepted Tradition** provides a proof on the basis of what is transmitted in a masoretic line from ancestors and scholars of the people. We include in this category the Torah and writings of the Prophets, those laws given directly to Moshe at Sinai (and not written in the Torah), and all the thirteen principles by which the Torah is interpreted, along with their rules. Thus, we have a proof that a statement is true when it is supported by a verse or by Talmudic law or by the statement of an

דֶּרֶךְ מָשָׁל, כְּשֶׁשָּׁנִינוּ (יבמות מ א): "וְאִם יֵשׁ שָׁם אָב – נְכָסִים שֶׁל אָב", אָמְרוּ עַל זֶה: "דַּאֲמַר מַר: אָב קוֹדֶם לְכָל יוֹצְאֵי יְרֵכוֹ";

וְכֵן כְּשֶׁאָמְרוּ (סנהדרין צ א): "כָּל יִשְׂרָאֵל יֵשׁ לָהֶם חֵלֶק לָעוֹלָם הַבָּא", אָמְתוּ מַאֲמָר זֶה בַּעֲבוּר הַכָּתוּב שֶׁנֶּאֱמַר (ישעיה ס כא): "וְעַמֵּךְ כֻּלָּם צַדִּיקִים לְעוֹלָם יִירְשׁוּ אָרֶץ". וְכֵן כֹּל כַּיוֹצֵא בָזֶה.

רְאָיָה מִצַּד הַהֶקֵּשׁ הִיא – שֶׁיִּתְבָּרֵר לָנוּ מֵהֱיוֹת מַאֲמָרֵנוּ תוֹלָדָה אֲמִתִּית שֶׁל הַקְדָּמָה מְאֻמֶּתֶת, וְהַיְנוּ שֶׁיִּוָּלֵד וְיִמָּשֵׁךְ זֶה הַמַּאֲמָר מִמַּאֲמָר אַחֵר מְאֻמָּת לָנוּ. וְזֶה בְּכֹחַ אֶחָד מִן הַהֶקֵּשִׁים שֶׁנִּתְבָּאֲרוּ לְמַעְלָה, דְּהַיְנוּ: הַהֶקֵּשׁ הַמּוֹפְתִי, הַמַּה־מָּצִינוּ, הַכָּל־שֶׁכֵּן, הַהֶקֵּשׁ הַתָּלוּי וְהַהֶקֵּשׁ הַמְּחַלֵּק.

וְצָרִיךְ שֶׁתֵּדַע, שֶׁכְּשֵׁם שֶׁיֶּאֱמַת מַאֲמָר אִם תָּבֹא לָנוּ רְאָיָה עָלָיו, כֵּן יֵאָמֵת אִם תָּבוֹא לָנוּ רְאָיָה עַל הֱיוֹת הִפְכּוֹ כּוֹזֵב, כִּי זֶה מְחַק

indisputable authority.

> *For example, when the Mishnah declares, (Ye-bamos 40a) "If the deceased brother is survived by his father as well as his brothers, his estate belongs to the father". The Talmud then brings a proof: "For the master has taught, in questions of inheritance, the father takes precedence over all his own children".*
>
> *Again, when the Talmud states, (Sanhedrin 90a) "Every Jew has a portion in the world to come", the truth of this statement is proven from the verse (Isaiah 60:21) "Your people shall be altogether righteous; they shall inherit the land forever. . .".*

A **Logical Proof** is adduced when a statement is clearly demonstrated to be a valid conclusion from a true premise. That is, the statement in question is deduced from some other statement which is already known to be true. This type of proof is based on one of the syllogisms which has been previously explained, namely: a classical syllogism, analogism, a fortiori, hypothetical syllogism, or disjunctive syllogism.

It is important to note that just as a statement is true if a proof can be brought to it (i.e., direct proof), so also it will be true if a proof can be brought that its opposite is false (i.e., indirect proof). For it is inherent in the nature of contradictory statements that whenever one is rejected the other must be accepted. However, they must be

הַהַפְכִּיִּים , כְּשֶׁאֶחָד יִשָּׁלֵל - הַשֵּׁנִי יָקוּם, וּבִלְבַד שֶׁלֹּא יִהְיוּ מֵאוֹתָם שֶׁיֵּשׁ בֵּינֵיהֶם אֶמְצָעִי, כִּי אָז שְׁנַיִם הֵם שֶׁיִּשָּׁלְלוּ וְיָקוּם הַשְּׁלִישִׁי.

וְאַרְאֶה לְךָ עַתָּה מָשָׁל אֶחָד עַל הָרְאָיָה שֶׁמִּצַּד הַמּוֹפֵת.

אָמְרוּ (יבמות סו א): "מִנַּיִן לַכֹּהֵן שֶׁנָּשָׂא אִשָּׁה וְקָנָה עֲבָדִים שֶׁיֹּאכְלוּ בַתְּרוּמָה? שֶׁנֶּאֱמַר (ויקרא כב יא): 'וְכֹהֵן כִּי יִקְנֶה נֶפֶשׁ קִנְיַן כַּסְפּוֹ הוּא יֹאכַל בּוֹ'". הִנֵּה הָיָה הַמַּאֲמָר שֶׁאֵשֶׁת כֹּהֵן אוֹכֶלֶת בַּתְּרוּמָה, וְהָרְאָיָה עַל זֶה מִכֹּחַ הַמּוֹפֵת, שֶׁהֲרֵי כְּבָר נִתְאַמֵּת לָנוּ שֶׁקִּנְיַן כַּסְפּוֹ שֶׁל הַכֹּהֵן אוֹכֵל בַּתְּרוּמָה, וְזֶה מִכֹּחַ הַכָּתוּב שֶׁכָּךְ מְפָרֵשׁ: "וְכֹהֵן כִּי-יִקְנֶה נֶפֶשׁ קִנְיַן כַּסְפּוֹ הוּא יֹאכַל בּוֹ", וְיָדַעְנוּ כְּמוֹ כֵן שֶׁאִשְׁתּוֹ שֶׁל הַכֹּהֵן הִיא קִנְיַן כַּסְפּוֹ, לְפִי שֶׁאִשָּׁה נִקְנֵית בְּכֶסֶף - אִם כֵּן מֻכְרָח שֶׁתֹּאכַל בַּתְּרוּמָה.

עוֹד אָמְרוּ (הוריות ט א): "וּמַאי שְׁנָא 'מֵאַחַת' דְּמַשְׁמַע לֵהּ? דִּכְתִיבֵהּ רַחֲמָנָא לְבַסּוֹף גַּבֵּי

genuine opposites and not the type of contradictory statements that have some mean term, for with the latter, it is possible to deny both contradictory terms and the mean term may be true.

I will now give an example of a proof through a classical syllogism.

> *The Talmud asks, (Yebamos 66a) "How is the law derived that the wife and slaves of a Cohen are permitted to eat terumah? It is written, (Leviticus 22:11) 'If a Cohen buys any person with money, he may eat of it [terumah]. . .'". It is proven through a syllogism that the wife of a Cohen may eat terumah. It is an accepted premise that anyone acquired with the Cohen's money may eat terumah. This is explicit in the verse "If a Cohen buys any person with money, he may eat of it [terumah]. . .". We know further that the Cohen's wife is considered his monetary acquisition for a woman is married by means of money. Thus, it is necessarily true that she may eat terumah. (This is a direct proof.)*
>
> *Another example may be found using a hypothetical syllogism where the Talmud discusses the question of whether a Cohen Gadol can, in principle, offer an oleh v'yored sacrifice. An oleh v'yored is a sin offering for certain transgressions which has a sliding scale of obli-*

עֲשִׂירִית הָאֵיפָה, לְמֵימְרָא דְכָל דְּמִחַיֵּיב
בַּעֲשִׂירִית הָאֵיפָה מִחַיֵּיב בְּכֻלָּן, דְּאִי סָלְקָא
דַעְתָּךְ מִתְחַיֵּיב בְּאַחַת אַף עַל פִּי שֶׁאֵין מִתְחַיֵּיב
בְּכֻלָּן, נִכְתְּבֵהּ רַחֲמָנָא לְהַאי 'מֵאַחַת' בְּדַלּוּת
אִי נַמִּי בַּעֲשִׂירוּת".

*gation. A rich man brings a female sheep, a poor man brings two doves, and the poorest brings a tenth of an ephah of wheat flour. The question about a Cohen Gadol arises because he is excluded by virtue of his office from offering a tenth of an ephah; and therefore, it is in doubt whether he can bring an oleh v'yored offering in one of its other forms. The Talmud states, (Horayos 9a) "Rabbi Akiva said, a Cohen Gadol is exempt from all forms of an oleh v'yored offering. Abaye and Rava both said that his proof is based on the verse [Leviticus 5:13] 'And the Cohen shall atone for him in regard to his sin that he has sinned with **any one** of these [offerings]. . .'. Since this verse is written after the last of the three oleh v'yored offerings, which is a tenth of an ephah, we are informed that only one who can sacrifice a tenth of an ephah can sacrifice one of the other forms of an oleh v'yored offering. Now **if** it can be said that the Cohen Gadol should be able to sacrifice one of the other oleh v'yored offerings even though he is not able to sacrifice the third one, **then** the Torah would have put this verse ["with **any one** of these [offerings]"] earlier in the paragraph, in proximity to the first two offerings of a poor man or a rich man".*

הִנֵּה הָיָה כָאן הַמַּאֲמָר שֶׁרַק הַמִּתְכַּפֵּר בָּאַחַת,
הוּא מִתְכַּפֵּר בְּכֻלָּן. וְהוּבְאָה רְאָיָה עַל זֶה מִכֹּחַ
מוֹפֵת כָּזֶה: אִם גַּם מִי שֶׁאֵינוֹ מִתְכַּפֵּר בָּאַחַת
הָיָה מִתְכַּפֵּר בְּכֻלָּן, הָיָה הַכָּתוּב אוֹמֵר "מֵאַחַת"
בְּדַלּוּת אוֹ בַּעֲשִׁירוּת, אָנוּ רוֹאִים שֶׁלֹּא אָמְרוּ
הַכָּתוּב לֹא בְּדַלּוּת וְלֹא בַּעֲשִׁירוּת – אִם כֵּן
מֻכְרָח, שֶׁמִּי שֶׁאֵינוֹ מִתְכַּפֵּר בָּאַחַת אֵינוֹ
מִתְכַּפֵּר בְּכֻלָּן, אֶלָּא הַמִּתְכַּפֵּר בָּאַחַת מִתְכַּפֵּר
בְּכֻלָּן. וְזֶה עַל יְדֵי הַהֶקֵּשׁ הַתָּלוּי שֶׁזָּכַרְנוּ
לְמַעְלָה. וְעַל דֶּרֶךְ זֶה כָּל שְׁאָר הַהֶקֵּשִׁים.

הָרְאָיָה עַל הֱיוֹת הַמַּאֲמָר כּוֹזֵב, גַּם הִיא עַל שְׁלֹשָׁה דְרָכִים,
וְהָיְנוּ: מִצַּד הַטֶּבַע, מִצַּד הַהַסְכָּמָה וּמִצַּד הַהֶקֵּשׁ.

*In this text, the statement in question is that only someone who gains atonement through a tenth of an ephah as an oleh v'yored offering can gain atonement through the other forms of an oleh v'yored offering. The proof for this is the following syllogism: **If** someone who has no atonement from one form of this offering is still able to bring some other form of oleh v'yored offering, **then** the verse "with **any one** of these [offerings]" would be found next to the oleh v'yored offering applicable to a rich man or poor man. We see that the verse is not found in proximity to the offerings of a rich man or poor man. Therefore, it follows that anyone who has no atonement through the offering of a tenth of an ephah is exempt from all other forms of oleh v'yored offering. (This is an indirect proof.) This conclusion is reached by way of a hypothetical syllogism which we have previously described, and, in a similar manner, the other syllogisms may be used to adduce a proof.*

## Disproofs of Statements

A disproof contending that a given statement is false operates in the same three ways as a proof; it may be postulatory, conventional or logical.

**מִצַּד הַטֶּבַע** – שֶׁיִּמָּצֵא אֶחָד מִן הָעִנְיָנִים הַמְאַמְּתִים בַּטֶּבַע
שֶׁזְּכַרְנוּ שֶׁיַּכְחִישׁוּ אֶת הַמַּאֲמָר.

דֶּרֶךְ מָשָׁל (ברכות נח ג): "וּגְמִירֵי דְּלָא עֲבַר
כִּסְלָא", הֵבִיאוּ רְאָיָה נֶגֶד הַמַּאֲמָר מִכֹּחַ הַחוּשׁ
וְאָמְרוּ: "וְהָא קָא חַזֵּינָן דַּעֲבַר".

**מִצַּד הַהַסְכָּמָה** – שֶׁיִּמָּצֵא כָּתוּב אוֹ מַאֲמָר, שֶׁאִי אֶפְשָׁר לַחֲלֹק
עֲלֵיהֶם, שֶׁיַּכְחִישׁוּ אֶת הַמַּאֲמָר.

דֶּרֶךְ מָשָׁל, כְּשֶׁאָמְרוּ (חגיגה ד א): "כָּל-זְכוּרְךָ –
לְרַבּוֹת אֶת הַקְּטַנִּים", הֵבִיאוּ רְאָיָה נֶגֶד זֶה מִן
הַמִּשְׁנָה "וְהָא אֲנַן תְּנַן: חוּץ מֵחֵרֵשׁ שׁוֹטֶה
וְקָטָן".

וְכֵן כְּשֶׁאָמְרוּ (בבא קמא פג ג): "סִמֵּא אֶת עֵינוֹ,
קָטַע אֶת יָדוֹ, שִׁבֵּר אֶת רַגְלוֹ – רוֹאִין אוֹתוֹ
כְּאִלּוּ הוּא עֶבֶד נִמְכָּר בַּשּׁוּק", הֵבִיאוּ רְאָיָה

A **Postulated Disproof** is concluded when it is found that axiomatic principles or direct sense perceptions contradict the statement in question.

> *For example, (Berachos 58b) "There is a tradition that shooting stars never pass through the constellation of Orion for if they did the world would be destroyed". The Talmud disproves this statement on the basis of direct sense perception: "But we have seen them pass through!"*

A **Disproof Through Convention** is concluded when we find a verse or a traditional text of undisputed authority which contradicts the statement in question.

> *For example, (Chagigah 4a) "In the verse [Exodus 23:17] 'Three times a year all your males shall appear before the Almighty God', 'all your males' includes even minors". The Talmud disproves this interpretation by referring to the Mishnah: "But we have learned in the Mishnah, with the exception of a deaf or insane person or a minor"!*

> *Another example is found in the Mishnah, (Babba Kamma 83b) "If someone is injured by another who blinded his eye, cut off his hand, or broke his foot, we evaluate the damage to the injured man as if he were a slave sold in the*

נֶגֶד זֶה מֵהַכָּתוּב "וְהָא כְּתִיב (ויקרא כד יז): וְאִישׁ
כִּי יַכֶּה כָּל־נֶפֶשׁ אָדָם מוֹת יוּמָת – עַיִן תַּחַת
עַיִן".

**מִצַּד הַהֶקֵּשׁ** – כְּשֶׁנִּרְאֶה הֱיוֹת הֵפֶךְ הַמַּאֲמָר אוֹ הַמִּתְחַלֵּף מִמֶּנּוּ
תוֹלָדָה אֲמִתִּית מֵהַקְדָּמָה מְאֻמֶּתֶת, אוֹ כְּשֶׁנִּרְאֶה צֵאת מִן הַמַּאֲמָר
תוֹלָדָה שֶׁכְּזָבָהּ מְפֻרְסָם, שֶׁאָז נָדִין שֶׁבְּהֶכְרֵחַ הַהַקְדָּמָה גַּם כֵּן כּוֹזֶבֶת,
וְזֶה בְּכֹחַ הַהֶקֵּשׁ הַתָּלוּי שֶׁזָּכַרְנוּ לְמַעְלָה. כִּי כֵּיוָן שֶׁנִּתְבָּרֵר לָנוּ הֱיוֹת
הַתּוֹלָדָה הַהִיא הֶמְשֵׁךְ שֶׁל מַאֲמָרֵנוּ, הִנֵּה מֵחֹק הַקּוֹדֵם וְהַנִּמְשָׁךְ הוּא,
שֶׁבְּהֶעְדֵּר הַנִּמְשָׁךְ יֻכְרַח הֶעְדֵּר הַקּוֹדֵם.

דֶּרֶךְ מָשָׁל, כְּשֶׁאָמְרוּ (בבא קמא פג ב): "אֵימָא
בְּמִיתָה מַמָּשׁ", סָתְרוּ הַסְּבָרָא הַזֹּאת בְּכֹחַ
רְאָיָה זֹאת: "לָא סָלְקָא דַעְתָּךְ – דְּהָא אִתְּקַשׁ
לְמַכֵּה בְּהֵמָה יְשַׁלְּמֶנָּה". הִנֵּה כָּאן סָתְרוּ

*market". The Talmud quotes a verse in apparent contradiction to this Mishnah in order to disprove it. "But is it not written [Leviticus 24:17] 'And he that kills any man shall surely be put to death. . . and if he maims his neighbor, as he has done, so shall it be done to him. . . an eye for an eye, etc. [implying physical retribution]'"?*

A **Logical Disproof** is concluded when the opposite or contrary of a given statement can be derived through a syllogism from a true premise (i.e., indirect disproof). Alternatively, if some logical consequence of the given statement is found to be patently false, then the premise in question is necessarily also false (reductio ad absurdum). This is a principle of consequent statements based on the hypothetical syllogism which we have earlier explained. Thus, when it is established that a certain conclusion is indeed drawn from the statement in question, then it follows that by denying the conclusion we must also deny the premise.

*Here is an example of the first type of logical disproof, which is an indirect disproof. The Talmud states, (Babba Kamma 83b) "Let us say that the punishment [for bodily injury] is actually physical retribution". This idea is disproven as follows: "You cannot say so, because the law concerning one who strikes a man is derived from a comparison with one who strikes an animal, and in the latter case he must **pay***

הַפֵּרוּשׁ שֶׁל "מִיתָה מַמָּשׁ", מִפְּנֵי הֱיוֹת מִתְחַלְּפוֹ
שֶׁהוּא "מָמוֹן", תּוֹלָדָה מֵהַקְדָּמָה אֲמִתִּית,
דְּהַיְנוּ שֶׁמַּכֶּה בְהֵמָה אֵינוֹ אֶלָּא בְמָמוֹן, וְזֶה עַל
יְדֵי הַמַּה-מָּצִינוּ שֶׁזְּכַרְנוּ לְמַעְלָה, מְיֻסָּד עַל
אַחַת מִן הַמְקֻבָּלוֹת אֶצְלֵנוּ, שֶׁהוּא –
שֶׁהַנּוֹשְׂאִים שֶׁהֻקְּשׁוּ זֶה לָזֶה בַּכְּתוּבִים, לְמֵדִים
זֶה מִזֶּה. עַתָּה נֹאמַר: מַכֵּה בְהֵמָה אֵינוֹ אֶלָּא
בְמָמוֹן, מַכֵּה אֵבֶר אָדָם לָמֵד מִמַּכֵּה בְהֵמָה
לְפִי שֶׁהֻקַּשׁ לוֹ – אִם כֵּן מַכֵּה אֵבֶר בָּאָדָם אֵינוֹ
אֶלָּא בְמָמוֹן; נִמְצָא זֶה הַפֵּרוּשׁ מְקֻיָּם, וְנִסְתָּר
מֵאֵלָיו פֵּרוּשׁ "בְּמִיתָה".

וּכְשֶׁאָמְרוּ (בבא קמא פד א): "אָמַר קְרָא: 'כֵּן יִנָּתֵן
בּוֹ', וְאֵין נְתִינָה אֶלָּא מָמוֹן", הֵבִיאוּ רְאָיָה נֶגֶד

*compensation". Here, the original explanation that the punishment should be physical retribution is disproven since the contrary law, namely monetary compensation, is shown to be a logical conclusion from a true premise. The premise is the verse stating that one who strikes an animal is only obligated to pay compensation. The conclusion is drawn by means of an analogism, i.e., whatever is said of one subject may also be said of any similar one. Although the two subjects, striking an animal and striking a man, are not inherently comparable, the Talmud associates their respective verses, and this is a sufficient basis of comparison. Now we may construct the following syllogism: One who strikes an animal is only required to pay compensation. The law for one who injures another man is derived from the law for one who strikes an animal since these two verses are associated. Therefore, one who injures another man is only required to pay compensation. By establishing the truth of this interpretation, the original explanation that the penalty should be physical retribution is disproven.*

*Here is an example of the second type of logical disproof, which is a reductio ad absurdum. It is written in the Torah, (Leviticus 24:20)*

זֶה בְּאָמְרָם: "אֶלָּא מֵעַתָּה: כַּאֲשֶׁר יִתֵּן מוּם
בָּאָדָם – הָכִי נַמֵּי דְּמָמוֹן הוּא". הִנֵּה הָיָה
הַמַּאֲמָר, שֶׁכָּל מָקוֹם שֶׁכָּתוּב "נְתִינָה" רְצוֹנוֹ
לוֹמַר – מָמוֹן; מִכָּאן יוֹצֵאת תּוֹלָדָה, שֶׁכְּשֶׁאָמַר
הַכָּתוּב "כַּאֲשֶׁר יִתֵּן מוּם בָּאָדָם" גַּם זֶה רְצוֹנוֹ
לוֹמַר – מָמוֹן, כִּי גַם זֶה לְשׁוֹן נְתִינָה, וְזֶה דָּבָר
שֶׁכְּזָבוֹ מְפֻרְסָם, אִם כֵּן וַדַּאי שֶׁהַהַקְדָּמָה
כּוֹזֶבֶת, וְזֶה מִכֹּחַ הַהֶקֵּשׁ הַתָּלוּי כָּזֶה: אִם כָּל
"נְתִינָה" שֶׁבַּתּוֹרָה הִיא מָמוֹן – גַּם "כַּאֲשֶׁר יִתֵּן
מוּם בָּאָדָם" הוּא מָמוֹן, "כַּאֲשֶׁר יִתֵּן מוּם"
וַדַּאי אֵינוֹ מָמוֹן – אִם כֵּן לֹא כָל "נְתִינָה"
שֶׁבַּתּוֹרָה מָמוֹן.

*". . . if someone [nosan] causes injury to another man, so shall it be [nosan] done to him". The Talmud states, (Babba Kamma 84a) "When the expression 'so shall it be [nosan] done to him' is used, the term 'nosan' can only refer to monetary compensation". This assertion is disproven as follows: "From this premise it would follow that also when the expression 'if someone [nosan] causes injury to another man' is used, even here the term 'nosan' refers merely to monetary damage". The statement in question is that wherever the term "nosan" is used, it refers to money. From this statement, the logical conclusion is that when the Torah states, "If someone [nosan] causes injury to another man", the reference is to monetary damage since the term "nosan" is used. Since this conclusion is evidently false, it follows that the premise is also false. This disproof may be stated as a hypothetical syllogism:* **If** *every "nosan" in the Torah refers to money,* **then** *this term also refers to money in the verse ". . . if someone [nosan] causes injury. . .". But in this verse, the correct interpretation is bodily damage and not monetary damage. Therefore, not every "nosan" in the Torah refers to money.*

וְיֵשׁ מִין מוֹפֵת מַכְחִישׁ שֶׁכּוֹחוֹ חָזָק מְאֹד, וְהוּא שֶׁנְּבָאֵר כָּל הַדְּרָכִים שֶׁאֶפְשָׁר לְהִתְפָּרֵשׁ בָּהֶם הַמַּאֲמָר, וְנִרְאֶה הֱיוֹתוֹ כוֹזֵב בְּכֻלָּם.

דֶּרֶךְ מָשָׁל, אָמְרוּ (בבא קמא כט א): "אָמַר רַבִּי אֲחָא: כְּגוֹן דְּעָבְרָא בְּמַיָּא דֶּרֶךְ שַׁרְעַתָּא דְּנַהֲרָא", וְסָתְרוּ זֶה בְּאָמְרָם: "הֵיכִי דָּמֵי? אִי דְּאִכָּא דַּרְכָּא אַחֲרִינָא – פּוֹשֵׁעַ הוּא! וְאִי דְּלֵכָּא דַּרְכָּא אַחֲרִינָא – אָנוּס הוּא!"

וְזֶה נִקְרָא גַּם כֵּן **מִמַּה־נַּפְשָׁךְ**.

וְאָמְנָם, בֵּין הָרְאָיָה הַמְאַמֶּתֶת וּבֵין הַמַּכְחֶשֶׁת תִּסְתַּתְרְנָה אִם יִמָּצֵא שֶׁאֵין הַדָּבָר כְּמוֹ שֶׁהֻזְכַּר בָּרְאָיָה, דְּהַיְנוּ שֶׁהַמֻּשְׂכָּל אוֹ הַחוּשׁ אוֹ

Aside from these two types of logical disproof, there is a classical rebuttal which is extremely powerful called a **Dilemma**. Its method is to enumerate all possible explanations of a given statement and then to demonstrate that the statement must be false no matter which explanation is chosen.

> *For example, the Talmud asks, (Babba Kamma 29a) "How can the owner be liable for damage caused when his camel falls? Rabbi Acha said, he will be liable if he leads his animal along a flooded path where the river has overflowed its banks". The Talmud rejects his answer, saying, "Under what circumstances did he take his camel there? If there was an alternate route, he would have been negligent [and we need not be told that he is liable]. If there was no other route, the damage was the result of circumstances beyond his control [and he is then exempt from liability]".*

## Rejection of Proofs and Disproofs

We have completed our discussion of all the particulars in the categories of proof and disproof, and now we will turn to the topic of contradictory arguments. A proof or disproof may be contradicted if it is shown that the substance of the proof is untrue. That is, the axiom, perception, convention, tradition, or verse which is the basis of the proof does not, in fact, support the truth of the statement in question. Alternatively, a proof or disproof from a syllogism may be

הַמְפָרְסֵם אוֹ הַמָּסֹרֶת אוֹ הַכָּתוּב אֵינוֹ מְאַמְּתוֹ אוֹ אֵינוֹ מַכְחִישׁוֹ; וְכֵן הַהֶקֵּשׁ, אוֹ שֶׁיִּסָּתֵר הַהֶקֵּשׁ וְתִבָּטֵל תּוֹלַדְתּוֹ.

דֶּרֶךְ מָשָׁל, כְּשֶׁהֵבִיאוּ רְאָיָה עַל מַאֲמַר רַבִּי יְהוּדָה שֶׁאָמַר (בבא קמא פח א): "הַחוֹבֵל בְּעֶבֶד כְּנַעֲנִי שֶׁלּוֹ פָּטוּר" מִן הַכָּתוּב (דברים כה יא): "כִּי יִנָּצוּ אֲנָשִׁים יַחְדָּו אִישׁ וְאָחִיו" –יָצָא עֶבֶד שֶׁאֵין לוֹ אַחֲוָה! סָתְרוּ לְדַעַת חֲכָמִים אֶת הָרְאָיָה בְּאָמְרָם: "אָחִיו הוּא בַּמִּצְוֹת"; וְנִמְצָא, שֶׁאֵין הַפָּסוּק הַזֶּה פּוֹטְרוֹ.

וְכֵן כְּשֶׁרָצָה לִסְתֹּר הַמַּאֲמָר (ברכות נח ב): "וּגְמִירֵי דְּלָא עָבַר כִּסְלָא" מִכֹּחַ הַחוּשׁ, בְּאָמְרוֹ: "וְהָא קָא חָזֵינַן דַּעֲבַר", סָתְרוּ הָרְאָיָה הַמַּכְחֶשֶׁת בְּאָמְרָם: "זִיוֵיהּ הוּא דַּעֲבַר", וְהַיְנוּ שֶׁאֵין הַחוּשׁ

contradicted if its conclusion does not, in fact, apply to the statement in question, or if the syllogism itself is refuted, and its conclusion is rejected.

*For example, the Talmud brings a proof to Rabbi Yehudah's statement (Babba Kamma 88a) "One who injures his own Canaanite slave is exempt [from liability]". The source for this law is the verse (Deuteronomy 25:11) "When two men strive together, a man against his brother. . .". This verse excludes a slave from the laws governing compensation, since he has no status of brotherhood. The Talmud then contradicts this proof, according to the view of the rabbis, by saying, "He is, however, a brother in the commandments". Thus, on the basis of this verse, it is impossible to exempt the master who injures his slave.*

*Similarly, when the statement is considered, (Berachos 58b) "There is a tradition that shooting stars never pass through the constellation of Orion", the Talmud brings a disproof from direct sense perception, saying, "But we have seen them pass through!" Afterwards the Talmud contradicts this disproof by saying, "It is only their light which appeared to pass through". That is, the sense perception does not*

מַכְחִישׁ הַמַּאֲמָר הַזֶּה.

וּכְשֶׁרָצוּ לְהוֹכִיחַ מִכֹּחַ קַל־וָחֹמֶר שֶׁנָּשִׂיא יָבִיא
אָשָׁם תָּלוּי סָתְרוּ הַקַּל־וָחֹמֶר, בְּאָמְרָם  (תורת
כהנים דיבורא דחטאת פרשה ה): "מָשִׁיחַ יוֹכִיחַ", וְנִמְצֵאת
הַתּוֹלָדָה מְבֻטֶּלֶת.

וּמִסּוֹתְרֵי הַמּוֹפֵת הַמַּכְחִישׁ הוּא, כְּשֶׁנַּחֲזֹר עַל דַּעַת הַחוֹלֵק אוֹתוֹ
הַקֹּשִׁי עַצְמוֹ שֶׁהִקְשָׁה עַל מַאֲמָרֵנוּ, אוֹ הַקֹּשִׁי אַחֵר שֶׁנִּרְאָה הֱיוֹת גַּם
דַּעַת הַחוֹלֵק מְכֻחֶשֶׁת בְּאֹפֶן שֶׁבְּהֶכְרֵחַ צָרִיךְ שֶׁיַּסְכִּים הַחוֹלֵק עַצְמוֹ
בְּאֵיזֶה תְנַאי אוֹ חִלּוּק, שֶׁבּוֹ תִּמָּלַטְנָה דַעְתּוֹ וְדַעְתֵּנוּ מִן הַקֹּשִׁי שֶׁהָיָה
בָּהֶן – וְזֶה נִקְרָא **וּלְטַעֲמֵיךְ** אוֹ **וּלְדִידָךְ**.

דֶּרֶךְ מָשָׁל, כְּשֶׁהִקְשׁוּ בַּשַּׁ"ס  (בבא קמא פח א): "אֶלָּא
מֵעַתָּה לְרַבָּנָן עֶבֶד יְהֵא כָּשֵׁר לַמַּלְכוּת?" הֵשִׁיבוּ

*actually disprove the statement in question.*

*Finally, when the Sifra sought to prove through an a fortiori that a prince may bring a doubtful guilt offering, it contradicted the proof by saying, (Toras Cohanim, Sin Offerings, Section 5) "The case of a Cohen Gadol proves otherwise". This example has been explained in Chapter Seven (see page 104). Since the argument a fortiori is refuted, the conclusion is therefore false.*

There is also a classical contradiction or defense against a disproof called **According to Your Reasoning**. This method is to reintroduce against the dissenting view the same difficulty that was originally presented against our statement, or to raise some other difficulty, so that the other view will be nullified just as ours appears nullified. To be a successful rebuttal, the difficulty which is chosen must force the acceptance of some qualification or distinction which will save not only the dissenting view but also our own.

*For example, in the passage mentioned earlier (page 134) Rabbi Yehuda stated that a Canaanite slave is not a "brother" to be entitled to compensation for damages, and the rabbis stated that he is a "brother" and should be entitled. The Talmud disproved their view as follows: (Babba Kamma 88a) "If a slave is really considered a 'brother', he should then be*

עַל זֶה: "אָמְרִי: וּלְטַעֲמֵיךְ תִּקְשֵׁי לָךְ גֵּר לִדְבָרֵי
הַכֹּל? אֶלָּא אָמַר קְרָא: 'מִקֶּרֶב אַחֶיךָ' –
הַמֻּבְחָר שֶׁבְּאַחֶיךָ!"

וְיוֹתֵר חָזָק יִהְיֶה מִזֶּה כְּשֶׁנָּסִיר הַקֹּשִׁי מִמַּאֲמָרֵנוּ וְנַשְׁלִיכֵהוּ עַל
דַּעַת הַחוֹלֵק אִתָּנוּ, אוֹ שֶׁהָרְאָיָה שֶׁהֵבִיא לְהַכְחִישׁ מַאֲמָרֵנוּ נַחֲזִירָהּ
רְאָיָה לְמַאֲמָרֵנוּ. וְזֶה נִקְרָא **אַדְּרַבָּא**, אוֹ הִיא **הַנּוֹתֶנֶת**, מִשָּׁם **רְאָיָה**.

*eligible for the kingship, and this is not so". The rabbis defended their view by saying, "**According to your reasoning** there is a difficulty because a convert is certainly considered a 'brother' and yet everyone agrees that he is not eligible for the kingship! Indeed, the verse states (Deuteronomy 17:15) 'one from among your brothers shall you appoint as a king over you', and this refers to the choicest among your brothers!" Just as this interpretation excludes converts, it also excludes slaves who were born Gentiles. In this way we contradict the disproof against the rabbis, for even Rabbi Yehudah must admit that the quality of "brother" needed to be eligible for the kingship has no bearing on the quality of "brother" needed to be eligible to receive compensation for injury.*

There is an even stronger defense which may be used to contradict the disproof brought by a dissenting view. This method is to resolve the difficulty posed to our statement, and at the same time employ that same difficulty against the dissenting view. Alternatively, it is possible to reject the disproof brought against our statement while using the same text as a positive proof. The first method is called **Just the Opposite!**, and the second is called **That Proves My Point!**, or **From There is a Proof.**

דֶּרֶךְ מָשָׁל, כְּשֶׁהִקְשׁוּ בַּשַׁ"ס (נצא קמא פנ נ): "דָּנִין נְזָקִין מִנְזָקִין וְאֵין דָּנִין נְזָקִין מִמִּיתָה", הֵשִׁיבוּ: "אַדְּרַבָּא! דָּנִין אָדָם מֵאָדָם וְאֵין דָּנִין אָדָם מִבְּהֵמָה".

וּכְשֶׁהֵבִיא (שנת פג א) רַבִּי מֵאִיר רְאָיָה לִדְבָרָיו מִפָּסוּק "לַחְתּוֹת אֵשׁ מִיָּקוּד" (ישעיה ל יד), הֵשִׁיב

*This method is used in the passage mentioned earlier (page 126) where the Talmud discusses the nature of liability for bodily injury. There, it is proven that a person who inflicts bodily injury on another is liable to pay compensation in accordance with the verse which states that one who causes injury to an animal must pay. An objection is raised: if any comparison can be made to derive this law, why should striking a man be compared to striking an animal? It is more appropriate to compare striking a man (causing injury) to manslaughter, proving by this comparison that one who causes injury to another should be punished with physical retribution. This is disproven as follows: (Babba Kamma 83b) "We derive one case of damage from another, and not a case of damage from a case involving the death penalty". The logic of this disproof is then employed to prove the other view: "It is just the opposite! It is more appropriate to compare one case dealing with human beings to another, than to compare a case dealing with human beings to a case dealing with animals".*

*Another example: (Shabbos 82a) "If one carries out a shard [on the Sabbath] what is the minimum measurement [for which he is guilty*

לוֹ רַבִּי יוֹסֵי: "מִשָּׁם רְאָיָה! – 'וְלַחְשׁוֹף מַיִם מִגֶּבֶא'" (שם).

וְהִנֵּה כָּל זְמַן שֶׁתִּסְתַּתֵּר הָרְאָיָה הַמְאַמֶּתֶת יָשׁוּב הַמַּאֲמָר מִסְפָּק, אִם לֹא תִהְיֶה עָלָיו רְאָיָה מַכְחֶשֶׁת. וְכֵן כְּשֶׁתִּסְתַּתֵּר הַמַּכְחֶשֶׁת יָשׁוּב מִסְפָּק, אִם לֹא תִהְיֶה עָלָיו רְאָיָה מְאַמֶּתֶת.

וְאָמְנָם יֵשׁ מִין רְאָיָה אַחֶרֶת שֶׁאֵינָהּ לֹא מְאַמֶּתֶת לְגַמְרֵי וְלֹא מַכְחֶשֶׁת לְגַמְרֵי, אֶלָּא מַטָּה הַדַּעַת לְאֶחָד מִן הַצְּדָדִים, וְנִקְרָא זֶה **סְבָרָא**, וְיִקָּרֵא זֶה בִּהְיוֹת הַטַּעֲנוֹת שְׁקוּלוֹת לְהֵן וּלְלָאו, אֶלָּא שֶׁהַדַּעַת תֵּטֶה יוֹתֵר לְצַד הָאֶחָד מִשֶּׁכְּנֶגְדּוֹ.

*of transgression]? Rabbi Meir said, large enough to scrape coals from the hearth. Rabbi Yosi said, large enough to contain a cup of water". Rabbi Meir brought a proof to his view from the verse (Isaiah 30:14) ". . . a shard sufficient for taking fire from the hearth. . .". Rabbi Yosi replied, "From there is a proof for my view for the end of the same verse states '. . . or for taking water out of the cistern'".*

## Theory

We stated at the beginning of the chapter that it is only possible to accept or reject any statement on the basis of proofs or disproofs which may be brought. Consequently, if a proof is contradicted, we do not necessarily reject the statement in question; rather we revert to our original position of doubt until a clear disproof is presented. Only then can we legitimately reject the statement in question. Similarly, when a disproof is contradicted, the statement remains in doubt until a positive proof can be brought to establish its validity.

However, there is an entirely different method of proof which inclines the understanding in favor of one side of the argument, when the proofs pro and con are equally balanced. This method of proof is called a **Theory**. Although it neither absolutely proves the statement in question nor disproves its opposite, nonetheless it is reasonable for the mind to lean more to one side than the other on the basis of a theory.

דֶּרֶךְ מָשָׁל (חולין יט ג): "אִכָּא דְאָמְרֵי: אַף מַחֲזִיר!
וְאִכָּא דְאָמְרֵי: מַחֲזִיר דַּוְקָא! וּמִסְתַּבְּרָא
כְּמַאן דְּאָמַר: אַף מַחֲזִיר!"

וּמִמַּה שֶּׁצָּרִיךְ שֶׁתֵּדַע, שֶׁלִּהְיוֹת הָרְאָיוֹת אֲמִתִּיּוֹת וְהַתּוֹלָדוֹת
צוֹדְקוֹת צָרִיךְ שֶׁיִּהְיֶה נִשְׁמָר הַיַּחַס הַנָּכוֹן בֵּין כָּל הַמַּאֲמָרִים
הַמּוֹלִידִים וְהַתּוֹלָדוֹת, הַמְאַמְּתִים וְהַמְאֻמָּתִים, הַנִּסְתָּרִים וְהַסּוֹתְרִים,
שֶׁיִּהְיוּ דוֹמִים זֶה לָזֶה. וְזֶה, כִּי הִנֵּה כָּל נוֹשֵׂא שֶׁיִּהְיֶה, אִי אֶפְשָׁר שֶׁלֹּא
יִבָּחֲנוּ בוֹ בְּחִינוֹת רַבּוֹת, אִם בְּמַה שֶּׁנּוֹגֵעַ בְּעַצְמוֹ שֶׁל נוֹשֵׂא וְאִם בְּמַה
שֶׁנּוֹגֵעַ בְּמַה שֶׁהוּא מִתְיַחֵס אֶל אֲחֵרִים, וְהַנְּשׂוּאִים שֶׁיֵּאָמְרוּ בוֹ אֶפְשָׁר
שֶׁיֵּאָמְרוּ לְפִי כָּל מַה שֶּׁבְּעַצְמוֹ, אוֹ לְפִי קְצָת מִמַּה שֶּׁבְּעַצְמוֹ, אוֹ לְפִי
אֵיזֶה יַחַס מִיְּחָסָיו. וּכְבָר מָנִינוּ בְּמִינֵי הַמַּאֲמָרִים הַמַּאֲמָר שֶׁהוּא לְפִי
בְּחִינָה אַחַת, שֶׁהוּא עַל פִּי הַשֹּׁרֶשׁ הַזֶּה.

דֶּרֶךְ מָשָׁל, אָמְרוּ בַּשַּׁ"ס (פסחים יט ג): "עֲזָרָה
רְשׁוּת הָרַבִּים הִיא", הִנֵּה מַאֲמָר זֶה, לֹא יוּבַן

*For example, (Chullin 19b) "The sons of Rabbi Chiyya said, the Cohen twists the throat around to the back of the bird's neck and then nips off the head. Some read 'may twist' and others, 'must twist'. It is more reasonable, however, to read 'may twist'".*

## Validity of Deductions and Proofs

We have completed our description of all the categories of deductions, proofs, disproofs and rebuttals according to their structural form. Now, let us examine the content of each term and statement. For if the deduction is to be valid, and the proof true, it is necessary to keep the proper relationship between all the terms in the premise and conclusion, the proof and what is desired to be proven and the rejected proofs and their supposed refutations. That is, in each part, all the terms must be used consistently. Every term used has various aspects of meaning; therefore, it is essential to be careful that the terms involved in any deduction or proof are used in a similar way. Thus the subject in any statement may be considered either in an absolute sense without regard to its context, or in relation to something else. Similarly, the predicate which is applied to the subject may be relevant to the subject in an absolute sense, or to a part of it, or to some relative aspect of the subject. These distinctions are particularly relevant to a conditional statement which is only predicated in a limited aspect, as we explained in Chapter Three.

*For example, the Talmud states, (Pesachim 19b) "The Temple court is a public domain". This statement cannot be understood absolutely, i.e.,*

בְּהֶחְלֵט שֶׁתִּהְיֶה הָעֲזָרָה רְשׁוּת הָרַבִּים לְכָל
הַבְּחִינוֹת אֶלָּא לְעִנְיַן סְפֵק טֻמְאָה; וְהַמַּאֲמָר
שֶׁנֶּאֱמַר לְפִי בְחִינָה אַחַת לֹא תַעֲשֵׂהוּ הַקְדָּמָה
לַתּוֹלָדָה בִּבְחִינָה אַחֶרֶת, כִּי אֵין הַדִּמְיוֹן
וְהַהַשְׁוָאָה בֵּינֵיהֶם אֲמִתִּיִּים אֶלָּא נִרְאִים.
וְנִמְצָא, שֶׁלֹּא תוּכַל לְהוֹלִיד מִן הַמַּאֲמָר
שֶׁזְּכַרְנוּ "עֲזָרָה – רְשׁוּת הָרַבִּים הִיא",
שֶׁהַמְטַלְטֵל בָּהּ בַּשַּׁבָּת חוּץ לְאַרְבַּע אַמּוֹת
יִהְיֶה חַיָּב, כִּי לְעִנְיַן טֻמְאָה לְבַד הִיא רְשׁוּת
הָרַבִּים, וּלְעִנְיַן שַׁבָּת הִיא רְשׁוּת הַיָּחִיד. וְכֵן
לֹא תַכְחִישׁ מַאֲמָר אוֹמֵר הֱיוֹתָהּ רְשׁוּת הַיָּחִיד
מִכֹּחַ הַמַּאֲמָר הַזֶּה שֶׁזְּכַרְנוּ, כִּי הָאוֹמֵר רְשׁוּת
הַיָּחִיד, יְדַבֵּר לְעִנְיַן שַׁבָּת, וְהַמַּאֲמָר הַזֶּה לְעִנְיַן
טֻמְאָה. וְכֵן כֹּל הַדּוֹמֶה לָזֶה.

*that the Temple court is a public domain in every aspect of law. Its intent is specifically in reference to a "doubtful uncleanness"; and therefore, the law is that any "doubtful uncleanness" in the Temple court is ruled to be clean, as with all cases of a public domain. Now, a statement which is understood in one respect cannot be used as a premise in order to reach a conclusion which is understood in a different respect since the common term does not indicate a true comparison. Thus, you cannot deduce from the above statement ("The Temple court is a public domain") that one who carries something beyond four cubits is guilty of violating the Sabbath. For the Temple court is only a public domain with respect to the law of "uncleanness", but with respect to Sabbath laws, it is not a public domain. Likewise, the hypothesis that the Temple court is a private domain and it is permissible to carry things there on the Sabbath cannot be disproved on the strength of the above-mentioned text. For the one who presents the hypothesis that it is a private domain could only be referring to the Sabbath laws, while the above text in the Talmud is referring to defilement.*

וְצָרִיךְ שֶׁתֵּדַע, שֶׁכְּלַל הַבְּחִינוֹת שֶׁאֶפְשָׁר שֶׁיִּבָּחֲנוּ בְּנוֹשֵׂא מִן הַנּוֹשְׂאִים - אַרְבַּע: מַה שֶּׁבְּעַצְמוֹ, מַה שֶּׁבְּסִגְלָתוֹ, מַה שֶּׁבְּמִקְרָיו וּמַה שֶּׁבְּיַחֲסוֹ אֶל זוּלָתוֹ.

**מַה שֶּׁבְּעַצְמוֹ** - הוּא מַה שֶּׁבּוֹ תְּלוּיָה הֲוָיַת הַנּוֹשֵׂא הַהוּא בֶּאֱמֶת, שֶׁאִלּוּ הָיָה נֶעְדָּר, לֹא הָיָה הַנּוֹשֵׂא הַהוּא מַה שֶּׁהוּא. דֶּרֶךְ מָשָׁל: הַסַּכִּין הֱיוֹתוֹ כְּלִי מְחַתֵּךְ - הוּא מַה שֶּׁבְּעַצְמוֹ, וְאִלּוּ לֹא הָיָה כָךְ, לֹא הָיָה הַסַּכִּין.

**מַה שֶּׁבְּסִגְלָתוֹ** - הוּא עִנְיָן שֶׁמִּתְלַוֶּה תָמִיד אֶל הַנּוֹשֵׂא וְלֹא יָסוּר מִמֶּנּוּ, אַךְ אֵין הֲוָיַת הַנּוֹשֵׂא תְּלוּיָה בּוֹ, שֶׁהֲרֵי אִלּוּ יְצָיַר הֶעְדֵּרוֹ, לֹא הָיָה חָדֵל הַנּוֹשֵׂא מִלִּהְיוֹת מַה שֶּׁהוּא.

דֶּרֶךְ מָשָׁל, כְּשֶׁאָמְרוּ (פריה פ״ט מ״ג): "חוּץ מִן הַחֻלְדָּה, מִפְּנֵי שֶׁהִיא מַלֶּקֶת", הִנֵּה זֶה דָבָר נִמְצָא תָמִיד בַּחֻלְדָּה שֶׁהִיא מַלֶּקֶת, אַךְ אֵין הֱיוֹתָהּ חֻלְדָּה תָּלוּי בָּזֶה.

In principle, there are four general aspects with which to define the frame of reference of the subject of any statement. Any predication applied to a subject must refer to what the subject is in itself, or to what is unique to it, or to its attributes, or to what it is in relation to something else.

**What it is in itself** – this is what the true essence of the subject depends on, and without which the subject would not be what it is. For example, a knife is a utensil for cutting. This is its essence, for if a knife did not have this function it would not be a knife.

**What is unique to it** – this is an attribute that always accompanies the subject, and although the essence of the subject does not depend on it, the subject is never without it. However, if you could imagine the subject without its unique attribute, it would not cease to be what it is.

> *For example, (Parah Chapter 9 Mishnah 3) "The weasel is an exception because it laps when it drinks". Other animals disqualify water for sprinkling, but a weasel does not. The attribute that it drinks by lapping is always found in a weasel, but its being a weasel does not depend on this unique quality. However, the predication of this Mishnah, that a weasel does not disqualify water for sprinkling, **does** depend on this unique quality.*

**מַה שֶּׁבְּמִקְרָיו** – הוּא מַה שֶּׁמִּתְלַוֶּה אֶל הַנּוֹשֵׂא בְּדֶרֶךְ מִקְרֶה; פֵּרוּשׁ, שֶׁכְּבָר הָיָה אֶפְשָׁר שֶׁלֹּא יִתְלַוֶּה לוֹ, אוֹ שֶׁיִּתְלַוֶּה לוֹ עִנְיָן מִתְחַלֵּף מִזֶּה, וַאֲפִלּוּ הַפְכִּי לוֹ, וְאַף עַל פִּי כֵן הָיָה הַנּוֹשֵׂא הַהוּא מַה שֶּׁהוּא. וְזֶה מַה שֶּׁנּוֹגֵעַ בְּצוּרַת הַנּוֹשֵׂא אוֹ בְמִדָּתוֹ, פֵּרוּשׁ    הֱיוֹתוֹ עָגֹל אוֹ מְרֻבָּע, אָרֹךְ אוֹ קָצָר, שֶׁהֲרֵי הָעָגֹל הָיָה אֶפְשָׁר שֶׁיִּהְיֶה מְרֻבָּע, הַמְרֻבָּע הָיָה אֶפְשָׁר שֶׁיִּהְיֶה עָגֹל, הָאָרֹךְ הָיָה אֶפְשָׁר שֶׁיִּהְיֶה קָצָר, וְהַקָּצָר אֶפְשָׁר שֶׁיִּהְיֶה אָרֹךְ, וְלֹא מִפְּנֵי זֶה הָיָה אוֹתוֹ הַנּוֹשֵׂא נוֹשֵׂא אַחֵר.

**מַה שֶּׁבְּיַחֲסוֹ אֶל זוּלָתוֹ** – הוּא עִנְיָן שֶׁאֵינוֹ בוֹ מִפְּנֵי עַצְמוֹ כְּלָל, אֶלָּא מִפְּנֵי שֶׁהוּא מִצְטָרֵף וּמִתְיַחֵס אֶל אַחֵר. דֶּרֶךְ מָשָׁל: הֱיוֹתוֹ דוֹמֶה אוֹ בִלְתִּי דוֹמֶה – זֶה אֵינוֹ עִנְיָן נִבְחָן בַּנּוֹשֵׂא מִצַּד עַצְמוֹ, אֶלָּא מִצַּד הֱיוֹתוֹ נֶעֱרָךְ עִם אַחֵר, הֱיוֹתוֹ פּוֹעֵל אוֹ הֱיוֹתוֹ נִפְעָל. וְכֵן כָּל כַּיּוֹצֵא בָּזֶה מִמַּה שֶּׁלֹּא יִשְׁתַּלֵּם בִּמְצִיאוּת נוֹשֵׂא אֶחָד לְבַד, אֶלָּא בִּמְצִיאוּת נוֹשְׂאִים שׁוֹנִים לִהְיוֹתָם מִתְיַחֲסִים זֶה לָזֶה.

וְאָמְנָם, בְּכָל בְּחִינָה שֶׁתִּהְיֶה, אֶפְשָׁר שֶׁיֵּאָמֵר נָשׂוּא בְּנוֹשֵׂא, וְלֹא מִפְּנֵי זֶה נָדִין אוֹתוֹ הַנָּשׂוּא עַצְמוֹ בְּאוֹתוֹ הַנּוֹשֵׂא עַצְמוֹ בִּבְחִינָה אַחֶרֶת.

**Its attributes** – this is whatever accompanies the subject according to circumstance. That is, from the start, it is conceivable that an attribute may or may not be found accompanying the subject, or that the subject may possess a contrary attribute or even an opposite attribute, and still the subject would be what it is. Thus, if a predication is made in reference to the form or dimension of the subject (i.e., its being round or square, long or short), then this is a factor upon which the predicate depends. Even though the subject will not be considered a different subject on account of a change in its attributes, the predicate, however, will not be true unless the subject happens to have that attribute upon which the predication depends.

**What it is in relation to something else** – this is a characteristic that has no bearing on the intrinsic nature of the subject; rather it is found only in conjunction with or in relation to something else. For example, similarity or dissimilarity is found not intrinsically in the subject, but only externally in connection with another subject. Similarly, a subject is an effective cause or a recipient of some effect only in relation to some other subject. Included in this category are all other accidents which cannot be considered in an isolated subject, such as Relation, Time, Situation, Acquisition, and Position. All of these imply a connection with some other subject.

If a statement is qualified in any way so that the predicate is applied to the subject in one particular aspect, it does not necessarily follow that the predicate can be applied to the same subject in any other aspect.

דֶּרֶךְ מָשָׁל, אָמְרוּ (ספרי פרשת נשא ה יג): "כְּשֶׁבָּא
אִסוּר הַקַּל עַל אִסוּר הַקַּל – אָסַר אֶת
אוֹסְרָיו", פֵּרוּשׁ: אֵשֶׁת אִישׁ נִקְרֵאת אִסוּר קַל
לְגַבֵּי חֲמוֹתוֹ בַּמֶּה שֶׁיֵּשׁ לָהּ הֶתֵּר, מַה שֶׁאֵין כֵּן
בַּחֲמוֹתוֹ; וְהִנֵּה מִצַּד אַחֵר אֵשֶׁת אִישׁ חֲמוּרָה
מֵחֲמוֹתוֹ, שֶׁזּוֹ בְּחֶנֶק וְזוֹ בִּכָרֵת, אָמְנָם בִּבְחִינַת

*For example, (Sifri, Naso 5:13) "What shall we say? When an adulterer lives with a married woman, we know that he causes her to be forbidden to her husband since it is through the husband's act of marrying his wife that the prohibition of adultery takes effect. Now, surely, does it not follow that when a man lives with his mother-in-law, which is a stronger prohibition, he should also become forbidden to his own wife, since this prohibition also takes effect through his act of marrying his wife"? The explanation of this a fortiori is that adultery is called a weak prohibition in comparison to incest because the former prohibition is nullified through divorce or death while the latter cannot be nullified under any circumstance; therefore, a law applicable to adultery would surely apply in the case of incest. However, from another point of view, (Yebamos 94b) adultery is a stricter prohibition than incest, because it is punishable by death through strangulation, and there is no instance where the death penalty is reduced to excision; while incest, on the other hand, is punishable by death through burning, and this death penalty is reduced to excision. According to this reasoning, the a fortiori argument is not valid. We*

הֱיוֹת לָהּ הֶתֵּר נִקְרֵאת אֵשֶׁת אִישׁ – קַלָּה,
וּבִבְחִינַת הָעֹנֶשׁ נִקְרֵאת אֵשֶׁת אִישׁ – חֲמוּרָה.

עוֹד צָרִיךְ שֶׁתֵּדַע, שֶׁהַנּוֹשֵׂא אֶפְשָׁר שֶׁיֵּאָמֵר בַּנּוֹשֵׂא בְּכֹחַ, וְאֶפְשָׁר
שֶׁיֵּאָמֵר בְּפֹעַל. פֵּרוּשׁ – אֶפְשָׁר שֶׁנֶּאֱמַר שֶׁאוֹתוֹ הַנּוֹשֵׂא הָיָה בְּפֹעַל
בְּאוֹתוֹ הַנּוֹשֵׂא,

דֶּרֶךְ מָשָׁל, אָמְרוּ (זבחים לט א): "כֹּהֵן הַמְחַטֵּא –
מְחַלֵּק, וְשֶׁאֵינוֹ מְחַטֵּא – אֵינוֹ מְחַלֵּק", וְהִקְשׁוּ:
"וּכְלָלָא הוּא? וַהֲרֵי מִשְׁמָרָה כֻּלָּהּ דְּאֵין
מְחַטְּאִין וּמְחַלְּקִין?" וְתֵרְצוּ: "רָאוּי לְחַטּוּיֵ
קָאָמְרִינַן". וְזֶה, שֶׁהַמַּקְשֶׁה הֵבִין בַּתְּחִלָּה "כֹּהֵן
הַמְחַטֵּא" – שֶׁמְּחַטֵּא בְּפֹעַל, וְעַל זֶה הֵבִיא

*see that adultery is call "weaker" in the aspect*
*that it is possible to nullify the prohibition, and*
*in the aspect of its punishment it is called*
*"stronger".*

Further, it is important to recognize that the predicate may be stated about the subject either potentially or actually. That is, confusion may arise as to whether a certain predicate has been stated as potentially true about the subject or actually true in fact. We have already seen that the aspects of the subject must be consistent for any deduction or proof to be sound, and the same is true about the aspects of potentiality and actuality in the predicate.

*For example, (Zevachim 99a) "The Cohen who*
*sprinkles the blood may eat a portion of the sin*
*offering, and one who does not may not eat*
*from it". The Talmud raises a difficulty, "Is this*
*a general rule? Surely, the entire shift of*
*Cohanim on duty may eat a portion even*
*though they did not all sprinkle the blood". It*
*resolved this difficulty by saying, "We were talk-*
*ing about any Cohen who may potentially*
*sprinkle the blood, and the entire shift of*
*Cohanim are able potentially to sprinkle the*
*blood of the sin offering". The one who raised*
*the difficulty ("Is this a general rule?") under-*
*stood that the phrase ("who sprinkles the*
*blood") refers to one who actually performs the*

רְאָיָה נֶגֶד זֶה הַמַּאֲמָר מִן הַמִּנְהָג הַנּוֹהֵג, שֶׁבְּנֵי הַמִּשְׁמָרָה אֵינָם מְחַטְּאִים בְּפֹעַל וְאַף עַל פִּי כֵן מְחַלְּקִים; וְתֵרֵץ הַמִּתְרֵץ, שֶׁאֵין לְהָבִין כָּאן מְחַטֵּא בְּפֹעַל אֶלָּא בְּכֹחַ וּבַהֲכָנָה, פֵּרוּשׁ – שֶׁרָאוּי לַחְטוֹי, וּבְנֵי הַמִּשְׁמָרָה כֻּלָּם רְאוּיִים לַחְטוֹי.

וְאָמְנָם כָּל הַחִלּוּקִים וְהַהֶבְדֵּלִים הָאֵלֶּה, צָרִיךְ לִשְׁמֹר בְּכָל הַמַּשָּׂא וּמַתָּן הָעִיּוּנִי, וְאָז יִהְיֶה אֲמִתִּי וְנָכוֹן.

וְהִנֵּה עַד הֵנָּה בֵּאַרְנוּ קַבָּלַת הַמַּאֲמָרִים אוֹ הַכְחָשָׁתָם בְּמַה שֶּׁיַּסְכִּים הַשֵּׂכֶל עִמָּהֶם אוֹ לֹא יַסְכִּים מִצַּד עִנְיָנָם. וְאוּלָם יֵשׁ עוֹד שֶׁיַּסְכִּים אוֹ לֹא יַסְכִּים עִם הַמַּאֲמָר לֹא מִצַּד עִנְיָנוֹ, אֶלָּא מִצַּד הַגָּדָתוֹ, וְזֶה בִּשְׁנֵי דְרָכִים: הָאֶחָד – מִצַּד כְּלַל כָּל הַהַגָּדָה, וְהַשֵּׁנִי – מִצַּד חֲלָקֶיהָ.

**מִצַּד כְּלַל כָּל הַהַגָּדָה** – הוּא, כִּי הִנֵּה מֵחֹק יֹשֶׁר הַסִּפּוּר הוּא שֶׁתִּהְיֶה בַּסִּפּוּר תּוֹעֶלֶת וְלֹא יִהְיֶה בּוֹ מוֹתָר וְדָבָר בָּטֵל. וְעַל פִּי הַשֹּׁרֶשׁ

*sprinkling of the blood. On this basis he brought a disproof against the statement in question. The accepted custom is against this ruling, for all members of the shift do not actually sprinkle the blood, and yet, they all eat a portion of the sin offering. The defender answers that the phrase ("who sprinkles") was meant not in the aspect of actual fact, but in the aspect of potential or ability. That is, we are dealing with all those Cohanim who are eligible to sprinkle the blood, and, in truth, all the members of the current shift are included.*

In conclusion, these distinctions and differences in both the subject and the predicate of statements must be maintained consistently throughout the dialectic investigation, and only then will the entire progression of the debate be true and correct.

## Stylistic Proofs and Disproofs

All of our discussion up to now has concentrated on how the mind proceeds to accept or reject statements with respect to their content. In addition to content, however, there is another basis upon which any statement can be accepted or rejected, and that is its form. Here, there are two considerations. We must evaluate the form of the statement as a whole and in terms of its parts.

**The statement as a whole** — it is a rule of proper speech that every sentence should have value and should not be repetitious or superfluous. Accordingly, if we hear a statement and what is said

הַזֶּה, אִם נִשְׁמַע סִפּוּר שֶׁיֵּרָאֶה לָנוּ הֱיוֹת הַגָּדָתוֹ בִּלְתִּי מֻצְרֶכֶת, נַקְשֶׁה עָלָיו: פְּשִׁיטָא! כִּי הַדָּבָר הַמְפֻרְסָם וְנוֹדַע לַכֹּל, אֵין צֹרֶךְ לְהַגִּידוֹ. וּתְרוּץ הַקֻּשִׁי הַזֶּה יִהְיֶה כְּשֶׁנִּמְצָא שֶׁיִּהְיֶה מָקוֹם לַחֲשֹׁב נֶגֶד מַה שֶּׁיֻּגַּד לָנוּ, וְנִקְרָא זֶה סָלְקָא דַעְתִּין.

**מִצַּד חֶלְקֵי הַהַגָּדָה** – הוּא, כִּי מֵחֵק הַסִּפּוּר הוּא גַם כֵּן, שֶׁלֹּא יִהְיֶה בְּשׁוּם חֵלֶק מִמֶּנּוּ דָּבָר מוֹתָר אוֹ נִכְפָּל לְלֹא צֹרֶךְ. וּמֵחֵקוֹ כְּמוֹ כֵן, שֶׁתִּהְיֶינָה הַמִּלּוֹת מְכֻוָּנוֹת עִם הָעִנְיָן וּמְכֻוָּנוֹת זוֹ עִם זוֹ. וּמֵחֵקוֹ כְּמוֹ כֵן, שֶׁיִּהְיֶה סִדְרוֹ הָגוּן וְנָאוֹת בְּחַלֵּק מַה שֶּׁצָּרִיךְ לְחַלֵּק וּבְחַבֵּר מַה שֶּׁצָּרִיךְ לְחַבֵּר. וְאִם נִמְצָא בַּמַּאֲמָר אֶחָד חֶסְרוֹן מֵאֵלֶּה הַתְּנָאִים, נַקְשֶׁה עָלָיו כְּפִי מַה שֶּׁנִּמְצָא שֶׁחָסֵר מִמֶּנּוּ. דֶּרֶךְ מָשָׁל: כְּשֶׁנִּמְצָא הֱיוֹת בִּדְבָרָיו כֶּפֶל, נַקְשֶׁה: הָא תּוּ לָמָּה לִי? כְּשֶׁנִּמְצָא הֱיוֹת הַמִּלּוֹת בִּלְתִּי מְכֻוָּנוֹת, נַקְשֶׁה עָלָיו הָא גוּפָא קַשְׁיָא! כְּשֶׁנִּמְצָא שֶׁאֵין הַסֵּדֶר הָגוּן, נַקְשֶׁה עָלָיו כְּפִי מַה שֶּׁחָסֵר מִמֶּנּוּ; דֶּרֶךְ מָשָׁל (ברכות נ א): "תַּנָּא הֵיכָא קָאֵי?" (גיטין פג): "לְעָרְבִינְהוּ וְלִיתְנִינְהוּ!" (בבא קמא כז א): "פָּתַח בְּכַד וְסִיֵּם בְּחָבִית!" וְכַיּוֹצֵא בָזֶה.

appears superfluous, we must raise the objection, "But this is obvious"! Generally, something which is well known and accepted by all need not be stated. This difficulty is resolved by finding some possibility of an opposite view, which is called "One might have thought to say". Thus the seemingly obvious sentence must be stated after all in order to exclude this opposing possibility.

**The statement in terms of its parts** – the parts of a sentence can be evaluated according to three rules of proper speech. First of all, no part of the sentence should be extraneous or repetitive. Secondly, the words which are chosen should be appropriate to the subject matter and internally consistent. Thirdly, the sentence should be logically and reasonably ordered, separating what needs to be separated and combining what needs to be combined. If any of these stipulations are found lacking in a sentence, an objection must be raised according to these principles. For example, the objection raised when any part appears repetitious is, "Why do I need this addition"? The objection raised when the words are not consistent is, "This is self-contradictory"! When the organization of the sentence is not logical we raise an objection according to whatever is lacking. For example, (Berachos 2a) "In what context is the Tanna speaking"? (Gittin 80b) "He should have combined the cases and taught them together". (Babba Kamma 27a) "At the beginning he referred to a jug, but at the end he switched and referred to a barrel"! There are many other objections based on concepts similar to these.

From Chapter Three until this point we have completed our description of all the natural first principles, which are inherent to our intellect, i.e., the method of understanding statements, building syllogisms and accepting or rejecting ideas. The structures of intensive study and investigation, as well as all Talmudic debate in all

כָּל אֵלֶּה יְסוֹדוֹת טִבְעִיִּים מְחֻקָּקִים בְּשִׂכְלֵנוּ, שֶׁעֲלֵיהֶם נִבְנִים בִּנְיְנֵי הָעִיּוּן וְהַחֲקִירָה וְכָל סוּגִיּוֹת הַתַּלְמוּד בְּכָל חֶלְקֵיהֶן.

עַתָּה נְבָאֵר חֶלְקֵי הַסּוּגִיּוֹת בִּפְרָט, שֶׁהֵם כְּלַל הַבִּנְיָנִים הַנִּבְנִים עַל הַיְסוֹדוֹת הָאֵלֶּה.

its aspects, are based on these principles.

In the coming chapter we will explain in detail all the elements of Talmudic debate.

# פרק ט

הִנֵּה חֶלְקֵי הַסּוּגְיוֹת בִּכְלָל כְּבָר זְכַרְנוּם, וְהֵם: מֵימְרָא, שְׁאֵלָה, תְּשׁוּבָה, סְתִירָה, רְאָיָה, קֻשְׁיָא וְתֵרוּץ. עַתָּה נַזְכִּיר פְּרָטֵיהֶם וּנְבָאֵר מִשְׁפְּטֵיהֶם.

הַמֵּימְרָא תִּתְחַלֵּק לְאַרְבָּעָה חֲלָקִים: הָאֶחָד – שְׁמוּעָה, הַשֵּׁנִי –פֵּרוּשׁ, הַשְּׁלִישִׁי – דִּיּוּק, הָרְבִיעִי- הַגָּדָה.

הַשְּׁמוּעָה הִיא – שֶׁיֹּאמַר אוֹמֵר מַאֲמָר אֶחָד, יוֹדִיעַ בּוֹ אֶחָד מִן הָעִנְיָנִים בְּדָבָר מִן הַהֲלָכוֹת, אוֹ מִן הַמּוּסָרִים, אוֹ בְּאֵיזֶה מִין מִשְׁכָּל שֶׁיִּהְיֶה.

דֶּרֶךְ מָשָׁל (ברכות כ ב): "אָמַר רַב אַדָּא בַּר אַהֲבָה: נָשִׁים חַיָּבוֹת בְּקִדּוּשׁ הַיּוֹם – דְּבַר תּוֹרָה".

וּמִשְׁפָּטֶיהָ מִשְׁפְּטֵי הַמַּאֲמָרִים שֶׁבֵּאַרְנוּ בְּפֶרֶק ג.

הַפֵּרוּשׁ הוּא – שֶׁיְּפָרֵשׁ אֶחָד מִן הַכְּתוּבִים אוֹ מִן הַמַּאֲמָרִים.

דֶּרֶךְ מָשָׁל (ברכות כג א): "אָמַר רַבִּי יְהוֹשֻׁעַ בֶּן לֵוִי: מַה טִיבָן שֶׁל טוֹבְלֵי שַׁחֲרִין?" פֵּרְשׁוּ אַחַר כָּךְ:

# Chapter Nine

We have already described the principle elements of debate in Chapter Two. They are: statement, question, answer, contradiction, proof, difficulty and resolution. Now we will describe their sub-categories and explain their basic rules.

## Statement

There are four types of statements: first-hand knowledge, explanation, inference, and reported information.

A statement of **First-hand Knowledge** – the speaker communicates a halachic or ethical principle or any other idea.

> *For example, (Berachos 20b) "Rav Ada bar Ahavah stated: Torah law obligates women to fulfill the mitzvah of kiddush."*

The rules governing statements of first-hand knowledge are the same as the principles governing statements, which have already been explained in Chapter Three.

**Explanation** – the speaker's purpose is to explain a verse or prior statement.

> *For example, (Berachos 22a) "Rabbi Yehoshua ben Levi asked, what is the value of the ritual bath for those accustomed to immerse in the morning? You ask, what value?! Rabbi Yehoshua himself stated that one who has a*

"הָכִי קָאָמַר: מַה טִיבָן בְּאַרְבָּעִים סְאָה –

אֶפְשָׁר בְּתִשְׁעָה קַבִּין? מַה טִיבָן בִּטְבִילָה –

אֶפְשָׁר בִּנְתִינָה?"

וְאָמְנָם מִשְׁפַּט הַפֵּרוּשׁ הוּא, שֶׁמִּלְּבַד הַסְכִּימוֹ עִם הָאֱמֶת בְּעֶצֶם עִנְיָנוֹ, צָרִיךְ שֶׁיַּסְכִּים עִם הַמַּאֲמָר הַמְפֹרָשׁ כְּפִי מִלּוֹתָיו וְסֵדֶר הַגָּדָתוֹ.

וְאוּלָם, אִם יַסְכִּים לְגַמְרֵי עִם הַמַּאֲמָר – יִקָּרֵא **פֵּרוּשׁ מְרֻוָּח**, וְאִם יַסְכִּים בְּעִקַּר הַמַּאֲמָר וְלֹא יֵאוֹת הֵיטֵב עִם כָּל הַמִּלּוֹת אוֹ עִם כָּל הַסֵּדֶר, עַד שֶׁנִּצְטָרֵךְ לוֹמַר שֶׁלֹּא דִּבֵּר בַּעַל הַמַּאֲמָר בְּדִקְדּוּק – יִקָּרֵא **פֵּרוּשׁ דָּחוּק**; וְאִם לֹא יַסְכִּים כְּלָל עִם הַמַּאֲמָר, נִדְחֵהוּ לְגַמְרֵי. וְהִנֵּה בִּכְלָל זֶה, יִכָּלֵל דֶּרֶךְ בֵּאוּר הַנִּקְרָא **אוֹקִימְתָּא**, וְהוּא בֵּאוּר תְּנָאֵי בַּמַּאֲמָר, דְּהַיְנוּ שֶׁלֹּא נְבָאֵר כְּלָל הַהַגָּדָה וּמִלּוֹתֶיהָ, אֶלָּא נַנִּיחֵם

*nocturnal emission may not engage in Torah activities until he immerses". The Talmud then offers an explanation: "This is what he meant. What is the value of a ritual bath containing forty se'ahs? It is possible to be purified with only nine kabs of water [note: one se'ah equals six kabs]. Why is immersion necessary? It is possible to be purified merely through pouring water over the body"! At first, Rabbi Yehoshua's question was not understood since it goes without saying that the ritual bath is beneficial. Afterwards it was explained that there is an alternative method of purification making the ritual bath unnecessary.*

The principles governing an explanation are that it must agree with the essential content of the statement, and with the explicit wording and formal structure of the statement.

When the explanation is in total agreement with the text, it is called a **Full Explanation**. However, when the explanation agrees with the essential message, but the wording and form of the statement are inappropriate, then it is called a **Forced Explanation** because it must be assumed that the author did not use his words precisely. However, if the explanation is completely foreign to the content and to the text of the statement, it cannot be accepted as an explanation at all. Another type of explanation is based on a method of clarification called **Presumption**. Here, the purpose of the explanation is not to deal with wording or formal structure but rather to clarify the

כְּמַשְׁמָעָן הַפָּשׁוּט, אֲבָל נַגְבִּיל הַמַּאֲמָר בְּאַחַד הַתְּנָאִים, וְהוּא כְּשֶׁנֶּאֱמַר: "הָכָא בְּמַאי עָסְקִינָן", אוֹ "הָא מָנִי? רַבִּי פְלוֹנִי הִיא".

דֶּרֶךְ מָשָׁל (ברכות כג): "הָכָא בְּמַאי עָסְקִינָן", וְכֵן (ברכות כד ב): "לָא שָׁנוּ אֶלָּא שֶׁיָּכוֹל לְכַוֵּן אֶת לִבּוֹ בַּלַּחַשׁ".

הַדִּיּוּק הוּא – שֶׁיְּדַיֵּק מִמַּאֲמָר אֶחָד אוֹ כָתוּב אֶחָד מַה שֶּׁלֹּא פֵּרֵשׁ בּוֹ, וּכְמוֹ שֶׁבֵּאַרְנוּ לְמַעְלָה.

דֶּרֶךְ מָשָׁל, עַל מִשְׁנַת (ברכות כד ב): "בַּעַל קֶרִי מְהַרְהֵר בְּלִבּוֹ" "אָמַר רָבִינָא: זֹאת אוֹמֶרֶת – הִרְהוּר כְּדִבּוּר דָּמֵי!"

וּמִשְׁפָּטָיו נִתְבָּאֲרוּ בְּפֶרֶק ה.

הַהַגָּדָה – שֶׁיַּגִּיד אֶחָד מַעֲשֶׂה אוֹ מַאֲמָר זוּלָתוֹ. וְכֵן נִכְלַל בַּמִּין הַזֶּה כְּשֶׁיַּגִּיד מַחֲשֶׁבֶת זוּלָתוֹ, פֵּרוּשׁ – כְּשֶׁיַּגִּיד אֶחָד מַה שֶּׁהִרְגִּישׁ אַחֵר לְפִי דַעְתּוֹ מִן הַקֻּשְׁיוֹת אוֹ מִן הַתֵּרוּצִים.

presumed or understood stipulations of a given statement. The text is left to be understood in its primary meaning; however, the explanation qualifies the statement by clarifying an unstated assumption. A presumption is commonly preceded in the Talmud by the phrase "Here, with what case are we dealing"? or "Whose opinion is represented here? It is Rabbi so-and-so".

> *For example, (Berachos 24b) those who say their prayers out loud are lacking faith. Rav Huna adds, "This only refers to those who are able to concentrate in a silent prayer".*

**Inference** – a statement which is derived from another statement or verse. The purpose of an inference is to make an assertion which is not explicit in the first statement .

> *For example, (Berachos 20b) "One who has a nocturnal emission should recite the words of Sh'ma Yisrael in his mind. Ravina said, this implies that reciting in one's mind is the same as reciting out loud".*

We have already explained inferences and their rules in detail in Chapter Five.

**Reported Information** – the speaker's purpose is to inform us about someone else's deed or statement. A reconstruction of someone else's opinion is also considered reported information. In this case, the speaker informs us of something that others should consider either a difficulty or a solution according to their stated view.

דֶּרֶךְ מָשָׁל, כְּשֶׁאָמְרוּ (שבת יט א): "אָמַר רַבִּי צָדוֹק:
כָּךְ הָיָה מִנְהָגוֹ שֶׁל בֵּית רַבָּן גַּמְלִיאֵל".

וּכְשֶׁאָמְרוּ (בבא קמא פג ב): "תּוּ קָא קַשְׁיָא לַתַּנָּא:
מַאי חָזֵית דִּילַפְתְּ מִמַּכֵּה בְהֵמָה – לֵילַף מִמַּכֵּה
אָדָם", הִנֵּה שָׁם מַגִּיד הַשַּׁ"ס מַה שֶּׁהִרְגִּישׁ
הַתַּנָּא לְפִי דַעְתּוֹ בְּדִבְרֵי עַצְמוֹ.

הַשְּׁאֵלָה תֵּחָלֵק לִשְׁנַיִם: הָאֶחָד – שְׁאֵלָה, הַשֵּׁנִי – אִבַּעְיָא.

הַשְּׁאֵלָה – כְּשֶׁיִּשְׁאַל שׁוֹאֵל עַל עִנְיָן אֶחָד, אִם הוּא – אִם אֵינוֹ,
אוֹ עַל תְּנַאי מִמֶּנּוּ, כְּגוֹן עַל מָקוֹם, אוֹ עַל זְמָן, אוֹ עַל טַעַם, וְכַיּוֹצֵא
בָּזֶה.

דֶּרֶךְ מָשָׁל (יבמות קב א): "אָמַרְתִּי לוֹ: כְּלוּם אַתָּה
בָּקִי בְּרַבִּי יְהוּדָה בֶּן בְּתֵירָא?"

וְכֵן כְּשֶׁאָמְרוּ (ברכות לה א): "כֵּיצַד מְבָרְכִין עַל
הַפֵּרוֹת ?"

*For example, (Shabbos 19a) "Rabbi Tzadok said, this was the custom in the school of Raban Gamliel".*

*(Babba Kamma 83b) "Furthermore, the difficulty which might have occurred to the Tanna is: Why is it preferable to derive the law from one who strikes an animal? It is better to derive it from one who strikes a man"! In this example, the Talmud reconstructs the Tanna's difficulty regarding the law of the Mishnah. (See page 216 for a complete discussion of this text.)*

## Question

The category of question has two parts: the first is a query (point of information) and the second is a question of principle.

**Query** – the speaker asks for confirmation or denial of a statement, or about some specific circumstance such as the place, time or cause.

*For example, (Yebamos 102a) "I asked him, are you familiar with the rulings of Rabbi Yehudah ben Bessairah"?*

*(Berachos 35a) "What is the proper blessing on fruits"?*

וְכֵן כְּשֶׁאָמְרוּ (יבמות קיג ב): "מַאי שְׁנָא חֵרֵשׁ
וְחֵרֶשֶׁת דְּתַקִּינוּ לְהוּ רַבָּנָן נִשּׂוּאִין, וּמַאי שְׁנָא
דְּשׁוֹטֶה וְשׁוֹטָה דְּלָא תַּקִּינוּ לְהוּ רַבָּנָן נִשּׂוּאִין?"

**הָאַבַּעְיָא** – כְּשֶׁיִּשָּׁאֵל שׁוֹאֵל עַל עִנְיָן אֶחָד שֶׁיֵּשׁ בּוֹ פָּנִים לִשְׁנֵי
צְדָדִים וִיבַקֵּשׁ עַל הַהַכְרָעָה לְאֶחָד מֵהֶם.

דֶּרֶךְ מָשָׁל (יבמות נח ג): "בְּעָא מִנֵּהּ רַבִּי חִיָּא בַר
יוֹסֵף מִשְּׁמוּאֵל: כֹּהֵן גָּדוֹל שֶׁקִּדֵּשׁ אֶת הַקְּטַנָּה
וּבָגְרָה תַחְתָּיו – מַהוּ? בָּתַר נִשּׂוּאִין אָזְלִינָן אוֹ
בָּתַר אֵרוּסִין אָזְלִינָן?"

> *(Yebamos 112b)* *"What is the difference between deaf-mutes, for whom the rabbis ordained that a marriage is valid, and the insane, for whom marriage is invalid"?*

**Question of Principle** – the speaker presents a certain topic which may be understood in one of two ways, and he asks for a decision.

> *For example, (Yebamos 58b) "Rabbi Chiyya bar Yosef presented the following question to Shmuel: What is the law when a girl is betrothed to the Cohen Gadol and she subsequently reaches adolescence? Let us understand the prohibition of an adolescent girl to the Cohen Gadol. Is he unable to marry her at the stage of adolescence even though he is already betrothed, or is betrothal forbidden and in the case that she is already betrothed to him before adolescence he is permitted to marry her"? In this question, adolescence refers to a certain stage of puberty during which it cannot be determined whether the girl is a virgin, and it is required by Torah law that the Cohen Gadol marry a virgin.*

**הַתְּשׁוּבָה** תֵּחָלֵק גַּם כֵּן לִשְׁנַיִם: הָאֶחָד – תְּשׁוּבַת הַשְּׁאֵלָה, הַשֵּׁנִי – תְּשׁוּבַת הָאִבַּעְיָא, וְנִקְרֵאת פְּשִׁיטוּת.

**הַתְּשׁוּבָה** – שֶׁיָּשִׁיב עַל הַשְּׁאֵלָה כְּפִי מַה שֶׁהִיא. אִם שָׁאַל עַל מְצִיאוּת עִנְיָן, אִם הוּא – אִם אֵינוֹ , יָשִׁיב לוֹ: הֵן! אוֹ לָאו! וְאִם טַעַם בִּקֵשׁ – יְשִׁיבֵהוּ הַטַּעַם.

דֶּרֶךְ מָשָׁל, עַל שָׁאֲלַת (יבמות קב א): "כְּלוּם אַתָּה בָּקִי בְּרַבִּי יְהוּדָה בֶן בְּתֵירָא?" הֵשִׁיב: "הֵן!"

עַל שָׁאֲלַת (יבמות קיב ב): "מַאי שְׁנָא חֵרֵשׁ וְחֵרֶשֶׁת?" הֵשִׁיב: "חֵרֵשׁ וְחֵרֶשֶׁת דְּקָיְמָא תַּקַּנְתָּא דְרַבָּנָן – תַּקִּינוּ לְהוּ רַבָּנָן נִשּׂוּאִין, שׁוֹטֶה וְשׁוֹטָה דְּלָא קָיְמָא תַּקַּנְתָּא דְרַבָּנָן – לָא תַּקִּינוּ רַבָּנָן נִשּׂוּאִין".

וְכֵן הַשְּׁאָר. וּמִשְׁפָּטָהּ לִהְיוֹת תְּשׁוּבָה עַל פִּי הַשְּׁאֵלָה וְלִהְיוֹת אֲמִתִּית.

**הַפְּשִׁיטוּת** הִיא – שֶׁיַּכְרִיעַ לְאֶחָד מִשְּׁנֵי צִדְדֵי הָאִבַּעְיָא.

# Answer

The third category, answer, is likewise divided into two parts: the answer to a query and the answer to a question of principle, which is called a determination.

**Answer** – the speaker responds to a query according to whatever is sought. If the query involves the affirmation or denial of a certain fact, the response must be yes or no. If the query is about the reason for something, the answer must give a reason.

> *For example, it was asked, (Yebamos 102a) "Are you familiar with the rulings of Rabbi Yehudah ben Basseirah"? The response was, "Yes"!*

> *The Talmud asked, (Yebamos 112b) "What is the difference between a deaf-mute and an insane person"? The response was, "Since deaf-mutes are capable of fulfilling rabbinical laws, the rabbis ordained that their marriage is valid. But the insane are incapable, and thus the rabbis did not validate their marriage".*

Similar examples may be found for the other types of questions. The requirements of an answer are that the response must be appropriate to the query and that it must be true.

**Determination** – the response decides the question of principle in one direction or the other.

דֶּרֶךְ מָשָׁל, עַל הַבַּעְיָא (יבמות נח ב): "כֹּהֵן גָּדוֹל
שֶׁקִּדֵּשׁ אֶת הַקְּטַנָּה וּבָגְרָה תַחְתָּיו – מַהוּ?"
פָּשַׁט שְׁמוּאֵל דְּבָתַר נִשּׂוּאִין אָזְלִינָן.

וּמִשְׁפָּטָהּ כְּמִשְׁפַּט הַתְּשׁוּבָה.

**הָרְאָיָה** תֵּחָלֵק לִשְׁנַיִם: הָאֶחָד הוֹכָחָה, וְהַשֵּׁנִי סִיַּעְתָּא.

**הַהוֹכָחָה הִיא** – שֶׁיָּבִיא רְאָיָה לְהוֹכִיחַ אֲמִתַּת מַאֲמָר שֶׁנֶּאֱמָר.

דֶּרֶךְ מָשָׁל (פסחים טז א): "רַבִּי אֶלְעָזָר אוֹמֵר: אֵין
טֻמְאָה לַמַּשְׁקִין כָּל עִקָּר! תֵּדַע, שֶׁהֲרֵי הֵעִיד
יוֹסֵי בֶן יוֹעֶזֶר אִישׁ צְרֵידָה עַל אֵיל קַמְצָא דָכָן
וְעַל מַשְׁקִין בֵּית מִטְבְּחַיָּא דָּכָן".

*For example, (Yebamos 58b) "Is the Cohen Ga-*
*dol permitted to marry an adolescent to whom*
*he was betrothed when she was a child"?*
*Shmuel determined that the prohibition of an*
*adolescent applies to him at the time of mar-*
*riage even though he was already betrothed,*
*and therefore he is not permitted to marry her*
*at the time of her adolescence.*

The rules governing a determination are the same as the rules for other answers.

## Proof

There are two kinds of proofs: one is demonstration and the other is validation.

**Demonstration** – a proof is adduced to demonstrate the truth of a given statement.

*For example, (Pesachim 16a) "Rabbi Eleazar*
*said: Liquids (e.g., water, blood, etc.) cannot be-*
*come unclean at all according to Torah law!*
*This can be construed from the fact that Yosi*
*ben Yo'ezer of Zeredah testified that the ayil lo-*
*cust is kosher, and also that the liquids (e.g.,*
*water, blood, etc.) of the Temple slaughterhouse*
*are clean". From the latter statement it is evi-*
*dent that if liquids are deemed unclean, it is*
*only a rabbinical law; however, the rabbis did*

וְכֵן כְּשֶׁשָּׁאֲלוּ "מְנָא הַנֵּי מִלֵּי" וְהֵשִׁיבוּ: "דְּתָנוּ רַבָּנָן". וּמִשְׁפָּטָהּ, שֶׁתּוֹכִיחַ בְּהֶכְרֵחַ אֲמִתַּת הַמַּאֲמָר עַל פִּי חֻקֵּי הָרְאָיָה הַמֻּכְרַחַת שֶׁפֵּרַשְׁתִּי. אָמְנָם גַּם מִכֹּחַ סְבָרָא נוּכַל לְהוֹכִיחַ, אַךְ אֵינָהּ כָּל כָּךְ חֲזָקָה.

**הַסִּיַּעְתָּא** – שֶׁיּוּבָא מַאֲמָר אֶחָד שֶׁיַּסְכִּים לְמַאֲמָר אַחֵר לְחַזֵּק הַדֵּעָה שֶׁנֶּאֶמְרָה בוֹ.

דֶּרֶךְ מָשָׁל (יבמות קב ג): "תַּנְיָא כְּוָתֵהּ דְּרָבָא! חָלְצָה בְּמִנְעָל הַנִּפְרָם, שֶׁחוֹפֶה אֶת רֹב הָרֶגֶל – חֲלִיצָתָהּ כְּשֵׁרָה".

וּמִשְׁפָּטָהּ כְּמִשְׁפַּט הַהוֹכָחָה.

**הַסְּתִירָה** תֵּחָלֵק לִשְׁנַיִם: הָאֶחָד – סְתִירָה, וְהַשֵּׁנִי – דְּחִיָּה.

> *not apply their enactment in the Temple in or-*
> *der not to disqualify the animals designated for*
> *sacrifice. By implication, liquids are not un-*
> *clean at all according to Torah law.*

Similarly, whenever the Talmud asks, "From where is this known"? and answers, "Thus our rabbis have taught", a demonstration is indicated. The rule of demonstration is that it must prove conclusively the truth of the given statement according to all the principles which I have explained in Chapter Eight. In addition, it is possible to demonstrate something on the strength of a theory, but this type of proof is not as binding.

**Validation** – in order to support a stated opinion, another statement is presented which agrees with this opinion.

> *For example, (Yebamos 102b) Rava said there is*
> *a distinction between a leather sock and a felt*
> *sock. "It has been taught in accordance with*
> *Rava's view: If a woman performed chalitzah*
> *with a torn shoe covering most of the foot or a*
> *leather sock, the chalitzah is valid; with a felt*
> *sock, it is invalid".*

The rule for a validation is the same as for a demonstration.

## Contradiction

Contradiction has two parts: one is a direct contradiction and the other is opposition.

**הַסְּתִירָה** – שֶׁיִּסְתֵּר מַאֲמָר שֶׁנֶּאֱמַר אוֹ רְאָיָה שֶׁהוּבָאת וְיֵרָאֶה הֱיוֹתָם מְבֻטָּלִים.

דֶּרֶךְ מָשָׁל (פסחים יז ג): "אָמַר רַב פַּפָּא: אֲפִלּוּ לְמָאן דְּאָמַר טֻמְאַת מַשְׁקִין דְּאוֹרַיְתָא – מַשְׁקֵי בֵּית מִטְבְּחַיָא הִלְכְתָא גְּמִירֵי לַהּ. אֲמַר לֵהּ רַב הוּנָא בְּרֵהּ דְּרַב נָתָן לְרַב פַּפָּא: וְאֶלָּא הָא דְּאָמַר רַבִּי אֶלְעָזָר אֵין טֻמְאָה לַמַּשְׁקִין כָּל עִקָּר, תֵּדַע שֶׁהֲרֵי הֵעִיד יוֹסֵי בֶּן יוֹעֶזֶר אִישׁ צְרֵידָה עַל מַשְׁקֵי בֵּית מִטְבְּחַיָא דָּכָן, וְאִי הִלְכְתָא גְּמִירֵי לַהּ– מַי גָּמְרִינָן מִנַּהּ?" הִנֵּה כָּאן סָתַר שְׁמוּעָתוֹ שֶׁל רַב פַּפָּא לַחֲלוּטִין מִכֹּחַ הַמּוֹפֵת שֶׁהֵבִיא שֶׁהֱגֶדָהּ.

וְהִנֵּה מִשְׁפַּט הַסְּתִירָה שֶׁתִּסְתּוֹר בְּכֹחַ חָזָק עַל פִּי חֻקּוֹת הָרְאָיָה הַמַּכְחֶשֶׁת שֶׁפֵּרַשְׁתִּי לְמַעְלָה.

**הַדְּחִיָּה** – שֶׁיְּדַחֶה הֶכְרֵחַ הַמַּאֲמָר, אַךְ לֹא יְבַטֵּל עִנְיָנוֹ לְגַמְרֵי, וְלֹא תְּכֻחַשׁ אֶפְשָׁרוּתוֹ. דֶּרֶךְ מָשָׁל, כְּשֶׁאָמְרוּ: "מַאי לָאו?" הֵשִׁיבוּ:

**Direct Contradiction** – the purpose is to contradict some statement or some proof and show how it can be nullified.

> *For example, (Pesachim 17b) "Rav Papa said: even those who say that liquids can become unclean according to Torah law would agree that there is a ruling handed down from Sinai that liquids of the Temple slaughterhouse cannot become unclean. Rav Huna ben Rav Nossan said to Rav Papa: But you are wrong, for the Tanna Rabbi Eleazar concluded that liquids have no uncleanness at all in Torah law on the basis of Yosi ben Yo'ezer of Zeredah, who testified that the liquids of the Temple slaughterhouse are clean. Now, if that fact is actually a ruling handed down from Sinai, then we could not deduce anything from it". Here, the statement of Rav Papa is absolutely contradicted on the basis of evidence brought against it.*

The rule for a contradiction is that it categorically destroys a statement or proof according to the laws of disproof which are explained above in Chapter Eight.

**Opposition** – the purpose of an opposition is to undermine the certainty of a given statement. However, an opposition neither nullifies the statement nor does it invalidate the possibility that it could be true. For example, the Talmud uses the expression "What else could it be but this"? and generally the response is, "Not necessarily so"!

"לָאו!" וְכֵן כְּשֶׁיֹּאמְרוּ: "וְדִלְמָא?" "וְאֵימָא?" הִנֵּה הוּא סִימָן דְּחִיָּה לְהֶכְרֵחַ הַמַּאֲמָר שֶׁנֶּאֱמַר. וְהִנֵּה הַדְּחִיָּה דַּי שֶׁתִּסְתֵּר הַהֶכְרֵחַ, אַף עַל פִּי שֶׁנִּשְׁאַר הַמַּאֲמָר אֶפְשָׁרִי, וְאָז נִשְׁאַר הַמַּאֲמָר מְסֻפָּק וּבִלְתִּי־מֻכְרָח. אָמְנָם צָרִיךְ עַל כָּל פָּנִים, שֶׁמַּה שֶׁיָּקִים עַל יָדָהּ יִהְיֶה לוֹ מָקוֹם בַּנּוֹשֵׂא אֲשֶׁר נָדוֹן עָלָיו וְלֹא יִהְיֶה דָּבָר רָחוֹק בְּתַכְלִית, כִּי אִלּוּ הָיָה כָּךְ, הָיָה נִשְׁאַר הַמַּאֲמָר מְקֻיָּם בְּכֹחַ הַסְּבָרָא, כְּמוֹ שֶׁאָמַרְנוּ לְמַעְלָה.

הַקֻּשְׁיָא תֵּחָלֵק לִשְׁלֹשָׁה: הָאֶחָד – פִּרְכָא, הַשֵּׁנִי – רְמִיָּא, הַשְּׁלִישִׁי – תְּיוּבְתָּא.

הַפִּרְכָא הִיא – כְּשֶׁיִּמָּצֵא בְּסֵדֶר הַמַּאֲמָר אוֹ הַגָּדָתוֹ דָּבָר בִּלְתִּי נָאוֹת. דֶּרֶךְ מָשָׁל, כְּשֶׁאָמְרוּ: "הָא גּוּפָא קַשְׁיָא!"

אוֹ כְּשֶׁאָמְרוּ (יבמות קיז ג): "שְׁנַיִם אוֹמְרִים: מֵת, וְעֵד אוֹמֵר: לֹא מֵת – מַאי קָא מַשְׁמַע לָן?

Similarly, when the Talmud says "And perhaps. . ." or "I might say. . .", all these expressions indicate an opposition to the certainty of the given statement. It is sufficient for an opposition to destroy the certainty of a given statement even though the statement remains a possibility, because, as a result, the given statement will remain in doubt and unproven. However, the opposing point of view must present a plausible understanding of the subject matter under discussion. An opposition cannot be based on just any possibility, no matter how farfetched, because, in that case, the statement in question will remain in place simply because it represents a more reasonable theory. We have already discussed this earlier in Chapter Eight.

## Difficulty

Difficulty can be divided into three parts: the first is an objection, the second is an apparent contradiction and the third is a refutation.

**Objection** – whenever the order or formal structure of the statement contains something inconsistent or inappropriate. An objection may be introduced by the expression "This is self-contradictory"!

> *Another instance of an objection is exemplified when the Talmud states, (Yebamos 117b) "A woman may remarry when two witnesses testify that her husband is dead and one testifies that he is not. What novel idea do we learn from this? Even where the two witnesses are technically disqualified, nonetheless we follow the testimony of the majority as Rabbi Neche-*

בִּפְסוּלֵי עֵדוּת, וְכִדְרַבִּי נְחֶמְיָה דְּאָזִיל בָּתַר רֹב
דֵּעוֹת. הַיְנוּ הָךְ!"

וְכֵן שָׁם ‎(יבמות קי״ח א‏)‎: ‏‏"וְלִפְלֹג רַבִּי מֵאִיר
בְּרֵישָׁא!"

וְכֵן כֹּל כַּיּוֹצֵא בָזֶה, קֻשְׁיוֹת שֶׁעַל סִדּוּרֵי הַמַּאֲמָרִים אוֹ צֹרֶךְ
הַהַגָּדָה בְּכֻלָּם אוֹ בְּחֶלְקֵיהֶם.

הָרֶמְיָא- כְּשֶׁיּוּבְאוּ שְׁנֵי מַאֲמָרִים, אוֹ שְׁנֵי כְתוּבִים הַפְּכִיִּים אוֹ
מִתְנַגְּדִים, לְבַקֵּשׁ יִשּׁוּבָם.

דֶּרֶךְ מָשָׁל ‎(יבמות קכ ב‏)‎: ‏‏"וּרְמִינְהִי: אָדָם אֵינוֹ
מְטַמֵּא עַד שֶׁתֵּצֵא נַפְשׁוֹ, אֲפִלּוּ מְגֻיָּד, וַאֲפִלּוּ
גוֹסֵס".

> *miah taught." Then the Talmud raises an ob-*
> *jection, "But this is exactly what was taught in*
> *the previous case of the Mishnah, and there is*
> *no need to repeat it"!*
>
> *Another example: (Yebamos 118a) "Rabbi Meir*
> *should also argue in the former case just as he*
> *did in the latter".*

Generally, an objection is raised whenever there is a difficulty in the order of statements or in the necessity for stating either the entire sentence or a part of it.

**Apparent Contradiction** – when two statements or two verses appear either opposite or contrary to one another and a solution is sought.

> *For example, (Yebamos 120b) "Even though*
> *witnesses have seen a man mortally wounded,*
> *they may not testify that he is dead unless they*
> *have seen that his soul has departed. This im-*
> *plies the possibility that a mortally wounded*
> *man may still live. But this contradicts the fol-*
> *lowing: A body is not unclean until the soul has*
> *departed, even if the man is mortally wounded*
> *or dying. This implies that we exclude the pos-*
> *sibility that a mortally wounded man may live,*
> *but nonetheless, the body is not unclean until*
> *the soul has departed".*

וְכֵן כְּשֶׁאָמְרוּ (ברכות ד א): "רַבִּי יַעֲקֹב בַּר אִידִי
רָמֵי, כְּתִיב (בראשית כח טו): 'וְהִנֵּה אָנֹכִי עִמָּךְ
וּשְׁמַרְתִּיךָ בְּכֹל אֲשֶׁר־תֵּלֵךְ', וּכְתִיב (בראשית לב ח):
'וַיִּירָא יַעֲקֹב מְאֹד'."

הַתֵּרוּץ יֵחָלֵק לִשְׁנַיִם: הָאֶחָד – הַיִּשּׁוּב, הַשֵּׁנִי – הַשִּׁנּוּי.

הַיִּשּׁוּב כְּשֶׁתִּתְרַץ הַפִּרְכָא אוֹ הָרַמְיָא בְּיִשּׁוּב נָכוֹן וַאֲמִתִּי,
שֶׁיַּאֲמִין בּוֹ הַמִּתְרָץ הֱיוֹת זֶה אֲמִתַּת הַדָּבָר.

דֶּרֶךְ מָשָׁל, כְּשֶׁתֵּרֵץ רַבִּי יַעֲקֹב בַּר אִידִי
לְרַמְיָתוֹ (ברכות ד א): "אָמַר, שֶׁמָּא יִגְרֹם הַחֵטְא".

וּמִשְׁפָּטוֹ שֶׁיִּהְיֶה אֲמִתִּי בְּעַצְמוֹ וְיַסְכִּים עִם הַמַּאֲמָר שֶׁעָלָיו הוּא בָּא.

*Similarly, (Berachos 4a) "Rabbi Ya'akov bar Idi pointed out this contradiction: It is written (Genesis 28:15) 'Behold I am with you and will protect you wherever you go', and it is also written: (Genesis 32:8) 'And Ya'akov was very much afraid'".*

(Translator's Note: **Refutation** is not defined.)

## Resolution

**Resolution** has two categories: the first is a settlement and the second is an alternative.

**Settlement** – when an objection or apparent contradiction is resolved through a valid and true solution, and also the one who proposes it believes that it is true.

*For example, to continue with the previous text, Rabbi Ya'akov bar Idi himself resolved the apparent contradiction which he raised. (Berachos 4a) "Ya'akov thought that perhaps sin may have some bearing on God's promise to him".*

The rules for a settlement are that it must be true in its own right, and it must agree with the statement in question which it was meant to defend.

**הַשִּׁנּוּי** – כְּשֶׁתִּתְרַץ הַקֻּשְׁיָא אוֹ הָרַמְיָא בְּמַה שֶׁאֵין הַכַּוָּנָה בּוֹ
לַמְתָרֵץ בְּהֶחְלֵט שֶׁתִּהְיֶה כֵן אֲמִתַּת הַדָּבָר, אֶלָּא שֶׁתִּדָּחֶה הַקֻּשְׁיָא.
וְהִנֵּה זֶה דּוֹמֶה לִדְחִיָּה בֶּאֱמֶת, אֶלָּא שֶׁהַדְּחִיָּה תִּהְיֶה עַל מַאֲמָר שֶׁהֻנַּח
אוֹ רְאָיָה שֶׁהוּבָאת, וְהַשִּׁנּוּי – דְּחִיָּה עַל קֻשְׁיָא.

דֶּרֶךְ מָשָׁל, כְּשֶׁהִקְשׁוּ עַל רָבָא, בְּאָמְרָם (יבמות קד)
ג) "חֵרֵשׁ שֶׁנֶּחְלַץ וְחֵרֶשֶׁת שֶׁחָלְצָה – חֲלִיצָתָהּ
פְּסוּלָה, מַאי טַעְמָא? לָאו מִשּׁוּם דְּלָאו בְּנֵי
קְרִיָּה נִינְהוּ?". דָּחוּ וְאָמְרוּ: "לָא! מִשּׁוּם דְּלָאו
בְּנֵי דֵעָה נִינְהוּ".

וּמִשְׁפַּט הַשִּׁנּוּי הוּא, שֶׁיּוּכַל לְהַסְכִּים עִם הַמַּאֲמָר שֶׁעָלָיו הוּבָא,
וַאֲפִלּוּ נִצְטָרֵךְ לְהַנִּיחַ בּוֹ קְצָת זָרוּת וְחֶסְרוֹן, אוֹ דָּבָר בִּלְתִּי נָאוֹת,
וְנֹאמַר שֶׁלֹּא דִקְדֵּק כָּל כָּךְ בַּעַל הַמַּאֲמָר בְּמִלּוֹתָיו. וְאוּלָם כְּפִי רִבּוּת

**Alternative** – when an objection or apparent contradiction is resolved, but the one who offers the resolution does not claim absolutely that his position is true. It is sufficient that his alternative defends the given statement and undermines the difficulty. We can see that this is very similar to an opposition, only an opposition applies to a statement or a proof and an alternative applies to a difficulty.

> *For example, (Yebamos 104b) Rava stated that chalitzah may be performed by a dumb man or woman since only their speech is impaired. The Talmud raised a difficulty, "We have learned that chalitzah is invalid in the case of a man or woman who is a deaf-mute. Now what is the reason? Is it not that their power of speech is impaired [and the same ruling should apply to a person who is dumb!]"? Then the following alternative is presented: "Not necessarily so! There is a possibility that the chalitzah is invalid because he lacks the power of understanding [but this only applies to a deaf-mute and not to one who is dumb]".*

The rule for an alternative is that it must offer a viable interpretation of the statement upon which a difficulty was raised, even if it is necessary to posit some extraneous fact or to accept something lacking or forced. At worst, we will only say that the author of the statement did not use his words precisely. However, the more information is lacking and must be supplied in order to understand the

הַחֶסְרוֹן שֶׁנִּצְטָרֵךְ לְהַנִּיחַ בּוֹ, כָּךְ יִהְיֶה הַשִּׁנּוּי יוֹתֵר דָּחוּק, וְאִם תִּרְבֶּה הַזָּרוּת כָּל כָּךְ שֶׁמְּלוֹתָיו בֶּאֱמֶת לֹא תִסְבַּלְנָה אוֹתוֹ, לֹא נִתֵּן לוֹ מָקוֹם כְּלָל.

statement, the more the alternative will be considered a forced explanation. If the text cannot bear such a forced interpretation, then the alternative will not be accepted to remove the difficulty.

# פרק י

הִנֵּה עַד הֵנָּה בֵּאַרְנוּ חֶלְקֵי הַסְּגִיּוֹת וְהַמְכֻוָּן בָּהֶם. עַתָּה נְבָאֵר סֵדֶר הָעִיּוּן בָּהֶן לְהַשִּׂיג כָּל דָּבָר לְפִי מַה שֶּׁהוּא.

כְּבָר הִקְדַּמְתִּי לְךָ, שֶׁדַּרְכֵי הַהַגָּדָה וְאָפְנֵי הַדִּבּוּר הֵם רַבִּים. וְאוּלָם זֶה נוֹלָד מִסִּבּוֹת שׁוֹנוֹת. הָרִאשׁוֹנָה – שֶׁטֶּבַע הָאֲנָשִׁים נוֹתֵן זֶה, שֶׁיִּהְיֶה לְכָל אֶחָד דֶּרֶךְ פְּרָטִי וּמְיֻחָד לְהַגִּיד מַחְשְׁבוֹתָיו וּלְבַטֵּא מַה שֶּׁבְּלִבּוֹ כְּכָל שְׁאָר הָעִנְיָנִים הַטִּבְעִיִּים שֶׁמִּתְחַלְּפִים בִּבְנֵי הָאָדָם כְּפִי מִזְגֵיהֶם וּתְכוּנָתָם וּנְטִיַּת שִׂכְלָם. הַשְּׁנִיָּה – מַה שֶּׁמְּלֶאכֶת הַמְּלִיצָה מְלַמֶּדֶת לְהַנְעִים הַהַגָּדָה וּלְיַפּוֹתָהּ, אוֹ לְהָקֵל הַהֲבָנָה לַשׁוֹמְעִים וּלְהַכְנִיס הַדְּבָרִים בְּלִבָּם. הַשְּׁלִישִׁית – מַה שֶּׁמִּנְהַג הַדּוֹרוֹת אוֹ הָאֲרָצוֹת גּוֹרֵם, כִּי יֵשׁ שֶׁנָּהֲגוּ לְדַבֵּר בְּדֶרֶךְ אֶחָד, וְיֵשׁ שֶׁנָּהֲגוּ לְדַבֵּר בְּדֶרֶךְ אַחֵר, וְעַל הָרֹב מִתְלַמְּדִים בְּנֵי הָאָדָם לְדַבֵּר כְּפִי מִנְהַג מְקוֹמָם בִּזְמַנָּם.

וְזֶה מִמַּה שֶּׁצָּרִיךְ כָּל קוֹרֵא בְחִבּוּר מִן הַחִבּוּרִים שֶׁיִּשְׁתַּדֵּל לְהַכִּיר לְשׁוֹן הַמְחַבֵּר הַהוּא וְדֶרֶךְ הַגָּדָתוֹ, כִּי מַה שֶּׁלְּפִי אַחַת הַלְּשׁוֹנוֹת אוֹ דַרְכֵי הַדִּבּוּר יִרְמֹז לָנוּ עִנְיָן אֶחָד וְנָבִין מִמֶּנּוּ הֲבָנָה אַחַת, אֶפְשָׁר שֶׁלְּפִי לָשׁוֹן אַחֶרֶת וְדֶרֶךְ אַחֵר יִרְמֹז לָנוּ עִנְיָן מִתְחַלֵּף מִזֶּה מְאֹד, וְנָבִין מִמֶּנּוּ הֲבָנָה רְחוֹקָה מִן הָאַחֶרֶת.

# Chapter Ten

Up to this point we have explained the principle elements of debate and how the purpose of every statement may be determined through them. Now we shall explain the sequence of steps necessary for an analysis of any discourse in order to understand the essence of each part.

We have already introduced the idea at the end of Chapter Three that there are many different manners of expression and styles of speech. These differences arise from various independent causes. The first is that each person has a unique way of choosing words to express his thoughts and what is in his heart. This is the same as any other natural manifestation that varies from one individual to another according to his temperament, character, and natural inclination. The second cause is the requirements of the art of rhetoric, which are needed either to enhance and beautify the expression used or to facilitate the understanding of the listeners and cause the words to penetrate their hearts. The third cause is the influence of the prevailing custom of the generation and country. Although there are individual differences, most people become accustomed to speak in the manner of their place and time.

It follows that the reader of any text must strive to be sensitive to the author's language and his particular manner of expression. For from the connotation and nuance of one style and manner of speech we construct our concept and understanding of what is being said, and yet it is possible that if the language and style are interpreted differently we will come to a radically different concept of the text.

וְהִנֵּה בְּבוֹאֲךָ לָעַיֵן בְּאַחַת מִן הַסְּגִיּוֹת, תַּתְחִיל בָּהּ מְעַט מְעַט, וְכָל דִּבּוּר שֶׁתִּקְרָא מִמֶּנָּה, תִּתְבּוֹנֵן בּוֹ תְּחִלָּה עַד שֶׁתַּבְחִין חֲלָקָיו הֵיטֵב, דְּהַיְנוּ הַנּוֹשֵׂא וְהַנָּשׂוּא וְהַדֶּרֶךְ שֶׁיֵּאָמֵר הָעִנְיָן הַהוּא, דְּהַיְנוּ הַנָּשׂוּא בְּאוֹתוֹ הַנּוֹשֵׂא. וְאוּלָם יִהְיֶה הַדִּבּוּר בְּאֵיזוֹ צוּרָה שֶׁיִּהְיֶה, צָרִיךְ שֶׁתְּצַיְּרֵהוּ בְּמַחְשַׁבְתְּךָ בְּצוּרַת הַמַּאֲמָרִים הַיְשָׁרָה; פֵּרוּשׁ – כִּי, אִם תִּמְצָא הַמַּאֲמָר בְּדֶרֶךְ תְּמִיהָה אוֹ בְּדֶרֶךְ קַשְׁיָא בְּאֵיזֶה דֶרֶךְ שֶׁיִּהְיֶה, הִנֵּה תּוֹצִיא תַּמְצִית כַּוָּנָתוֹ בְּמַחְשַׁבְתְּךָ, וְהַיְנוּ הָעִנְיָן שֶׁרָצָה לוֹמַר בַּעַל הַמַּאֲמָר הַהוּא, וְהַנּוֹשֵׂא שֶׁבּוֹ רָצָה לוֹמַר הָעִנְיָן הַהוּא, וְאָז תְּצַיְּרֵהוּ בְּשִׂכְלְךָ עַל הַצּוּרָה הַיְשָׁרָה, שֶׁהִיא: הַנּוֹשֵׂא פְּלוֹנִי יֵשׁ בּוֹ עִנְיָן פְּלוֹנִי.

דֶּרֶךְ מָשָׁל, כְּשֶׁמָּצָאתָ הַדִּבּוּר (פסחים ז ג): "אַבִי הַבֵּן מַאי אִכָּא לְמֵימַר?" הִנֵּה זֶה הַדִּבּוּר בְּדֶרֶךְ קַשְׁיָא. וּכְשֶׁתּוֹצִיא תַּמְצִית כַּוָּנָתוֹ, תִּמְצָא שֶׁהוּא מִתְכַּוֵּן לוֹמַר, שֶׁאֲבִי הַבֵּן צָרִיךְ שֶׁיֹּאמַר:

After you have taken into account these rules of style, here is the procedure to follow when you investigate any section of the Talmud. Start by dividing each statement that you read into its smallest parts. Think about it until you understand clearly the subject and predicate and the type of predication, i.e., how the particular predicate is related to its subject, as we described in Chapter Three. Consequently, no matter what form the particular statement takes, you must translate it in your mind to formulate a complete thought. In other words, if you find a statement phrased in the form of a question or difficulty, you must mentally extract its intention and find the predicate which the author wants to communicate and the subject about which he is speaking. You will then have formulated a complete thought, that is, such-and-such a subject has such-and-such a concept predicated on it.

> For example, take the statement (Pesachim 7b) "But concerning the father of the boy, what is there to say"? The topic of the Gemorah is the contention that the proper blessing for circumcision is "who has commanded us **concerning circumcision.**" The above statement raises the difficulty that the father is an exception to this ruling. This statement is phrased in the form of a difficulty, but if you extract its full intention, you will see that the author's meaning is this: The father of the son must indeed bless "who has commanded us **to circumcise the son**". This formulation of the statement is a complete thought containing a subject and a

"לָמוּל אֶת הַבֵּן". וְזוֹ הִיא הַצּוּרָה הַיְשָׁרָה שֶׁל
הַמַּאֲמָר הַזֶּה, וְכֵן תְּצַיְּרֵהוּ בְמַחֲשַׁבְתְּךָ.

וְאָמְנָם, אַחֲרֵי הַכִּירְךָ הַמַּאֲמָר בַּחֲלָקָיו, אָז צָרִיךְ שֶׁתִּתְבּוֹנֵן
לְהַכִּיר, מַהִי הַתַּכְלִית בַּאֲמִירַת אוֹתוֹ הַמַּאֲמָר, אִם הוּא עִנְיָן בִּפְנֵי
עַצְמוֹ, דְּהַיְנוּ לְהוֹדִיעַ הֱיוֹת הָעִנְיָן הַהוּא בַּנּוֹשֵׂא הַהוּא, אוֹ לִשְׁאֹל אִם
יֵשׁ עִנְיָן בְּנוֹשֵׂא אֶחָד, אוֹ אִם הוּא מִתְחַבֵּר וּמִתְיַחֵס אֶל מַאֲמָר
אַחֵר שֶׁנֶּאֱמַר, וְיִהְיֶה, אוֹ לְפָרְשׁוֹ, אוֹ לְהוֹכִיחַ עָלָיו, אוֹ לְהַקְשׁוֹת עָלָיו
אוֹ לְתָרֵץ קֻשְׁיָא שֶׁהֻקְשֵׁית עָלָיו, אוֹ לְהָשִׁיב עַל שְׁאֵלָה. כְּשֶׁתִּמְצָא
וְתַכִּיר תַּכְלִית כַּוָּנָתוֹ, אָז צָרִיךְ שֶׁתִּתְבּוֹנֵן, אֵיךְ הוּא מַסְכִּים עִם
הַתַּכְלִית בֶּאֱמֶת; פֵּרוּשׁ – אֵיךְ מִכֹּחַ הַמַּאֲמָר הַזֶּה יְפֹרַשׁ הָרִאשׁוֹן, אוֹ
נוֹכִיחַ עָלָיו, אוֹ יִתְבָּאֵר הֱיוֹת בּוֹ קֹשִׁי, אוֹ יוּסַר הַקֹּשִׁי מִמֶּנּוּ, אוֹ תִהְיֶה
תְּשׁוּבָה לִשְׁאֵלָה.

וְאָמְנָם מִמַּה שֶּׁצָּרִיךְ שֶׁתִּתְבּוֹנֵן הוּא, כִּי הִנֵּה כָּל מַאֲמָר וְכָל
הַקְדָּמָה צָרִיךְ שֶׁיִּהְיוּ מְאֻמָּתִים, וּכְמוֹ שֶׁאָמַרְתִּי לְמַעְלָה. אַךְ הַאֲמָתַת
מַאֲמָר אֶחָד, לִפְעָמִים תִּהְיֶה מִכֹּחַ מוֹפְתִים רַבִּים נִמְשָׁכִים זֶה אַחַר
זֶה. כִּי הִנֵּה תִּמָּצֵא הַקְדָּמָה אַחַת מְאֻמֶּתֶת מַאֲמָר אֶחָד, וְהַהַקְדָּמָה
הַהִיא תֵּאָמֵת מִכֹּחַ הַקְדָּמָה אַחֶרֶת, וְהָאַחֶרֶת מֵאַחֶרֶת, עַד שֶׁיַּגִּיעַ
הַדָּבָר אֶל הַמְאֻמָּתִים מִצַּד עַצְמָם אוֹ אֶל הַהַסְכָּמָה שֶׁפֵּרַשְׁתִּי לְמַעְלָה,
וְאָז נָשׁוּב לְמַפְרֵעַ עַל כָּל הַהַקְדָּמוֹת שֶׁהִזְכַּרְנוּ עַד הָרִאשׁוֹנָה, כִּי נֶאֱמַר:

*predicate, and this is what you must mentally
reconstruct from the text.*

After you have identified the subject and predicate of the statement, the next step is to determine the purpose of the statement. Ask yourself, is it opening a new topic by informing us of what may be said about a certain subject (Statement) or asking whether something may be said about that subject (Question)? Or, is it connected or related to a prior statement and its purpose is to offer an Explanation, or to bring a Proof or Disproof, or to present a Difficulty or a Resolution to a problem, or give an Answer to a question? Once you have discovered the intended purpose, the next step is to ascertain whether that purpose is actually served by the statement in question. That is, exactly how does this statement explain the first one? How strong is the proof which it presents in support of that statement? Does the statement in question successfully bring to light a difficulty in the earlier statement, or does it succeed in removing a difficulty from it? Is the answer an answer to the question?

The next step to consider is that every statement and every premise must be established as true, as we explained earlier in Chapter Eight. However, just to establish the truth of one statement sometimes requires a long chain of syllogisms. For when a certain premise is granted in order to verify a statement, that premise in turn is verified on the strength of another prior premise, and that other one on the basis of yet another until a statement is reached which is inherently true or acceptable on account of tradition or common sense, as we have explained above. From this point we can retrace all the premises that have been established in support of the last one, which verified the statement in question. If the third (axiomatic)

אִם הַשְּׁלִישִׁית אֱמֶת – מֻכְרָח שֶׁהַשְּׁנִיָּה תִּהְיֶה אֱמֶת, וְאִם הַשְּׁנִיָּה אֱמֶת
– מֻכְרָח שֶׁהָרִאשׁוֹנָה תִּהְיֶה אֱמֶת, כֵּיוָן שֶׁכֻּלָּן תְּלוּיוֹת זוֹ בָזוֹ, וְזֶה בֵּין
בְּהַנָּחוֹת וּבֵין בִּקְשָׁיוֹת.

וְהִנֵּה נִמְצָא, שֶׁיֵּשׁ מַאֲמָרִים, וּרְאָיוֹת הַמַּאֲמָרִים, וּרְאָיוֹת
הָרְאָיוֹת, וּרְאָיוֹת רְאָיוֹת הָרְאָיוֹת, וְעַל דֶּרֶךְ זֶה יוּכַל הַדָּבָר לְמֶשֶׁךְ
וְלָלֶכֶת בְּהֶמְשֵׁךְ גָּדוֹל. וּכְבָר יֵאָמְרוּ אֵלֶּה הַדְּבָרִים בְּדֶרֶךְ קָצָר כְּפִי
לְשׁוֹן הַתַּלְמוּד, וְאַתָּה צָרִיךְ שֶׁתְּצַיֵּר וְתִתְבּוֹנֵן בְּמַחֲשַׁבְתְּךָ אֶת הַכֹּל
בְּצוּרָה הַיְשָׁרָה, דְּהַיְנוּ צָרִיךְ שֶׁתַּכִּיר וְתַבְחִין מַה שֶׁהוּא הַמַּאֲמָר
הַנִּרְצֶה, וּמַה שֶׁהִיא הָרְאָיָה שֶׁעָלָיו, וּמָה רְאָיוֹת הָרְאָיָה, וְכֵן עַד הַסּוֹף.

עוֹד יֵשׁ בֵּאוּר הַמַּאֲמָרִים, וְהַיְנוּ שֶׁדָּבָר אֶחָד יֵאָמֵר בְּקִצְרָה אוֹ
בִרְמִיזָה וְאַחַר כָּךְ יְבֹאַר בְּיוֹתֵר הַרְחָבָה, וְהִנֵּה אֵין הַבֵּאוּר אֶלָּא
הַדָּבָר הָאֶחָד בְּעַצְמוֹ, אָמְנָם הוּא בְּדֶרֶךְ יוֹתֵר רָחָב מִן הָרִאשׁוֹן. וְגַם
זֶה צָרִיךְ שֶׁתַּבְחִין, מַהוּ מַאֲמָר וּמַהוּ בֵּאוּר מַאֲמָר.

דֶּרֶךְ מָשָׁל, כְּשֶׁמָּצָאתָ שֶׁאָמְרוּ (שבת ה ג): "הֵיכָא
אַשְׁכְּחָנָא כְּהַאי גַוְנָא דְּחַיָּב? אָמַר רַב סַפְרָא
אָמַר רַבִּי אַמִּי אָמַר רַבִּי יוֹחָנָן: מִדֵּי דַהֲוָה

premise is given, then the second must be true, and if the second is true then the first must also be true since all the premises are dependent on one another in turn. In this manner we can verify the premises of any statement, regardless of whether it was phrased originally as a statement or a question.

Thus we may have statements, proofs of statements, proofs of proofs, proofs of proofs of proofs, and so on, continuing even at great length. However, the style of a Talmudic text is that all these things are often set down very briefly and many of the actual steps are unstated. Therefore, it is up to us to reconstruct and determine all the steps in the entire chain. The key step is to identify the premise which will establish the statement in question, and then determine the proof for that premise, and the proof for the proof, and so on until the end.

An additional precaution involves distinguishing between the text itself and the subsequent elucidation. The text may be brief and even obscure and the purpose of the elucidation is to explain it at greater length. The elucidation, in fact, adds nothing to the message of the text other than greater clarity. Nonetheless, it is necessary at all times to identify the substance of the text and that of the elucidation.

*Here is an example of the analytical procedure we have explained. (Shabbos 5b) "Our rabbis have taught: One who carries something on the Sabbath from a store out into the street and passes through a colonnade is liable. Have you ever heard of such a case being liable? Rav Safra said that Rabbi Ami reported in the*

אַמַּעֲבִיר חֵפֶץ בִּרְשׁוּת הָרַבִּים, הָתָם לָאו אַף עַל גַּב דְּכָמָה דְנָקִיט לֵהּ וְאָזֵיל – פָּטוּר, כִּי מַנַּח לֵהּ – חַיָּב, הָכָא נַמִּי לָא שְׁנָא". וְהִקְשׁוּ עוֹד: " מִי דָּמֵי? הָתָם כָּל הֵיכָא דְּמַנַּח לֵהּ – מְקוֹם חִיּוּב הוּא , הָכָא אִי מַנַּח לֵהּ בַּסְּטָיו – מְקוֹם פְּטוֹר הוּא".

הִנֵּה בַּתְּחִלָּה הָיָה הַמַּאֲמָר, שֶׁ"הַמּוֹצִיא מֵחֲנוּת לִפְלַטְיָא דֶּרֶךְ סְטָיו – חַיָּב". וְהִקְשָׁה הַשַּׁ"ס עַל זֶה בְּאָמְרוֹ: "הֵיכָא אַשְׁכַּחְנָא כְּהַאי גַּוְנָא דְּחַיְּבִי?" כַּוָּנַת זֶה שְׁמּוֹצִיא מֵחֲנוּת לִפְלַטְיָא דֶּרֶךְ סְטָיו, הַדַּעַת נוֹתֶנֶת שֶׁלֹּא יִהְיֶה חַיָּב, וְזֶה לְפִי שֶׁמּוֹצִיא מֵרְשׁוּת לִרְשׁוּת שֶׁהוּא חַיָּב– הוּא כְּשֶׁמּוֹצִיא מֵרְשׁוּת הַיָּחִיד לִרְשׁוּת הָרַבִּים אוֹ אִפְּכָא, וְאֵין בֵּין הָעֲקִירָה וְהַהַנָּחָה עִנְיָן פְּטוּר;

*name of Rabbi Yochanan: It is the same princi-
ple as in the case of one who moves something
more than four cubits in a public domain.
There, even though he is exempt as long as he
holds the object and keeps walking, nonetheless
when he brings it to rest he is liable. So here in
our case the law is no different". The Talmud
continues with another objection, "What is the
comparison!? There, every spot where he may
bring it to rest is a place in which he would be
liable, but here if he happened to stop in the
colonnade, it is a place in which he would be
exempt."*

*At the beginning of the above text the Talmud
presents a statement (One who carries from a
store into the street through a colonnade is
liable) and an objection raised to this statement (Have you ever heard of such a case being
liable?). The essential thought intended by this
objection is that one who carries something
from a store into the street through a colonnade
should **not** logically be liable. This is based on
the presumption that carrying something from
one domain to another (that is, from a private
to a public domain or vice versa) is liable only
when there is no intervening area of exemption
between the place where he picked up the object*

אַךְ כְּשֶׁיֵּשׁ בֵּין הָעֲקִירָה וְהַהַנָּחָה אֶמְצָעִיּוּת שֶׁל
פְּטוֹר – אֵין לָנוּ שֶׁיִּהְיֶה חַיָּב.

וְהִנֵּה נִכְלְלוּ בָזֶה מַאֲמָר, וּרְאָיָה עָלָיו, וּרְאָיָה
עַל הָרְאָיָה, לְפִי שֶׁכַּוָּנַת "הֵיכָא אַשְׁכַּחְנָא כְּהַאי
גַּוְנָא דְּחַיָּב" הוּא שֶׁלֹּא מָצָאנוּ מוֹצִיא מֵרְשׁוּת
לִרְשׁוּת כְּגוֹן זֶה שֶׁיִּהְיֶה חַיָּב, וּמוּבָן מִזֶּה, שֶׁאִם
כֵּן אֵין פֵּרוּשׁ "מוֹצִיא מֵרְשׁוּת לִרְשׁוּת" כְּמוֹ זֶה
אֶלָּא הַמּוֹצִיא מֵרְשׁוּת לִרְשׁוּת בְּלִי אֶמְצָעִיּוּת
פְּטוֹר כְּלָל, וּמִזֶּה נוֹצִיא שֶׁהַמּוֹצִיא הַזֶּה רָאוּי
שֶׁלֹּא יִהְיֶה חַיָּב.

*and the place where he put it down. However, when there is an intervening area of exemption between the place where he picked up the object and the place where he put it down, then we should not consider him liable.*

*Thus, included in this single sentence of the Talmud ("Have you ever heard of such a case being liable?") there is a proposition, which is understood from the difficulty, and a proof, which is the presumption prior to this proposition, and a proof of the proof, which is the basis of this presumption. The basis of the argument is that there is no other case which is liable when someone carries something from one domain to another through an area of exemption, such as the colonnade in our case. This is a proof for the following presumption. The law that one who carries something from one domain to another on the Sabbath is liable does not apply in a case like ours, but rather only when one carries an object from one domain to another without passing through any area of exemption. From this proof we derive the desired proposition. One who carries an object from a store into the street through a colonnade should not, in fact, be liable.*

וְאוּלָם אַתָּה תְצַיֵּר כָּל זֶה בְּמַחֲשַׁבְתְּךָ בְּצוּרָה
הַפְּשׁוּטָה הַיְשָׁרָה, וְהַיְנוּ שֶׁהַמּוֹצִיא מֵחֲנוּת
לִפְלַטְיָא דֶּרֶךְ סְטָיו אֵין לָנוּ לְחַיְּבוֹ, וּרְאָיָה
לָזֶה: אִם אֵין אָנוּ מוֹצְאִים בְּפֵרוּשׁ שֶׁהַמּוֹצִיא
מֵרְשׁוּת לִרְשׁוּת בְּהֶפְסֵק עִנְיָן פָּטוּר בָּאֶמְצַע
יִהְיֶה חַיָּב – אֵין לָנוּ לְחַיְּבוֹ, בֶּאֱמֶת אֵין אָנוּ
מוֹצְאִים בְּפֵרוּשׁ שֶׁיִּהְיֶה חַיָּב – אִם כֵּן אֵין לָנוּ
לְחַיְּבוֹ; רְאָיָה עַל הַהַקְדָּמָה, שֶׁאִם אֵין אָנוּ
מוֹצְאִים בְּפֵרוּשׁ שֶׁהַמּוֹצִיא מֵרְשׁוּת לִרְשׁוּת
בְּהֶפְסֵק עִנְיָן פָּטוּר בָּאֶמְצַע יִהְיֶה חַיָּב, אֵין לָנוּ
לְחַיְּבוֹ, לְפִי שֶׁכֹּל שֶׁאֵינוֹ בִּכְלַל הַהֲבָנָה
הָרִאשׁוֹנָה שֶׁל אֶחָד מֵהַדִּינִים, אֵין לָנוּ
לְהַכְנִיסוֹ בַּכְּלָל הַהוּא אֶלָּא אִם כֵּן יֵשׁ לָנוּ
רְאָיָה בְּרוּרָה עַל זֶה. מוֹצִיא מֵרְשׁוּת לִרְשׁוּת

*However, you must proceed further from these three statements to reconstruct the entire argument in your thoughts in a clear, orderly way, tracing each statement to its first premises.*

*One who carries something from a store into the street through a colonnade should not be liable. The proof for this statement is a hypothetical syllogism.*

*1a. If we have no explicit case where one is liable for carrying on the Sabbath in which an area of exemption intervenes, **then** our case should not be liable.*

*1b. In fact, we find no such explicit case.*

*1c. Therefore, we should not consider our case to be liable.*

*The proof of the major premise used in this syllogism (1a. if we have no other explicit case, then we cannot consider our case liable) is a classical syllogism, as follows:*

*2a. Everything which is not included in the primary understanding of any law needs a clear proof in order that it should be included.*

בְּהֶפְסֵק פָּטוֹר, אֵינוֹ בִּכְלַל הַהֲבָנָה הָרִאשׁוֹנָה
שֶׁל "הַמּוֹצִיא מֵרְשׁוּת לִרְשׁוּת" – אִם כֵּן אֵין
לָנוּ לְהַכְנִיסוֹ בַּכְּלָל הַהוּא אֶלָּא אִם כֵּן יֵשׁ לָנוּ
רְאָיָה בְּרוּרָה, וְהַיְנוּ: אֵין לָנוּ לְחַיְּבוֹ. הַהַקְדָּמָה
שֶׁכֹּל שֶׁאֵינוֹ בִּכְלַל הַהֲבָנָה הָרִאשׁוֹנָה שֶׁל אַחַד
הַדִּינִים אֵין לָנוּ לְהַכְנִיסוֹ בַּכְּלָל הַהוּא, וְכֵן
הַשְּׁנִיָּה שֶׁמּוֹצִיא מֵרְשׁוּת לִרְשׁוּת בְּהֶפְסֵק עִנְיַן
פָּטוֹר בָּאֶמְצַע אֵינוֹ בִּכְלַל הַהֲבָנָה הָרִאשׁוֹנָה
שֶׁל "הַמּוֹצִיא מֵרְשׁוּת לִרְשׁוּת", אֵינָן צְרִיכוֹת
רְאָיָה אַחֶרֶת, כִּי הֵן מִן הַמֻּשְׂכָּלוֹת. נִמְצֵינוּ
לְמֵדִים, שֶׁהַמּוֹצִיא מֵרְשׁוּת לִרְשׁוּת בְּהֶפְסֵק
פָּטוֹר בָּאֶמְצַע אֵין לָנוּ לְחַיְּבוֹ, הַמּוֹצִיא מֵחֲנוּת
לִפְלַטְיָא דֶּרֶךְ סְטָיו הוּא מוֹצִיא מֵרְשׁוּת

*2b. Carrying something on the Sabbath where there is an intervening area of exemption is not included in the primary understanding of the law.*

*2c. (1a.) Therefore, we cannot say that it should be included without having a clear proof.*

*This now validates the conclusion of the hypothetical syllogism which we stated first (1c. we should not consider our case to be liable).*

*Now, the major premise of the second syllogism (2a. that we should not add anything in a law which is not included in its primary understanding) and the minor premise (2b. that carrying through an area of exemption is not in the primary understanding of carrying from one domain to another on the Sabbath, which is liable) do not need any further proof for they are both accepted concepts. Thus we are left with the following definition:*

*3a. Carrying an object through an area of exemption should not be liable.*

*3b. Carrying an object from a store into the street through a colonnade is equivalent to carrying through an area of exemption.*

לִרְשׁוּת בְּהֶפְסֵק פְּטוֹר בָּאֶמְצַע – אִם כֵּן אֵין לָנוּ לְחַיְּבוֹ.

וְהִנֵּה כָּל זֶה תּוּכַל לִכְלֹל בְּקֶשֶׁר אֶחָד שֶׁתִּמָּצֵאֶנָּה בּוֹ כָּל הַהַקְדָּמוֹת מִתְקַשְּׁרוֹת זוֹ בָּזוֹ לְפָנֶיךָ עַד צֵאת הַתּוֹלָדָה הַמְבֻקֶּשֶׁת, וְתֹאמַר: מוֹצִיא מֵחָנוּת לִפְלַטְיָא דֶּרֶךְ סְטָיו הוּא מוֹצִיא מֵרְשׁוּת לִרְשׁוּת בְּהֶפְסֵק פְּטוֹר בָּאֶמְצַע, מוֹצִיא מֵרְשׁוּת לִרְשׁוּת בְּהֶפְסֵק פְּטוֹר בָּאֶמְצַע אֵינוֹ בִּכְלַל הַהֲבָנָה הָרִאשׁוֹנָה שֶׁל "הַמּוֹצִיא מֵרְשׁוּת לִרְשׁוּת", וְגַם אֵין לָנוּ רְאָיָה שֶׁיִּכָּלֵל בּוֹ מַה שֶּׁאֵינוֹ בַּהֲבָנָה הָרִאשׁוֹנָה שֶׁל "הַמּוֹצִיא מֵרְשׁוּת לִרְשׁוּת", [וְאִם] אֵין רְאָיָה שֶׁיִּכָּלֵל בּוֹ אֵין לָנוּ לְחַיְּבוֹ מִשְּׁמוֹ – אִם כֵּן מוֹצִיא מֵחָנוּת לִפְלַטְיָא דֶּרֶךְ סְטָיו אֵין לָנוּ לְחַיְּבוֹ מִשּׁוּם "מוֹצִיא מֵרְשׁוּת לִרְשׁוּת".

*3c. On this basis we conclude that carrying through a colonnade should not be liable.*

*Now this entire argument may be tied together in a single chain by joining the essential premises of each of the above syllogisms in order to arrive at the desired conclusion. You may reason as follows:*

*Carrying an object from a store into the street through a colonnade is equivalent to carrying an object through an area of exemption.*

*Carrying through an area of exemption is not included in the primary understanding of the law of carrying on the Sabbath.*

*We have no explicit source from which to prove that such a case should be included which is not in the primary understanding of the law.*

*Thus, if the proof is lacking, we should not say that carrying through an area of exemption is liable under the law of carrying on the Sabbath.*

*Finally, carrying an object from a store into the street through a colonnade should not be liable under this law.*

אַחַר כָּךְ הֵשִׁיבוּ עַל זֶה: "מִדֵּי דַהֲוָה אַמַּעֲבִיר
חֵפֶץ בִּרְשׁוּת הָרַבִּים", כַּוָּנַת זֶה, שֶׁרָאוּי
שֶׁהַמּוֹצִיא מֵרְשׁוּת לִרְשׁוּת בְּהֶפְסֵק פָּטוּר יִהְיֶה
חַיָּב, הֵפֶךְ מַה שֶּׁחָשַׁבְנוּ רָאוּי שֶׁלֹּא יִהְיֶה חַיָּב,
רְאָיָה עַל זֶה הַמַּעֲבִיר חֵפֶץ בִּרְשׁוּת הָרַבִּים;
וּבֵאוּר זֶה, שֶׁהַמַּעֲבִיר בִּרְשׁוּת הָרַבִּים, הִנֵּה בֵּין
הָעֲקִירָה וְהַהֲנָחָה יֵשׁ עִנְיָן פָּטוּר שֶׁהוּא כָּל זְמַן
שֶׁמּוֹלִיכוֹ, וְאַחַר כָּךְ כְּשֶׁמַּנִּיחַ מִתְחַיֵּב, אִם כֵּן
גַּם כֵּן נוּכַל לוֹמַר שֶׁיִּהְיֶה חַיָּב, אַף עַל פִּי שֶׁיֵּשׁ
הַהַעֲבָרָה דֶּרֶךְ סְטָיו בָּאֶמְצַע. וְנִמְצָא, שֶׁיֵּשׁ

*After we have understood the difficulty thoroughly, let us now turn to the resolution offered in the Talmud: "The principle exemplified in this case is the same as in the case of one who carries something more than four cubits in a public domain". The intention of this statement is that carrying an object from one domain to another when an area of exemption intervenes should be liable. This is in opposition to what we previously thought, i.e., that such a case should not be liable. The disproof of our original contention is based on a comparison with the case of carrying something in a public domain. The elucidation of this comparison is that when one carries an object in the public domain there is an intervening area of exemption between the place where he picked up the object and put it down, namely the area through which he passes while he continues to carry the object. A person is only liable when he finally puts down the object, but he is not liable during the time that he is actually carrying it. If so, we may also say in our case that one should be liable even for carrying an object through a colonnade which intervenes between a private domain and the street. We have reconstructed a statement and a proof and an*

כָּאן מַאֲמָר וּרְאָיָה. וּבֵאוּר הַמַּאֲמָר הוּא,
שֶׁהַמוֹצִיא מֵרְשׁוּת לִרְשׁוּת בְּהֶפְסֵק פָּטוּר שֶׁהוּא
חַיָּב, רְאָיָה עַל זֶה מִכֹּחַ דִּמְיוֹן: הַמוֹצִיא
מֵרְשׁוּת לִרְשׁוּת הוּא דוֹמֶה לְמַעֲבִיר בִּרְשׁוּת
הָרַבִּים, מַעֲבִיר בִּרְשׁוּת הָרַבִּים הוּא חַיָּב אַף
עַל פִּי שֶׁיֵּשׁ הֶפְסֵק פָּטוּר בֵּין עֲקִירָה לְהַנָּחָה-
אִם כֵּן גַּם הַמוֹצִיא מֵרְשׁוּת לִרְשׁוּת. בֵּאוּר
הַהַקְדָּמָה, שֶׁהַמַּעֲבִיר בִּרְשׁוּת הָרַבִּים יֵשׁ בּוֹ
הֶפְסֵק פָּטוּר בֵּין הָעֲקִירָה וְהַהַנָּחָה: שֶׁכָּל זְמַן
שֶׁהוּא מְהַלֵּךְ הוּא פָּטוּר.

*elucidation of a principle from the single sentence of the Talmud which we quoted above.*

*The statement is that someone who carries something from one domain to another through an area of exemption should be liable. The proof is an analogism:*

*4a. Carrying from one domain to another through an area of exemption is like carrying an object four cubits in a public domain.*

*4b. Carrying an object in a public domain is liable on the Sabbath even though there is an intervening area of exemption between his picking up and putting down the object.*

*4c. Therefore, carrying an object from one domain to another should also be liable even though there is an intervening area of exemption.*

*The elucidation is that when one carries an object in a public domain, there is what may be termed an intervening area of exemption between his picking up the object and putting it down because as long as he continues to carry it he is exempt from liability.*

הִנְּךָ רוֹאֶה, כַּמָּה לְשׁוֹנָם שֶׁל חֲכָמִים קְצָרָה וְכַמָּה מִן הַהִתְבּוֹנְנוּת נִכְלָל בָּהֶם. וְאוּלָם כָּל זֶה צָרִיךְ שֶׁיִּצְטַיֵּר בְּשִׂכְלְךָ מִכֹּחַ הַמִּלּוֹת הָהֵן. כִּי, אִם קְצָת מִזֶּה יֶעְדַּר מִצִּיּוּרְךָ, הִנֵּה לֹא צִיַּרְתָּ מַה שֶּׁכִּוְּנוּ הֵם לוֹמַר.

וּמַה שֶּׁצָּרִיךְ שֶׁתִּתְבּוֹנֵן עוֹד, הוּא לְהַכִּיר הַשֵּׁמוֹת הַנִּרְדָּפִים שֶׁנִּתְבָּאֲרוּ אֵצֶל הַמְדַקְדְּקִים, וְכֵן הַמַּאֲמָרִים הַנִּרְדָּפִים, דְּהַיְנוּ שֶׁמִּלּוֹתֵיהֶם שׁוֹנוֹת וְעִנְיָנָם אֶחָד. כִּי הִנֵּה יִקְרֶה לִפְעָמִים, שֶׁיִּהְיוּ שְׁנֵי מַאֲמָרִים סוֹתְרִים זֶה אֶת זֶה אוֹ מוֹכִיחִים זֶה עַל זֶה, וְלֹא יַרְגִּישׁ בָּהֶם הַשֵּׂכֶל בִּתְחִלַּת הִתְבּוֹנְנוּתוֹ מִפְּנֵי הֱיוֹת נוֹשְׂאֵיהֶם אוֹ עִנְיְנֵיהֶם מֻזְכָּרִים בְּמִלּוֹת שׁוֹנוֹת, אַף עַל פִּי שֶׁהֵם אֶחָד בֶּאֱמֶת, אוֹ סִדְרֵי מִלּוֹתֵיהֶם מִתְחַלְּפִים; אָמְנָם כְּשֶׁיִּסְתַּכֵּל בָּהֶם הֵיטֵב וְיַשִּׂיג סוֹף כַּוָּנָתָם, יִמְצָא הֱיוֹתָם בֶּאֱמֶת מִתְיַחֲסִים זֶה לָזֶה.

דֶּרֶךְ מָשָׁל, אִם יֹאמַר אֶחָד: "קָדְשֵׁי מִזְבֵּחַ אֵין לָהֶם פִּדְיוֹן", וְיֹאמַר אַחֵר: "הַקָּרְבָּנוֹת יֵשׁ לָהֶם פִּדְיוֹן", הִנֵּה שְׁנֵי הַמַּאֲמָרִים הַפְכִּיִּים וַדַּאי. וְכֵן כְּשֶׁיֹּאמַר אֶחָד (פסחים יז א): "מַשְׁקֵי בֵי מַדְבְּחַיָּא דְכָן", וְיֹאמַר אַחֵר: "הַדָּם וְהַיַּיִן וְהַשֶּׁמֶן וְהַמַּיִם וְהַמַּיִם טְהוֹרִים", הִנֵּה שְׁנֵי הַמַּאֲמָרִים שָׁוִים, כִּי אֶחָד הִזְכִּיר הַסּוּג, וְאֶחָד הִזְכִּיר הַמִּינִים. וְכֹל כַּיּוֹצֵא בָזֶה.

Consider how concise is the language of our rabbis and how much thought lies behind every word! Yet every step of the argument must be reconstructed in your mind on the basis of their few brief words, for even if only a small step of reasoning is left out, you have not understood their full meaning.

A further precaution in the procedure of investigation is to recognize whether terms are synonymous or not, for there are many types of synonymous terms, as explained in the science of grammar. Similarly, one must consider whether two statements are synonymous or not, for even if their words are different, their intent may be the same. It can happen that two statements, in fact, contradict one another and the mind does not recognize this at first, either because their subjects or predicates are not expressed in the same terms, or because the syntax of the two statements is reversed. However, with sufficient concentration one can penetrate the true meaning of the statements under investigation and determine that they are, in fact, related.

> *For example, one text says, "No redemption is applicable to those things which are sanctified upon the altar", and another text states, "Sacrifices may be redeemed". We can see that these statements are clearly opposites. Similarly, one text states, (Pesachim 17a) "Liquids of the Temple altar are always considered clean", and another text states, "Blood, wine, oil and water are ritually pure". These two statements are synonymous, for one refers to the category and the other to its members.*

וְהִנֵּה צָרִיךְ שֶׁתְּדַקְדֵּק בְּכָל דִּבּוּר וְדִבּוּר לִרְאוֹת אֵיזֶה חֵלֶק מֵחֶלְקֵי הַסֻּגְיוֹת הוּא, וּכְמוֹ שֶׁהִצַּעְתִּי לְפָנֶיךָ לְמַעְלָה, וְנִמְצָא שֶׁלִּפְעָמִים נִרְכָּבִים שְׁנַיִם מִן הַחֲלָקִים כְּאֶחָד. דֶּרֶךְ מָשָׁל, כְּשֶׁתּוּבָא לִרְאָיָה עַל מַאֲמָר שֶׁנֶּאֱמַר הַגָּדַת אֶחָד מִן הַחֲכָמִים שֶׁמַּגִּיד מַעֲשֶׂה שֶׁאֵרַע אוֹ מַאֲמָר אַחֵר שֶׁנֶּאֱמַר, הִנֵּה תַּבְחִין שָׁם שְׁנֵי חֲלָקִים נִרְכָּבִים כְּאֶחָד, וְהַיְנוּ: הוֹכָחָה וְהַגָּדָה, כִּי נוֹכִיחַ בְּכֹחַ הַמַּאֲמָר בְּכֹחַ הַהַגָּדָה שֶׁהֻגְּדָה. וְצָרִיךְ שֶׁתָּבִין תְּחִלָּה הַהַגָּדָה בִּפְנֵי עַצְמָהּ, וְאַחַר כָּךְ תָּבִין הַהוֹכָחָה, פֵּרוּשׁ – אֵיךְ הַהַגָּדָה הַהִיא תִּהְיֶה הוֹכָחָה לַמַּאֲמָר שֶׁנִּרְצָה לְהוֹכִיחַ. וּכְבָר אֶפְשָׁר שֶׁתִּסְתַּתֵּר הַהוֹכָחָה וְיִקְשֶׁה עָלֶיהָ, וְלֹא מִפְּנֵי זֶה יִקְשֶׁה עַל הַהַגָּדָה, אֶלָּא שֶׁנִּרְאֶה הֱיוֹת הַהַגָּדָה זֹאת בִּלְתִּי מוֹכַחַת הַמַּאֲמָר שֶׁחָשַׁבְנוּ לְהוֹכִיחַ מִמֶּנָּה, וְאֶפְשָׁר שֶׁתִּסְתַּתֵּר הַהַגָּדָה עַצְמָהּ וְיִקְשֶׁה עָלֶיהָ, אֲפִילוּ שֶׁנּוֹדֶה עַל הַמַּאֲמָר הָרִאשׁוֹן, וְאֶפְשָׁר שֶׁנּוֹדֶה אֲפִלוּ עַל הַהוֹכָחָה, וְאַף עַל פִּי כֵן נַקְשֶׁה עַל הַהַגָּדָה, עַל מִלּוֹתֶיהָ אוֹ עַל אֵיזֶה עִנְיָן מִמֶּנָּה.

וְכֵן כְּשֶׁיִּרְצֶה אֶחָד מִן הַחֲכָמִים לְפָרֵשׁ טַעֲנָה אַחַת שֶׁהִרְגִּישׁ חָכָם אֶחָד בְּאֶחָד מִמַּאֲמָרָיו, הִנֵּה יַזְכִּיר הַקֻּשְׁיָא הַהִיא שֶׁהִקְשֵׁית לְפִי דַעְתּוֹ שֶׁל הֶחָכָם בַּעַל הַמַּאֲמָר, וְתִקָּרֵא זֹאת **קֻשְׁיָא מֻגֶּדֶת**, כִּי אֵינָהּ קֻשְׁיָא

Another precaution is to be precise about the purpose or function of each and every statement in a section of the Talmud under investigation, as I have instructed you at the beginning of the chapter. It is also possible that a single statement may sometimes combine two elements of debate together. For example, on a given statement, a proof may be brought in the form of reported information. This is called an **Ascribed Proof.** The basis of proof is either an event which took place, as it is reported by one of the rabbis, or a statement which is being quoted. In such a situation you can discern two elements of debate, one superimposed on the other, for the statement in question is proven on the strength of the reported information which is quoted. In a case such as this, you must first understand the reported statement on its own, and only afterwards proceed to understand the proof, that is to say, how the reported statement actually proves the statement in question. You will immediately see that it is possible to remove the proof or find fault with it, and this will not entail any difficulty with the reported statement itself. The sole contention is that this reported statement does not prove the statement in question as we thought it did. It is also possible to contradict the reported statement or find it difficult, and yet the statement which we set out to prove is admittedly true. Alternatively, it is possible to admit the validity of the proof and yet find some internal difficulties in the reported statement, either with its words or with some part of its content.

Another example is a difficulty ascribed to some other view which combines the two functions of reported information and difficulty. One of the rabbis raises an objection which he perceives as implicit in another rabbi's point of view. His understanding is that this is the implicit problem to which the other rabbi must have been responding when he made his statement. This is called an **Ascribed**

יַקְשֶׁה אוֹתוֹ הֶחָכָם עַל מַאֲמַר חֲבֵרוֹ, אֶלָּא זֶה הֶחָכָם מַגִּיד מַה שֶׁהִקְשָׁה לַחֲבֵרוֹ, וּכְבָר יִקְרֶה, שֶׁאוֹתוֹ חָכָם שֶׁהִגִּיד הַקַּשְׁיָא לֹא יַסְכִּים בָּהּ. וְאֶפְשָׁר שֶׁמַּקְשָׁן אֶחָד יַקְשֶׁה עַל הַמַּגִּיד עַל הַגָּדָתוֹ, שֶׁיֵּרָאֶה לוֹ הֱיוֹת בִּלְתִּי אֶפְשָׁר שֶׁבַּעַל הַמַּאֲמָר יְכַוֵּן לְמַה שֶׁחָשַׁב הוּא וְלֹא מִפְּנֵי זֶה יִסְתֹּר קֻשְׁיָתוֹ, אֶלָּא יִסְתֹּר הַגָּדָתוֹ; וְאֶפְשָׁר שֶׁיַּקְשֶׁה מַקְשֶׁה עַל הַקַּשְׁיָא עַצְמָהּ שֶׁהִגִּיד הַמַּגִּיד וְיִסְתֹּר אוֹתָהּ. וְכֵן אֶפְשָׁר שֶׁיַּקְשֶׁה עַל הַהַגָּדָה אוֹ עַל הַקַּשְׁיָא, וְלֹא מִפְּנֵי זֶה יַכְנִיס עַצְמוֹ בַּמַּאֲמָר הָאֶחָד, לֹא לְאַמְּתוֹ וְלֹא לְכַזְּבוֹ.

עַל כֵּן צָרִיךְ שֶׁתִּתְבּוֹנֵן מְאֹד לְהַבְדִּיל בֵּין מַה שֶׁיֹּאמַר אוֹמֵר מִדַּעַת עַצְמוֹ וּבֵין מַה שֶׁיַּגִּיד מַגִּיד מִזּוּלָתוֹ.

דֶּרֶךְ מָשָׁל, כְּשֶׁאָמְרוּ בַּשַּׁ"ס (בבא קמא פג ג): "וּמַאי אִם נַפְשְׁךָ לוֹמַר", הֵשִׁיב "תּוּ קָא קַשְׁיָא לַתַּנָּא",

**Difficulty** because it is not an objection which the speaker raises against his friend's statement, but rather he is telling us what should be a difficulty according to the other's view. Thus it can happen that the rabbi who tells us that there is a difficulty may not himself agree that it is a problem at all. Alternatively, someone else may raise a difficulty specifically against the speaker that it is impossible for the author of the statement in question to have had in mind the difficulty ascribed to him. However, this does not diminish the strength of the objection in and of itself. In addition, a difficulty may be raised specifically against the reported objection itself without questioning the fact that this difficulty is properly ascribed to the author of the statement in question. In this case, the problem is with the objection itself. Finally, the one who raises these objections against either the assignation of the difficulty or the difficulty itself may only be involved with the speaker. He is not necessarily entering into a discussion of whether the statement in question is true or false.

In light of this, you must be careful to distinguish between what the speaker says from his own point of view and what he reports as the view of other rabbis.

*Here is an example of an ascribed difficulty. (Babba Kamma 83b) The Tanna teaches that bodily damage is compensated by monetary payment and not physical punishment because we compare the case of one who injures a man to the case of one who injures an animal and in the latter case monetary compensation is applicable. Alternatively, we may derive this law from the verse "You shall take no monetary*

הִנֵּה זוֹ קֻשְׁיָא מְגֻדֶּת, שֶׁהַגִּיד הַמַּגִּיד שֶׁהַתַּנָּא
הִרְגִּישׁ קֻשְׁיָא זוֹ עַל דִּבְרֵי עַצְמוֹ, וְהִקְשׁוּ:
"אָמְרֵי, דָּנִין נִזָּקִין מִנִּזָּקִין וְאֵין דָּנִין נִזָּקִין
מִמִּיתָה", הִנֵּה הִיא קֻשְׁיָא עַל הַגָּדַת הַמַּגִּיד,
מַרְאֶה שֶׁאִי אֶפְשָׁר שֶׁתִּהְיֶה זֹאת כַּוָּנַת הַתַּנָּא
כְּמוֹ שֶׁבֵּאֵר הוּא בְּהַגָּדָתוֹ.

וּבְכָל הַדְּבָרִים הָאֵלֶּה צָרִיךְ שֶׁתִּשָּׁמֵר מְאֹד, כְּדֵי שֶׁתִּנָּקֶה מִן הַטָּעֻיּוֹת
וְהָעִרְבּוּבִים.

*compensation for a murder". By implication, monetary compensation is applicable to cases of bodily injury. The Talmud asks, "What was his problem that an alternative derivation needed to be offered"? and then answered, "This was the Tanna's difficulty: Why should the law for one who strikes a man be derived from the case of striking an animal rather than from another case of one who strikes a man [and kills him]". This is an ascribed difficulty. The speaker informs us that the Tanna must have recognized this difficulty in his first explanation of the law, and this is why he offered an alternative derivation. The Talmud continues with this objection: "But we could easily undermine this difficulty by saying we derive damages from cases of damages and not from cases of murder"! This objection is raised specifically against the speaker. Since there is an obvious resolution, it is clear that it would be impossible for the Tanna to have had in mind this difficulty which is ascribed to him by the speaker.*

In all these cases where two of the elements of debate are combined together we see that great care must be taken to separate the different points of view in order to avoid errors and confusion.

וְהִנֵּה אַחַר שֶׁהִשַּׂגְתָּ כַּוָּנַת הַסֻּגְיָא אֲשֶׁר לְפָנֶיךָ עַל פִּי כָל הַכְּלָלִים הָאֵלֶּה, אָז תָּשׁוּב לְהִתְבּוֹנֵן עַל כָּל חֵלֶק מֵחֲלָקֶיהָ, וְאִם יֵרָאֶה לְךָ שֶׁכֻּלָּם עוֹמְדִים בִּגְבוּלָם הָרָאוּי עַל פִּי הַמִּשְׁפָּטִים הַטִּבְעִיִּים שֶׁזָּכַרְתִּי לְמַעְלָה – הִנֵּה טוֹב מְאֹד, וְאִם יֵרָאֶה לְךָ בְּחֵלֶק מֵחֲלָקֶיהָ שֶׁלֹּא יִשְׁמֹר הַגְּבוּל הָרָאוּי לוֹ – אָז תִּטְרַח וְתַעֲמֹל עַד שֶׁתִּמְצָא לוֹ הַיִּשׁוּב הֶהָגוּן וְהָרָאוּי, שֶׁיַּסְכִּים עִם הַלָּשׁוֹן שֶׁלְּפָנֶיךָ וְיַסְכִּים עִם הָאֱמֶת אוֹ הַמְפֻרְסָם.

Now after you have finally grasped the meaning of any section of the Talmud by following all the steps of this procedure, you must review and reconsider each statement according to its function. If it appears to you that all of them fit neatly in place according to the natural first principles which I have described, you are exceedingly fortunate, but if you find that some of the statements do not keep to a form which is pleasing to the mind – then you must toil and strain until you find a satisfactory and appropriate solution which agrees with the words of the text on the one hand and with what is proven or what is common sense on the other.

# פרק יא

עַד הֵנָּה בֵּאַרְנוּ דֶּרֶךְ הֲבָנַת הַסּוּגְיוֹת, עַתָּה נְבָאֵר הַהַבְחָנוֹת שֶׁיֵּשׁ לְהַבְחִין בַּנּוֹשְׂאִים שֶׁנִּרְצֶה לָדוּן כְּפִי הַסּוּגְיוֹת וְהַהֲלָכוֹת אוֹ כְּפִי הַשֵּׂכֶל.

כְּלָלֵי הַהַבְחָנוֹת שֶׁאֶפְשָׁר לְהַבְחִין בַּנּוֹשְׂאִים – עֶשְׂרִים וְאַרְבַּע, וְאֵלּוּ הֵן:

הַבְחָנָה רִאשׁוֹנָה – **הַמַּהוּת**, וְהִיא כְּלַל עִנְיָנוֹ שֶׁל הַנּוֹשֵׂא כְּפִי מַה שֶׁהוּא בֶּאֱמֶת, שֶׁבּוֹ תַבְחִינֵהוּ בְּמַחֲשַׁבְתְּךָ מִכָּל שְׁאָר הַנּוֹשְׂאִים הַמְצוּיָרִים בָּהּ. וּבֵאוּר הָעִנְיָן הַכְּלָלִי הַזֶּה כָּרָאוּי, נִקְרָא **גֶּדֶר**.

דֶּרֶךְ מָשָׁל, כְּשֶׁאָמְרוּ (פאה פ"ז מ"ד): "אֵיזוֹהִי עוֹלֶלֶת? כָּל שֶׁאֵין לָהּ לֹא כָתֵף וְלֹא נָטֵף" – זֶה נִקְרָא גִדְרָהּ שֶׁל עוֹלֶלֶת, וְהַיְנוּ אֶשְׁכּוֹל שֶׁאֵין לוֹ לֹא כָתֵף וְלֹא נָטֵף.

וּמִשְׁפַּט הַגֶּדֶר הוּא שֶׁיְּבָאֵר הָעִקָּר מַה שֶׁבְּעַצְמוּתוֹ שֶׁל הַנּוֹשֵׂא, שֶׁהוּא מַה שֶׁעוֹשֶׂה אוֹתוֹ מַה שֶׁהוּא . פֵּרוּשׁ – שֶׁאִלּוּ הָיָה זֶה דָבָר זֶה נֶעְדָּר מִמֶּנּוּ, לֹא הָיָה זֶה הַנּוֹשֵׂא אֶלָּא נוֹשֵׂא אַחֵר.

הַבְחָנָה שְׁנִיָּה – **הַחֲלָקִים**. דֶּרֶךְ מָשָׁל (חולין מג א): "שְׁנֵי עוֹרוֹת יֵשׁ לוֹ לַוֶּשֶׁט". וְכֵן (שביעית פ"ט מ"ב): "גָּלִיל הָעֶלְיוֹן, גָּלִיל הַתַּחְתּוֹן, וְהָעֵמֶק".

# Chapter Eleven

Thus far we have explained how to reconstruct a complete understanding of every text of the Talmud. Now we will turn to the logical terms and distinctions which may be applicable when any subject is evaluated abstractly or in terms of Talmudic law.

There are twenty-four general logical terms that may be used in the analysis of subjects:

1. **Essence** is the all-encompassing identity of the subject as it truly is and its uniqueness, which makes this subject distinct from all other subjects which are formally identified in your mind. The enunciation of this encompassing identity is called a **Definition**. The rule for a definition is that it must state the essential point which substantially identifies the subject and makes it what it is. In other words, if this point would be removed we would no longer have this particular subject but some other one.

> For example, (Pe'ah Chapter 7 Mishnah 4) "What is a gleaning? Any bunch of grapes which has no shoulders and no grapes hanging down from the stalk". This is the definition of a "gleaning": a cluster without shoulders and without grapes hanging down.

2. **Parts.** For example, (Chullin 43a) "The food pipe has two skins." Similarly, (Shevi'is Chapter 9 Mishnah 2) "There are three counties, the Upper Galilee, the Lower Galilee, and the Jezreel

הַבְחָנָה שְׁלִישִׁית – הָאֵיכוּת, וְהִיא תְּכוּנַת הַנּוֹשֵׂא וּמִזְגּוֹ, כְּגוֹן אִם הוּא קַר וְאִם הוּא חַם, אִם הוּא לַח וְאִם יָבֵשׁ, הַמַּרְאֶה שֶׁבּוֹ, חָזְקוֹ אוֹ חֻלְשָׁתוֹ, וְכַיּוֹצֵא בָזֶה.

דֶּרֶךְ מָשָׁל (חולין מג א): "חִיצוֹן אָדֹם, וּפְנִימִי לָבָן";

וְכֵן (חולין עו א): "אֲשׁוּנֵי הָווּ צֻמֶּת הַגִּידִין, רְכִיכֵי לָא הָווּ צֻמֶּת הַגִּידִין".

הַבְחָנָה רְבִיעִית – הַכַּמּוּת, וְהִיא הַמִּדָּה בְּמַה שֶּׁשַּׁיָּךְ מִדָּה, וּמִנְיָן בְּמַה שֶּׁשַּׁיָּךְ מִנְיָן.

דֶּרֶךְ מָשָׁל (כלאים פ״ה מ״ה): "הֲרֵי זֶה מְקַדֵּשׁ שֵׁשׁ-עֶשְׂרֵה אַמָּה לְכָל רוּחַ",

אוֹ (שם): "הֲרֵי זֶה מְקַדֵּשׁ אַרְבָּעִים וַחֲמִשָּׁה גְּפָנִים". וְכֵן כֹּל כַּיּוֹצֵא בָזֶה.

223

Valley".

3. **Quality** is the character and constitution of the subject, such as whether its elements are primarily cold or hot, wet or dry. Also included is its appearance, strength or weakness, and the like.

> *For example, (Chullin 43a) "The outer skin of the food pipe is red, and the inner one is white". Color is a quality.*

> *Also, (Chullin 76a) "The part that is hard is called the juncture of the thigh sinews, and from the part that is soft onwards it is no longer called the juncture of the thigh sinews". Hardness and softness are qualities.*

4. **Quantity** is the *measurement* of things which are measured and the *number* of things which are counted.

> *For example, (Kil'ayim Chapter 5 Mishnah 5) "If one plants a forbidden plant in a vineyard, the vines are prohibited because of intermingling for a distance of sixteen cubits in every direction".*

> *Another example: (Kil'ayim Chapter 5 Mishnah 5) "When the vines are planted at intervals of four or five cubits, a total of forty-five vines will become prohibited".*

הַבְחָנָה חֲמִישִׁית – הַחֹמֶר, וְהוּא מַה שֶּׁמִּמֶּנּוּ נַעֲשָׂה הַנּוֹשֵׂא. דֶּרֶךְ מָשָׁל: כְּלֵי מַתֶּכֶת – חָמְרוֹ הוּא מַתֶּכֶת, כְּלֵי חֶרֶס – חָמְרוֹ חָרֶס.

הַבְחָנָה שִׁשִּׁית – הַצּוּרָה, וְהִיא מִשְּׁנֵי מִינִים: הָאַחַת – עַצְמִית, וְהַשְּׁנִיָּה – מֻרְגֶּשֶׁת. הָעַצְמִית הִיא מַהוּתוֹ שֶׁל הַנּוֹשֵׂא, דֶּרֶךְ מָשָׁל: צוּרַת הָאָדָם הִיא הֱיוֹתוֹ בַּעַל־חַי מְדַבֵּר; אָמְנָם זֶה עִנְיָן מֻשְׂכָּל בָּאָדָם, לֹא מֻרְגָּשׁ וְנִרְאֶה בּוֹ. הַמֻּרְגֶּשֶׁת הִיא תַּבְנִית הַנּוֹשֵׂא כְּמוֹ שֶׁיִּרְאוּהוּ הָעֵינַיִם.

דֶּרֶךְ מָשָׁל (מנחות לד ב): "כְּמִין תֵּבָה פְּרוּצָה",

(כלים פכ״ח מ״ז): "כְּמִין גַּם".

הַבְחָנָה שְׁבִיעִית – הַפְּעֻלָּה, וְהִיא מַה שֶּׁהוּא פּוֹעֵל בְּזוּלָתוֹ, וְיֵשׁ בָּהּ שְׁנֵי מִינִים: הָאַחַת – טִבְעִית, וְהִיא מַה שֶּׁפּוֹעֲלִים הַנִּמְצָאִים זֶה בָּזֶה בַּטֶּבַע, דֶּרֶךְ מָשָׁל: "דִּמְנַקְרָא לְהוּ לְמֵעַיָּא"; וְהַשְּׁנִיָּה – רְצוֹנִית, וְהִיא מַה שֶּׁפּוֹעֲלִים הַבְּנֵי־אָדָם בִּרְצוֹנָם, דֶּרֶךְ מָשָׁל (ברכות טו א): "הַקּוֹרֵא אֶת שְׁמַע".

הַבְחָנָה שְׁמִינִית – הָהִפָּעֵל, וְהוּא רֹשֶׁם שֶׁנִּרְשָׁם בַּנּוֹשֵׂא מִמַּה שֶּׁפּוֹעֲלִים בּוֹ אֲחֵרִים,

In the first case the extent of the prohibition is described with a measurement and in the second case with a number.

5. **Material** is what the subject is made from. For example, the material of metal tools is metal and the material of pottery is clay.

6. **Form.** There are two aspects of form. One is the abstract definitive form of a subject and the other is its concrete physical form. The **Definitive Form** is the essence of the thing; for example, the definitive form of a man is a creature with the power of speech. Note that this is a conceptual or intelligible definition and not a sensible or apparent one. The **Physical Form** is the profile of the subject as it appears to the eye.

> *For example, (Menachos 94b) "The 'show bread' was in the shape of an open ended box."*
>
> *(Kaylim Chapter 28 Mishnah 7) "If the attached piece of cloth is sewn on two sides in the form of a Greek gamma, Rabbi Akiva declares it unclean."*

7. **Action** is how one subject affects another. There are two types of action; one is involuntary and the other is voluntary. An **Involuntary Action** is done by any object or creation in its natural state, for example, "something which cleanses the bowels". A **Voluntary Action** is done by human beings exercising their will. For example, (Berachos 15a) "He recites the Sh'ma".

8. **Affection** is the impression left on a subject as a result of something else which acts upon it.

דֶּרֶךְ מָשָׁל (חולין נ א): "בְּנֵי מֵעַיִן שֶׁנִּקְּבוּ וְלֵחָה סוֹתַמְתָּן",

(שבת מ ב): "שֶׁהַיָּד סוֹלֶדֶת בּוֹ",

(פסחים עד א): "חַם מִקְצָתוֹ - חַם כֻּלּוֹ".

הַבְחָנָה תְּשִׁיעִית - **הַסּוּג וְהַמִּין**, דְּהַיְנוּ מֵאֵיזֶה סוּג הוּא הַנּוֹשֵׂא אוֹ מֵאֵיזֶה מִין. וּכְבָר נִתְבָּאֵר עִנְיַן הַסּוּג וְהַמִּין אֵצֶל בַּעֲלֵי הַדִּקְדּוּק, וְהוּא שֶׁכְּלָל הַרְבֵּה נוֹשְׂאִים מִשְׁתַּתְּפִים בְּעִנְיָן אֶחָד נִקְרָא מִין, דֶּרֶךְ מָשָׁל, אָדָם הוּא מִין כּוֹלֵל כָּל הָאֲנָשִׁים לִהְיוֹתָם מִשְׁתַּתְּפִים בְּעִנְיַן הָאֱנוֹשִׁיּוּת; וְאוּלָם מַה שֶּׁיִּכְלוֹל מִינִים רַבִּים יִקָּרֵא סוּג, דֶּרֶךְ מָשָׁל: "בַּעַל-חַי" הוּא סוּג שֶׁכּוֹלֵל מִין הָאָדָם, מִין הַבְּהֵמוֹת, מִין הָעוֹפוֹת, מִין הָרְמָשִׂים, מִין הַדָּגִים. וּכְשֶׁיִּהְיֶה עוֹד כְּלָל אַחֵר שֶׁיִּכְלוֹל סוּגִים רַבִּים יִקָּרֵא **סוּג הַסּוּג**, וְהַסּוּגִים הַנִּכְלָלִים בּוֹ יִקָּרְאוּ לְגַבֵּהּ מִינִים, וּלְגַבֵּי הַמִּינִים הַנִּכְלָלִים בָּהֶם יִקָּרְאוּ סוּגִים. דֶּרֶךְ מָשָׁל: "גֶּשֶׁם", הוּא סוּג כּוֹלֵל הַבַּעֲלֵי-חַיִּים וּבִלְתִּי בַּעֲלֵי-חַיִּים; וְכָל אֶחָד מִשְּׁנַיִם אֵלֶּה, הֵם סוּגִים שֶׁכּוֹלְלִים מִינִים הַרְבֵּה, דֶּרֶךְ מָשָׁל: "הַבַּעַל-חַי" כּוֹלֵל הַמְדַבֵּר וּבִלְתִּי מְדַבֵּר, "הַבִּלְתִּי בַּעַל-חַי" כּוֹלֵל הָאֲבָנִים, הַמַּתָּכוֹת וְהַצְּמָחִים.

For example, (Chullin 50a) "Rabbi Shimon ben
Gamliel said if the intestines were punctured
and the hole was sealed by fluids, the animal is
kosher".

(Shabbos 40b) "Raba and Rav Yosef said, in
this case, the oil is permitted even though it
reaches the temperature at which one's hand is
involuntarily withdrawn".

(Pesachim 74a) "A metal spit conducts heat,
and when one part is heated it will all become
hot".

9. **Kind** and **Species**. These terms are understood by asking, to
what kind does our subject belong, or what species is it? The
concepts of kind and species are explained in the science of grammar. When we include many related subjects under one heading this
is called a **Species**. For example, *Man* is a species which includes all
people by virtue of their shared humanity. Further, many species may
be classified together and this is called a **Kind**. For example, *Living
Things* is a kind which includes the species of *Man* and the species
of *Animals*, *Birds*, *Reptiles*, and *Fish*. When we find a further
generalization which includes many kinds, this is called a **Higher Kind**.
The intermediate kinds are called species relative to the higher kind
under which they are included, and they are called kinds relative to
the sub-species included under them. For example, *Material Things*
is a higher kind which includes both *Animate* and *Inanimate* objects.
Each of these is itself a kind including many species. *Animate*
includes both *intelligent* and *non-intelligent* creatures, while

וְאָמְנָם בַּעֲלֵי־חַי לְגַבֵּי גֶשֶׁם נִקְרָא מִין, וּלְגַבֵּי מְדַבֵּר נִקְרָא סוּג. "כְּלֵי עֵץ" הוּא סוּג כּוֹלֵל שְׁנֵי מִינִים, שֶׁהֵם פְּשׁוּטֵי כְּלֵי עֵץ וּמְקַבְּלֵי כְּלֵי עֵץ. וְכֵן כֹּל כַּיּוֹצֵא בָזֶה.

הַבְחָנָה עֲשִׂירִית – **הַסִּבָּה**, וְהִיא מַה שֶׁמִּכֹּחָהּ נוֹלַד וְנִמְצָא הַמְסֻבָּב. וְיֵשׁ בָּהּ שְׁנֵי מִינִים: הָאַחַת – **סִבָּה מוֹלֶדֶת**, וְהַשְּׁנִיָּה – **סִבָּה פּוֹעֶלֶת**. דֶּרֶךְ מָשָׁל: הָעֵץ לַפְּרִי הַיּוֹצֵא מִמֶּנּוּ – הוּא סִבָּה מוֹלֶדֶת, וַהֲרֵי זֶה כְּמוֹ הָאָב שֶׁהוּא סִבָּה לִבְנוֹ, שֶׁהוּא הֶמְשֵׁךְ נִמְשָׁךְ מִמֶּנּוּ. אַךְ (בבא מציעא חד ב): "דָּאֲזְלָא מֵחֲמָתֵהּ" – הוּא סִבָּה פּוֹעֶלֶת, וְכֵן (יומא עוד ב): "חַמְרָא וְרֵיחָנֵי פִּקְחִין" הֵם סִבָּה פּוֹעֶלֶת, וַהֲרֵי זֶה כְּכָל אֻמָּן לַכֵּלִים שֶׁהוּא עוֹשֶׂה, שֶׁאֵינָם הֶמְשֵׁךְ נִמְשָׁךְ מִמֶּנּוּ, אַךְ נִפְעָלִים מִמֶּנּוּ.

הַבְחָנָה אַחַת־עֶשְׂרֵה – **הָאֶמְצָעִי**, שֶׁעַל יָדוֹ פּוֹעֶלֶת הַסִּבָּה אֶת פְּעֻלָּתָהּ. דֶּרֶךְ מָשָׁל (כתובות עה א): "אֶפְשָׁר לְעַבְּרָהּ בְּקִיּוּהָא דְחַמְרָא".

הַבְחָנָה שְׁתֵּים־עֶשְׂרֵה – **הַמְּעוֹרֵר**, וְהוּא מַה שֶׁמְּעוֹרֵר אֶת הַפּוֹעֵל בִּרְצוֹן שֶׁיִּפְעַל. דֶּרֶךְ מָשָׁל (זבחים קטז א): "מַה שְּׁמוּעָה שָׁמַע וּבָא וְנִתְגַּיֵּר? קְרִיעַת יַם סוּף שָׁמַע וּבָא!" שְׁמוּעַת קְרִיעַת יַם סוּף הָיְתָה שֶׁהֶעִירָה אֶת יִתְרוֹ לְשֶׁיָּבוֹא.

הַבְחָנָה שְׁלֹשׁ־עֶשְׂרֵה – **הַתַּכְלִית**, וְהִיא הַכַּוָּנָה שֶׁמִּתְכַּוֵּן הַפּוֹעֵל בִּפְעֻלָּתוֹ, פֵּרוּשׁ – מַה שֶׁהוּא מְבַקֵּשׁ לְהַשִּׂיג עַל יְדֵי פְּעֻלָּתוֹ. דֶּרֶךְ מָשָׁל: הַלָּמֵד עַל מְנָת לַעֲשׂוֹת – תַּכְלִיתוֹ בַלִּמּוּד הִיא לְהַשִּׂיג הֱיוֹתוֹ עוֹשֶׂה מַעֲשִׂים טוֹבִים.

*Inanimate* includes *stones, metals,* and *plants.* Thus, *Animate Objects* in relation to *Material Things* is called a species and in relation to *intelligent* creatures it is called a kind. A kind such as *wooden vessels* may be divided into two species, such as *flat* vessels and *concave* ones.

10. **Cause** is that from which the effect emanates or comes into being. There are two divisions: the first is the generative cause and the second is the effective cause. For example, the tree is the **Generative Cause** of the fruit which grows from it. In this way the father is the cause of his son, for the son is a continuation following after his father. In contrast, (Babba Metzia 8b) "The one who leads an animal acquires it since it is walking because of him". This is an example of an **Effective Cause**. Also, (Yoma 76b) "Wine and smelling spices have made me smart". These are also an effective cause. In this way a craftsman is the cause of the utensils which he makes, for they are not an extension of him but rather they are his products.

11. **Means** is that which is instrumental for the cause to effect its action. For example, (Kesubos 75a) "It is possible for the Cohen to remove filth before the Temple service by means of wine vinegar".

12. **Motive** is what arouses a voluntary agent to act. For example, (Zevachim 116a) "What news did Yisro hear that he came to convert? He heard about the splitting of the sea and he came". From hearing about the splitting of the Red Sea, Yisro was motivated to come.

13. **Purpose** is the intent of the agent in his action, that is, what he desires to accomplish by his action. For example, when one studies in order to practice what he has learned, his purpose in studying is that he will be a person whose deeds are righteous.

הַבְחָנָה אַרְבַּע־עֶשְׂרֵה – **הַמְסֻבָּב,** וְהוּא הַנּוֹלָד מִן הַנּוֹשֵׂא, שֶׁנִּמְצָא הַנּוֹשֵׂא סִבָּה לוֹ. דֶּרֶךְ מָשָׁל (בבא מציעא ח ג): "דְּאָזְלָא מֵחֲמָתֵהּ", הַהֲלִיכָה הִיא הַמְסֻבָּב שֶׁלּוֹ, הַבֵּן הוּא מְסֻבָּב שֶׁל הָאָב, הַכְּלִי מְסֻבָּב שֶׁל הָאֻמָּן.

הַבְחָנָה חֲמֵשׁ־עֶשְׂרֵה – **הַמִּתְחַבֵּר,** וְהוּא כָּל מִקְרֶה שֶׁיִּתְלַוֶּה וְיִתְחַבֵּר לַנּוֹשֵׂא, נוֹסָף עַל עַצְמוּתוֹ. וְיֵחָלֵק לִשְׁלֹשָׁה מִינִים:

הָאֶחָד – מַה שֶּׁמִּתְחַבֵּר בְּעַצְמוֹ שֶׁל הַנּוֹשֵׂא, אוֹ עָלָיו, אוֹ אֵלָיו, כְּגוֹן הַחָכְמָה בֶּחָכָם, הַקַּלּוּת בְּדָבָר קַל, הַכָּבוֹד בַּנִּכְבָּד; הַצִּפּוּי עַל הַכְּלִי, הַלְּבוּשׁ עַל הָאָדָם. דֶּרֶךְ מָשָׁל: בְּהֵמָה מִסְכֶּנֶת – שֶׁיֵּשׁ בָּהּ מִקְרֶה הַסַּכָּנָה, מִטְפַּחַת שְׁרוּיָה בַּמַּיִם – שֶׁיֵּשׁ בָּהּ מִקְרֶה זֶה שֶׁל הֱיוֹתָהּ שְׁרוּיָה בַּמָּיִם.

הַשֵּׁנִי – עִנְיָן שֶׁנִּמְצָא עִם הַנּוֹשֵׂא בִּזְמַן אֶחָד. דֶּרֶךְ מָשָׁל (פסחים עו ג): "פַּת שֶׁאֲפָאָהּ עִם צָלִי", וְכֵן (ברכות לה ג): "כָּל שֶׁהוּא עִקָּר וְעִמּוֹ טְפֵלָה".

הַשְּׁלִישִׁי – הוּא הַקּוֹדֵם וְהַמְאֻחָר, וְהוּא מַה שֶּׁיִּקְדַּם לַנּוֹשֵׂא אוֹ שֶׁיָּבוֹא אַחֲרָיו. דֶּרֶךְ מָשָׁל (ברכות נא ג): "נוֹטְלִין לַיָּדַיִם וְאַחַר כָּךְ מוֹזְגִין אֶת הַכּוֹס", הִנֵּה נְטִילַת יָדַיִם הִיא קוֹדֶמֶת לִמְזִיגַת הַכּוֹס, וּמְזִיגַת הַכּוֹס הִיא הַבָּאָה אַחַר נְטִילַת יָדָיִם.

14. **Result** is that which results from something else when that thing is its cause. For example, (Babba Metzia 8b) "The animal walks because of the one who leads it". The animal's walking is the result of its being led. The son is the result of the father. The utensil is the result of the craftsman.

15. **Attribute** is any accident that is associated or attached to a subject superimposed on its essence. There are three types of attributes.

The first type includes attributes which are found inherent in the subject itself or found resting on it or associated with it. For example, a wise man has wisdom, something which is lightweight has lightness, a man who is respected has honor. Another example is the coating found on a vessel or the clothing on a man. Another example is an animal at the point of death, that is, an animal with the attribute that its life is endangered. Another example is a rag saturated with water, that is, a rag which has the attribute that it is soaked with water.

The second type of attribute is inherent in the subject only incidentally. For example, (Pesachim 76b) "Bread which is baked with meat", or (Berachos 35b) "Any food which has with it a spice or other minor ingredient".

The third type of attribute is not co-existent with the subject to which it is attached; it either precedes or follows it in time. For example, (Berachos 51b) "They should wash hands and afterwards pour the wine". The washing of the hands is an attribute which precedes pouring the cup of wine, and alternatively, pouring the wine is an attribute which follows after the act of washing hands.

הַבְחָנָה שֵׁשׁ-עֶשְׂרֵה – הַמָּקוֹם. דֶּרֶךְ מָשָׁל (עירובין פו ב): "שְׁתֵּי גְזוּזְטְרָאוֹת זוֹ לְמַעֲלָה מִזּוֹ", "שְׁתֵּי עֲיָרוֹת זוֹ סְמוּכָה לָזוֹ", (עירובין עה ב): "עֲשָׂרָה בָתִּים זֶה לִפְנִים מִזֶּה".

הַבְחָנָה שְׁבַע-עֶשְׂרֵה – הַמַּצָּב, וְהוּא תְּכוּנַת הִתְיַצֵּב הַנּוֹשֵׂא בִּמְקוֹמוֹ. דֶּרֶךְ מָשָׁל (מגילה כא א): "הַקּוֹרֵא אֶת הַמְּגִלָּה עוֹמֵד וְיוֹשֵׁב", (ברכות י ב): "בָּעֶרֶב כָּל אָדָם יַטֶּה וְיִקְרָא וּבַבֹּקֶר יַעֲמֹד".

הַבְחָנָה שְׁמוֹנֶה-עֶשְׂרֵה – הַתְּנוּעָה, וְהוּא מַה שֶׁיַּעְתֵּק הַנּוֹשֵׂא מִמָּקוֹם אֶל מָקוֹם. דֶּרֶךְ מָשָׁל (פסחים נא א): "הַהוֹלֵךְ מִמָּקוֹם שֶׁאֵין עוֹשִׂים לְמָקוֹם שֶׁעוֹשִׂים".

הַבְחָנָה תְּשַׁע-עֶשְׂרֵה – הַזְּמָן. דֶּרֶךְ מָשָׁל (ברכות ב א): "מֵאֵימָתַי קוֹרִין אֶת שְׁמַע?" (ברכות י ב): "בָּעֶרֶב כָּל אָדָם יַטֶּה וְיִקְרָא וּבַבֹּקֶר יַעֲמֹד".

הַבְחָנָה עֶשְׂרִים – הַיַּחַס, וְהוּא מַה שֶׁאֶחָד מִתְיַחֵס לְזוּלָתוֹ. דֶּרֶךְ מָשָׁל: דּוֹרוֹ שֶׁל מֹשֶׁה, זַרְעוֹ שֶׁל אַבְרָהָם.

הַבְחָנָה עֶשְׂרִים וְאַחַת – הַנּוֹשֵׂא, וְהַיְנוּ כְּשֶׁהַנִּדּוֹן שֶׁלְּפָנֵינוּ הוּא מִקְרֶה מִן הַמִּקְרִים שֶׁיִּהְיֶה נָשׂוּא עַל אֶחָד מִן הַנּוֹשְׂאִים, הִנֵּה נְבַקֵּשׁ מִי הוּא נוֹשְׂאוֹ. דֶּרֶךְ מָשָׁל, כְּשֶׁאָמְרוּ (פסחים יד ב): "אֵיזֶהוּ דָבָר שֶׁחֲלוּקָה טֻמְאָתוֹ בֵּין טֻמְאַת מֵת לְשֶׁרֶץ? הֱוֵי אוֹמֵר, זֶה מַתֶּכֶת!"

הַבְחָנָה עֶשְׂרִים וּשְׁתַּיִם – הַדִּמְיוֹן. דֶּרֶךְ מָשָׁל (חולין יז ג): "דָּמְיָא

16. **Position.** (Eruvin 87b) "Two balconies, one above the other", "two cities, one next to the other", and (Eruvin 75b) "ten houses, one in front of the other".

17. **Situation** is the manner in which the subject is oriented in its place. For example, (Megillah 21a) "The one who reads the Megillah may be standing or sitting". (Berachos 10b) "In the evening a man must recite the Sh'ma lying down, and in the morning he must recite it while standing".

18. **Movement** is the ability of a single subject to be moved from one place to another. For example, (Pesachim 50a) "A person who travels from a place where work is not done on the eve of Passover, and arrives in a place where work is done, should not work".

19. **Time.** For example, (Berachos 2a) "From what time may one begin to recite the Sh'ma"? (Berachos 10b) "In the evening a man must recite the Sh'ma lying down, and in the morning he must recite it while standing".

20. **Relation** is the relationship that one subject has to another. For example, the generation of Moshe, the descendants of Avraham.

21. **Subject** is the thing which is sought when the topic of discussion is a certain accident or attribute which must be predicated on some case, and we ask, what is the subject of this predication? For example, (Pesachim 14b) "We must be dealing with something whose uncleanness is not the same when the source of uncleanness is a corpse or a reptile. What should this be? It is metal".

22. **Comparison.** For example, (Chullin 17b) "A knife which is rough like an ear of grain [that is, only in one direction]". (Shabbos 101b) "A sword may acquire the same uncleanness as a corpse itself".

לְסָאסְאָה", (שבת קמ"ב): "חֶרֶב הֲרֵי הוּא כְּחָלָל", (כתובות ס"א): "אַדֵּי וְאַדֵּי חַד שְׁעוּרָא הוּא".

הַבְחָנָה עֶשְׂרִים וְשָׁלֹשׁ – **הַהֶבְדֵּל,** וְהוּא הֶעְדֵּר הַדִּמְיוֹן. דֶּרֶךְ מָשָׁל (פסחים כב"א): "שָׁאנֵי דָם דְּאִתְּקַשׁ לְמַיִם", (פסחים כב"ב): "שָׁאנֵי אֵבֶר מִן הַחַי דְּאִתְּקַשׁ לְדָם".

הַבְחָנָה עֶשְׂרִים וְאַרְבַּע – **הַנִּגּוּד,** וְהוּא הֵפֶךְ הַדִּמְיוֹן, וּכְבָר נִתְפָּרֵשׁ לְמַעֲלָה הַנִּגּוּד בְּכָל מִינָיו וְהֵבֵאנוּ מִשְׁלֵיהֶם, עַיֵּן שָׁם.

וְצָרִיךְ שֶׁתֵּדַע, שֶׁיֵּשׁ קְדִימָה וְאָחוֹר מִשְּׁלֹשָׁה מִינִים: הָאֶחָד – זְמַנִּי, הַשֵּׁנִי – שִׂכְלִי, וְהַשְּׁלִישִׁי – טִבְעִי. **זְמַנִּי –** הוּא מַה שֶׁיַּקְדִּים לְזוּלָתוֹ בַּזְּמַן. **שִׂכְלִי –** הוּא מַה שֶׁלֹּא יַקְדַּם בַּזְּמָן אֶלָּא בַּמַּעֲלָה, שֶׁנִּתַּן לוֹ קְדִימָה בַּשֵּׂכֶל; דֶּרֶךְ מָשָׁל: הַמֶּלֶךְ וְהָעָם – הַמֶּלֶךְ קוֹדֵם וְהָעָם מְאָחָר, הָעֶלְיוֹנִים קוֹדְמִים לַתַּחְתּוֹנִים, וְכֵן כַּיּוֹצֵא בָזֶה. **הַטִּבְעִי –** הוּא מִי שֶׁמְּצִיאוּתוֹ תְּלוּיָה בִּמְצִיאוּת חֲבֵרוֹ, אַף עַל פִּי שֶׁיִּמָּצְאוּ שְׁנֵיהֶם כְּאֶחָד, אוֹתוֹ שֶׁהוּא סִבָּה לַחֲבֵרוֹ יִקָּרֵא – קוֹדֵם, וְהַמְּסֻבָּב מִמֶּנּוּ – מְאָחָר.

(Kesubos 60a) "Rabbi Yehoshua said a child may nurse from his mother until the age of four or five. But has it not been taught, he said a child may nurse from his mother even with his pack slung over his shoulder? Both of these represent the same period of time".

23. **Difference** is the absence of comparison between two subjects. For example, (Pesachim 22a) "Blood is different since it is analogous to water in the verse". Therefore, it is permitted to derive benefit from it, whereas from leaven on Passover it is forbidden to derive any benefit. (Pesachim 22b) "The limb of a living animal is different from leaven on Passover since, in the verse, it is analogous to blood".

24. **Contrast** is the opposite of comparison. We have already explained it and brought examples in Chapter Four (see page 52).

In order to describe further the procedure for understanding any concept or subject we must introduce the idea of prior and anterior, which has three different senses. **Priority** may be understood in the sense of time, conceptual importance, or logic. The first is **Temporal Priority** – that is, when one thing precedes another in time. The second is **Conceptual Priority** – that is, something which takes precedence because of its higher importance rather than because it is first in time. For example, between the king and the people, the king is prior and the people anterior. The heavenly creatures are prior to the earthly creatures, and so on. The third sense is **Logical Priority** – that is, something which is, in reality, dependent on something else even though they exist together simultaneously. The one which is the cause of the other is prior, and the other, which is its effect, is anterior.

וּמַה שֶּׁעוֹזֵר אֶל הַהַשְׂכָּלָה עֵזֶר גָּדוֹל וּמֵקֵל לָהּ אֶת הַטֹּרַח הוּא הַסֵּדֶר, וְזֶה בֵּין לִלְמֹד וּבֵין לְלַמֵּד, כִּי הִנֵּה בָּזֶה מְסַקֵּל אֶת הַמְּסִלָּה לִפְנֵי הַשֵּׂכֶל שֶׁיּוּכַל לָלֶכֶת בְּדַרְכֵי הַהִתְבּוֹנְנוּת בְּלִי מִכְשׁוֹלוֹת. וְאִם לוֹמֵד הוּא – יַשִּׂיג הַמֻּשְׂכָּלוֹת שֶׁהוּא מְבַקֵּשׁ עַל נָכוֹן, וְאִם מְלַמֵּד הוּא – יְבָאֵר מַה שֶּׁבְּדַעְתּוֹ לְבָאֵר בְּאוֹר מַסְפִּיק וְיָקֵל אֶל הַלָּמֵד מִמֶּנּוּ לְהַשִּׂיג מַה שֶּׁיְּלַמְּדֵהוּ.

עִקְּרֵי הַסֵּדֶר – שְׁלֹשָׁה: הַסִּדּוּר, הַגְּדָרִים וְהַחִלּוּק.

**הַסִּדּוּר**– הוּא סִדּוּר הָעִנְיָנִים מַה שֶּׁרָאוּי לִהְיוֹת בִּתְחִלָּתָם וּמַה שֶּׁרָאוּי לִהְיוֹת אַחַר כָּךְ. וְהִנֵּה הַסִּדּוּר הַנָּאוֹת הוּא הִתְהַלֵּךְ תָּמִיד מִן הָעִנְיָנִים הַקּוֹדְמִים אֶל הַמְּאֻחָרִים, מֵהַיּוֹתֵר נוֹדָעִים אֶל הַנֶּעְלָמִים יוֹתֵר. פֵּרוּשׁ, הַכּוֹלְלִים הֵם תָּמִיד קוֹדְמִים, וְיוֹתֵר נוֹדָעִים מֵהַפְּרָטִים; הַפְּשׁוּטִים – יוֹתֵר נוֹדָעִים מֵהַמֻּרְכָּבִים. דֶּרֶךְ מָשָׁל, בְּחָכְמַת הַדִּקְדּוּק, הִנֵּה מַה שֶּׁרָאוּי שֶׁיְּדֻבַּר תְּחִלָּה הוּא בְּעִנְיָן הָאוֹתִיּוֹת, אַחַר כָּךְ עַל הַתֵּבוֹת וְהַנְּקֻדּוֹת, אַחַר כָּךְ עַל חֶלְקֵי הַדִּבּוּר, דְּהַיְנוּ הַשֵּׁמוֹת, הַפְּעָלִים, וְהַמִּלּוֹת, אַחַר כָּךְ עַל חִבּוּרֵי הַמַּאֲמָרִים אֵלֶּה עִם אֵלֶּה.

וְאָמְנָם צָרִיךְ שֶׁתֵּדַע, כִּי הִנֵּה מִינֵי הַחָכְמוֹת שְׁנַיִם, וְהֵם: הַשִּׂכְלִיּוֹת וְהַמַּעֲשִׂיּוֹת.

**שִׂכְלִיּוֹת** – מַה שֶּׁעִנְיָנָן יְדִיעַת מַדָּע אֶחָד, **מַעֲשִׂיּוֹת** – מַה שֶּׁעִנְיָנָן יְדִיעַת מְלָאכָה אֶחָת. דֶּרֶךְ מָשָׁל: חָכְמַת הַתְּכוּנָה הִיא יְדִיעַת הַגַּלְגַּלִּים וְכוֹכְבֵיהֶם בִּסְבוּבֵיהֶם, וְחָכְמַת הַדִּקְדּוּק הִיא יְדִיעַת מַעֲשֵׂה

We are now ready to discuss **Order**, which is a fundamental intellectual tool, used both in learning and in teaching, to lighten the burden of achieving clear understanding. This is the tool which will clear away all obstacles so that the intellect may proceed towards understanding without impediment. If one is learning, he will grasp the concepts he desires without error. If he is teaching, he will convey what is in his mind clearly, making it easier for the student to understand what is taught.

There are three fundamental principles of Order: Arrangement, Definitions, and Analysis.

**Arrangement** is the proper presentation of topics, placing what must be introduced first at the beginning and subsequent topics later. The most pleasing order is to go from things which are prior to those which are anterior. Proceed from what is more known to what is more unknown. The general is always prior and more known than the particular, and the simple is more known than the complex. For example, in the science of grammar it is proper that the first topic to be spoken about should be the letters of the alphabet. Afterwards should come words and vocalization, and after that, all the parts of speech, such as nouns, verbs, conjunctions, and prepositions, and finally the syntax of sentences.

In order to proceed further with the rules of Order one must distinguish between the two branches of knowledge: theoretical and practical.

The **Theoretical** is defined as the knowledge of a certain science. The **Practical** is defined as the knowledge of a certain art. For example, the field of astronomy is the knowledge of the heavenly spheres, their stars and their respective movements. The study of grammar is the practical knowledge of proper speech. The science of

238

הַדְּבּוּר הַמְּתֻקָּן. חָכְמַת הַתְּכוּנָה תִּקָּרֵא שִׂכְלִית, שֶׁאֵין בָּהּ אֶלָּא הַשְׂכָּלַת אֶחָד מִן הָעִנְיָנִים שֶׁבַּמְּצִיאוּת כְּמוֹ שֶׁהוּא בָּהּ, וְחָכְמַת הַדִּקְדּוּק תִּקָּרֵא מַעֲשִׂית, שֶׁהֲרֵי תַכְלִיתָהּ הִיא לְלַמֵּד אֵיךְ רָאוּי שֶׁיְּדַבֵּר בַּלָּשׁוֹן הַהִיא.

וְאוּלָם הַסֵּדֶר הָרָאוּי בְּלִמּוּדִים הַשִּׂכְלִיִּים הוּא תְּחִלַּת הַכֹּל יְדִיעַת הַנּוֹשֵׂא שֶׁעָלָיו נַעֲסֹק, אַחַר כָּךְ יְדִיעַת חֲלָקָיו, אַחַר כָּךְ יְדִיעַת סִבּוֹתָיו, אַחַר כָּךְ יְדִיעַת מִקְרָיו לְפִי הַהַדְרָגָה, דְּהַיְנוּ בַּתְּחִלָּה הַכּוֹלְלִים וְאַחַר כָּךְ הַפְּרָטִים, בַּתְּחִלָּה הַפְּשׁוּטִים וְאַחַר כָּךְ הַמֻּרְכָּבִים, וּכְמוֹ שֶׁאָמַרְתִּי לְמָעְלָה.

וְהַסֵּדֶר הָרָאוּי בְּלִמּוּדִים הַמַּעֲשִׂיִּים הוּא, תְּחִלַּת הַכֹּל יְדִיעַת הַתַּכְלִית אֲשֶׁר נִרְצֶה לְהַשִּׂיג, אַחַר כָּךְ יְדִיעַת הָאֶמְצָעִים הַמִּצְטָרְכִים לְהַשָּׂגַת הַתַּכְלִית הַהִיא לְפִי הַהַדְרָגָה. דֶּרֶךְ מָשָׁל, כְּשֶׁנִּרְצֶה לְלַמֵּד קְבִיעוּת חָדְשֵׁי הַשָּׁנָה, הִנֵּה צָרִיךְ שֶׁנְּבָאֵר בַּתְּחִלָּה הַתַּכְלִית, וְהִיא קְבִיעוּת רָאשֵׁי הֶחֳדָשִׁים בַּזְּמַן הָרָאוּי, אַחַר כָּךְ נְבָאֵר הָאֶמְצָעִים הַמִּצְטָרְכִים לָזֶה, וְהִיא יְדִיעַת עִנְיַן הֶחֳדָשִׁים הַחֲסֵרִים וְהַמְּלֵאִים וְהַשָּׁנִים הַסְּדוּרוֹת וְהַחֲסֵרוֹת וְהַשְּׁלֵמוֹת, עִנְיַן הַפְּשׁוּטוֹת וְהַמְּעֻבָּרוֹת, חֶשְׁבּוֹן הַמּוֹלָדוֹת וִידִיעַת הַדְּחִיּוֹת.

astronomy is called theoretical because it involves only the abstract knowledge of some element of reality. The art of grammar is called practical for its goal is to teach one how to speak a certain language properly.

Now the rules of Order are different when the subject matter is theoretical or practical. In the theoretical branch of knowledge, first understand the subject of discussion as a whole, and then understand its parts. After that you must know its causes, and then you must study its attributes according to their levels, as we described earlier. That is, general before particular and simple before complex.

By contrast, the practical branch of knowledge has these rules: First of all, it is necessary to understand the purpose which is the desired end of practicing the particular art. Afterwards it is necessary to understand all the necessary means of achieving this end according to their levels, proceeding from general to particular and from simple to complex. For example, when it is desired to teach the fixed regulation of the Jewish calendar, the purpose must be explained first, which is to determine the day which begins each lunar month. Afterwards, it is necessary to explain the means which are required. The first step is to know which of the months have a full complement of thirty days and which months are short. Afterwards, which years are of normal length, and which are either short or long. Then we must explain which years are simple years of twelve months and which are leap years with thirteen months. Finally, the calculation of the mean interval between new moons must be explained and also the days on which it is required to delay the beginning of a new month.

וּמִמָּה שֶׁצָּרִיךְ שֶׁתִּזָּהֵר מְאֹד בַּסִּדּוּר הוּא, שֶׁלֹּא תַזְכִּיר הָעִנְיָנִים חוּץ לִמְקוֹמָם וּמַדְרֵגָתָם, וְהַיְנוּ שֶׁלֹּא תְבָאֵר הַמְאֻחָר לִפְנֵי הַקּוֹדֵם, כִּי יִהְיֶה בִּלְתִּי אֶפְשָׁר לְהָבִין אֶת אֲשֶׁר תְּלַמְּדֵהוּ, מִפְּנֵי שֶׁתֶּחְסַר יְדִיעַת עִנְיַן מַה שֶׁרָאוּי שֶׁיִּקְדַּם, אוֹ שֶׁלֹּא תַזְכִּיר דָּבָר אֲשֶׁר לֹא בֵאַרְתּוֹ, כִּי זֶה יְבַלְבֵּל דַּעַת הַשּׁוֹמֵעַ וְיִמְנָעֵהוּ מֵהַשִּׂיג מַה שֶׁתְּלַמְּדֵהוּ, אֶלָּא אִם תֻּכְרַח לְהָבִיא דָּבָר אֲשֶׁר לֹא בֵאַרְתּוֹ עֲדַיִן, הִנֵּה תַזְכִּיר אֶצְלוֹ מִיָּד שֶׁעוֹד לְפָנִים תְּבָאֲרֵהוּ, כִּי זֶה מִמָּה שֶׁמַּשְׁקִיט דַּעַת הַשּׁוֹמֵעַ שֶׁלֹּא יְשׁוֹטֵט לְבַקֵּשׁ יְדִיעַת הַדָּבָר הַהוּא שֶׁאִי אֶפְשָׁר לוֹ לִמְצֹא אוֹתָהּ. דֶּרֶךְ מָשָׁל, אִלּוּ הָיִיתָ מְבָאֵר בְּלִמּוּד קְבִיעוּת הֶחָדָשִׁים שֶׁזָּכַרְנוּ עִנְיַן הַשָּׁנִים הַסְּדוּרוֹת וְהַחֲסֵרוֹת וְהַשְּׁלֵמוֹת קֹדֶם עִנְיַן הֶחָדָשִׁים הַחֲסֵרִים וְהַמְלֵאִים, הִנֵּה זֶה חִסָּרוֹן סֵדֶר, כִּי עִנְיַן הַסְּדוּרוֹת, הַחֲסֵרוֹת וְהַשְּׁלֵמוֹת תָּלוּי בְּעִנְיַן חִסָּרוֹן הֶחָדָשִׁים וּמְלוּאָם. וְאִי אֶפְשָׁר שֶׁתּוּכַל לְבָאֲרוֹ כָּרָאוּי קֹדֶם שֶׁתְּבָאֵר חִסָּרוֹן הֶחָדָשִׁים וּמְלוּאָם.

**הַגְּדָרִים** – הוּא שֶׁתִּתְבּוֹנֵן מְאֹד בְּכָל הָעִנְיָנִים שֶׁתַּזְכִּיר, לִגְדֹּר אוֹתָם לַאֲמִתָּם בִּגְדֵר שָׁלֵם שֶׁיִּכְלֹל כָּל עִקַּר עִנְיָנָם, עַד שֶׁיְּצַיֵּר צִיּוּרָם הֵיטֵב בְּדַעַת הַשּׁוֹמֵעַ, וְלֹא תִקַּח הָעִנְיָנִים הַמִּקְרִיִּים תַּחַת הָעַצְמִיִּים לִגְדֹּר בָּהֶם עִנְיָנְךָ, כִּי לֹא יִתֵּן זֶה צִיּוּר שָׁלֵם אֶל שׁוֹמְעֶיךָ.

**הַחִלּוּק** – הוּא גַם כֵּן עִקָּר גָּדוֹל לְהָקֵל לַלָּמֵד הַשָּׂגַת מְבֻקָּשׁוֹ, כִּי כָּל זְמַן שֶׁאֵין הַשֵּׂכֶל מַשִּׂיג אֶלָּא הַכְּלָלִים – אֵין הַשָּׂגָתוֹ שְׁלֵמָה. וּכְדֵי

There is a cardinal rule in arranging a proper order of presentation: do not discuss any topic out of place or without respect to its appropriate gradation. Thus, one should never explain a later concept before the prior one, because it will be impossible for the student to understand what is taught since he lacks any prior knowledge of the concept. Nor should one introduce some new concept which has not been explained, because this will confuse the listener and prevent him from understanding what is taught. If it is unavoidable to bring in a concept that has not yet been explained, one should always mention immediately that it will be explained farther on, because this will save the student needless speculation about something which he cannot find by going over what he has studied. For example, in teaching the regulation of the Jewish calendar, if you were to explain the topic of normal, short and long years before the topic of full and short months, this would be an improper order. For the years are either normal, short or long, depending on how many months are full and how many are short. Therefore, you will not be able to explain the different types of years properly until you have first explained that some months are short (twenty-nine days) and some are long (thirty days).

**Definitions** – You must give careful thought to defining your topic with true and complete definitions which do not leave out any essential parts. The goal is to create an accurate image in the mind of the listener of the concepts at hand. Do not use incidentals in place of essentials to formulate a definition of your terms, for by their nature, incidentals do not give a complete picture of what a thing is.

**Analysis** – This is also an essential tool to ease the burden of the student in attaining the understanding he desires. As long as the mind only considers generalities one's knowledge is necessarily limited. In order to complete our understanding, it is necessary to dissect

שֶׁיִּשְׁתַּלֵּם, צָרִיךְ שֶׁיָּנֻתַּח לְפָנָיו הַנּוֹשֵׂא לִנְתָחָיו, כְּדֵי שֶׁיּוּכַל לְהַבִּיט עַל כֻּלָּם וּלְהַכִּירָם כְּמוֹ שֶׁהֵם, וְאָז יִקָּרֵא שֶׁנִּצְטַיֵּר בּוֹ הַנּוֹשֵׂא צִיּוּר שָׁלֵם.

וְאָמְנָם מַה שֶּׁצָּרִיךְ שֶׁתִּשָּׁמֵר בָּזֶה הוּא, שֶׁיִּהְיוּ הַחֲלָקִים אֲשֶׁר תַּבְחִין, כּוֹלְלִים כָּל נוֹשְׂאֶיךָ בֶּאֱמֶת, לֹא פָּחוֹת וְלֹא יוֹתֵר, פֵּרוּשׁ – שֶׁלֹּא תַנִּיחַ חֵלֶק מִנּוֹשְׂאֶיךָ אֲשֶׁר לֹא תִמְנֵהוּ, וְכֵן לֹא תִמְנֶה יוֹתֵר עַל מַה שֶׁיֵּשׁ בּוֹ בֶּאֱמֶת. וְהַמֻּבְחָר שֶׁבַּחֲלוּק הוּא, שֶׁתְּחַלֵּק נוֹשְׂאֲךָ לַחֲלָקִים כּוֹלְלִים, וְאַחַר כָּךְ תָּשׁוּב וּתְחַלֵּק כָּל חֵלֶק מֵחֲלָקָיו לַחֲלָקִים שְׁנִיִּים, פְּרָטִיִּים מֵהָרִאשׁוֹנִים, וְכָל אֶחָד מִן הַשְּׁנִיִּים לִשְׁלִישִׁיִּים, וְכֵן עַל דֶּרֶךְ זֶה. וְטוֹב שֶׁתִּתְמַעֵט בְּמִסְפַּר הַחֲלָקִים כָּל מַה שֶׁאֶפְשָׁר לְךָ, וְתַרְבֶּה בְּחִלּוּק כָּל מַה שֶׁאֶפְשָׁר, פֵּרוּשׁ, שֶׁאִם תּוּכַל תִּשְׁתַּדֵּל לִכְלוֹל כָּל נוֹשְׂאֲךָ בִּשְׁנֵי חֲלָקִים אוֹ שְׁלֹשָׁה, וְכֵן עַל דֶּרֶךְ זֶה.

דֶּרֶךְ מָשָׁל (שבת ב א): "יְצִיאוֹת הַשַּׁבָּת שְׁתַּיִם שֶׁהֵן אַרְבַּע בִּפְנִים, וּשְׁתַּיִם שֶׁהֵן אַרְבַּע בַּחוּץ", הִנֵּה כָּאן חִלֵּק כְּלַל כָּל יְצִיאוֹת הַשַּׁבָּת לִשְׁנֵי חֲלָקִים, וְהַיְנוּ בִּפְנִים וּבַחוּץ, וְאַחַר כָּךְ חִלֵּק כָּל אֶחָד מִשְׁנֵי הַחֲלָקִים לִשְׁנַיִם. וְכָל אֶחָד מֵאֵלֶּה

the topic into its sections before the eyes of the student so that he can behold all of them and become familiar with each one. Then we may say that the topic at hand is understood with complete clarity.

The rules for correct analysis are as follows: The parts into which you divide your topic should be all-inclusive, covering the whole subject matter, nothing more and nothing less. That is, do not leave out any point of your topic which is not taken into consideration in the parts which you have made, and do not include anything as a section which extends beyond the bounds of your subject matter. The best analysis is one in which you divide your subject matter into parts which are as general as possible. Afterwards, divide each of the parts into sub-sections which are more particular than the first. Then each of the sub-sections should be sub-divided one step further, and so on. It is preferable to choose the smallest number of divisions possible, and to extend the process of sub-division to the greatest detail possible. That is, if possible, try to encompass the entire topic in two or three sections. Similarly, with the secondary and tertiary divisions, it is better to keep them down to a small number.

> *For example, (Shabbos 2a) "The liable acts of carrying on the Sabbath are two which are four inside, and two which are four outside". We see in this Mishnah that all acts of carrying on the Sabbath are divided into two sections: those for which a person inside a private domain is liable, and those for which a person standing in the public domain is liable. Then each of these sections has two sub-sections, and each sub-section has two tertiary divisions, that is, a*

הַשָּׁנִים לְשָׁנִים אֲחֵרִים, וְנִמְצְאוּ אַרְבָּעָה, וְזֶהוּ
"שְׁתַּיִם שֶׁהֵן אַרְבַּע".

וְהִנֵּה תִּזָּהֵר בָּזֶה לְהִתְהַלֵּךְ בְּהַדְרָגָה הָרְאוּיָה, וְלֹא תַזְכִּיר חֵלֶק
שְׁנִיִּי עִם הָרִאשׁוֹנִים, וְלֹא שְׁלִישִׁיִּי עִם הַשְּׁנִיִּים, וְכֵן כַּיּוֹצֵא בָּזֶה, אֶלָּא
כָּל דָּבָר בִּמְקוֹמוֹ וּמַדְרֵגָתוֹ, וְיִהְיוּ הַחֲלָקִים כָּל אֶחָד שׁוֹנֶה מֵחֲבֵרוֹ
וְנִבְדָּל מִמֶּנּוּ בֶּאֱמֶת, שֶׁלֹּא תִמְנֶה עִנְיָן אֶחָד שְׁתֵּי פְעָמִים.

זֶה כְּלַל דֶּרֶךְ הָעִיּוּן וְהַהִתְבּוֹנְנוּת לְהָבִין וּלְהַשִּׂיג כָּל מֻשְׂכָּל
שֶׁיִּהְיֶה לַאֲמִתּוֹ.

וַה' יִתֵּן חָכְמָה, מִפִּיו דַּעַת וּתְבוּנָה

תַּם וְנִשְׁלַם שֶׁבַח לָאֵל בּוֹרֵא עוֹלָם

*total of four divisions inside and four divisions outside. This is what is meant by "two which are four".*

It is important in analysis to remain consistent within each level of division. Do not discuss a sub-section together with the more general major sections of your topic, and do not bring in a lower-level division together with the sub-sections above it. Take care that each one is in its proper place with the other divisions of the same level. In addition, take care that each division is separate and independent from each other one, so that they do not overlap and cause you to count the same part of your subject twice.

This is, in totality, the procedure for investigating any text and understanding any subject, which will allow you to comprehend and penetrate the truth of intelligible reality.

May the Almighty grant wisdom; from His mouth shall come knowledge and understanding.

Finished and complete with praise to the Almighty, Creator of the universe.

# Appendix:

I     Chapter Outlines

II    General Index

III   Term Index

IV   Source Index

# Chapter Outlines

I. CHAPTER ONE: The Talmudic method defined (pg. 10)

  A. Dialectic investigation defined
  B. Parties in debate
     1. Group
     2. Individual
     3. Talmud

II. CHAPTER TWO: The seven principal elements of debate and their foundations (pg. 14)

  A. The principal elements of debate
     1. Statement
     2. Question
     3. Answer
     4. Contradiction
     5. Proof
     6. Difficulty
     7. Resolution
  B. The foundations of the elements
     1. Understanding statements
     2. Creating syllogisms
     3. Acceptance and rejection of ideas

III. CHAPTER THREE: Statements defined (pg. 22)

  A. Subject and predicate defined
  B. Statements divided according to their subjects
     1. Categorical
     2. Particular
     3. Partial
  C. Statements divided according to their predicates
     1. Simple statement
     2. Qualified statement
       a. Certain
       b. Possible
       c. Doubtful
       d. Impossible
     3. Statement of exclusion
     4. Statement of exception
     5. Conditional statement
     6. Hypothetical statement

       7. Compound statement
         a. Simple compound
           (1) Equal (both parts novel)
           (2) Unequal (only one part novel)
              (a) Not only. . . but even. . .
              (b) This. . . and needless to say. . .
         b. Disjunction
       8. Preclusive statement
       9. Statement of discrepancy
      10. Comparative statement
      11. Consequent statement
    D. Statements divided according to their style
       1. Extensive
       2. Concise
       3. Literal
       4. Rhetorical
       5. Metaphorical

IV. CHAPTER FOUR: Juxtaposition of statements (pg. 48)

    A. Equivalent statements
    B. Variant statements
    C. Opposite statements
       1. Diametrically opposed
       2. Contradictory
    D. Converse statements
       1. Complete converse
       2. Limited converse
       3. Contrapositive converse
    E. Obverse statements
    F. Incongruent statements

V. CHAPTER FIVE: Inferences (pg. 66)

    A. Inference defined
    B. Inferences which are not logically necessary
    C. Logically necessary inferences
       1. Inferences of categorical affirmative statements
         a. Contrapositive
         b. Limited converse
       2. Inference of categorical negative statements
         a. Complete converse
       3. Inferences of partial affirmative statements
         a. Absolute opposite
         b. Limited contrapositive
         c. Limited converse

    4. Inferences of partial negative statements
      a. Absolute opposite
      b. Limited contrapositive
      c. Limited converse

VI. CHAPTER SIX: Truth and falsity of statements and ultimate intention (pg. 76)

A. Figurative or hyperbolic statements
B. Literal statements
  1. Simple statement
    a. Simple predication must be true
  2. Qualified statement
    a. Qualification must be true
  3. Statement of exclusion
    a. Exclusion must be true
  4. Statement of exception
    a. Simple predication must be true
    b. Exceptional case must be true (Denial of the exceptional case does not deny the simple predication)
  5. Conditional statement
    a. Simple predication must be true
    b. Condition must be true (Denial of the condition does not deny the simple predication)
  6. Hypothetical statement
    a. Dependency must be true
  7. Compound statement
    a. Combination of simple predications must be true
  8. Preclusive statement
    a. Combination of affirmative and negative predications must be true
  9. Statement of discrepancy
    a. Combination of apparently contradictory predications must be true
  10. Comparative statement
    a. Combination of similar predications must be true
  11. Consequent statement
    a. Antecedent must be true
    b. Consequent must be true
    c. Dependency must be true

VII. CHAPTER SEVEN: Syllogisms (pg. 92)

A. Classical syllogism
  1. Syllogism defined
  2. Premise defined
  3. Conclusion defined
  4. Invalidity of the classical syllogism

.

B. Analogism
1. Analogism
2. A fortiori
3. Invalidity of an analogism or a fortiori
   a. Subjects not similar
   b. Subjects not greater or lesser
   c. Another similar subject exists without the given predicate
C. Hypothetical syllogism
D. Disjunctive syllogism

VIII. CHAPTER EIGHT: Statements: accepted, rejected or in doubt (pg. 112)

A. Proofs for acceptance of statements
1. Postulated proof
   a. Axiomatic principles
   b. Sense perceptions
2. Proof through convention
   a. Common sense
   b. Accepted tradition
3. Logical proof
4. Proof that the opposite statement is false
B. Proofs for rejection of statements
1. Postulated disproof
   a. Axiomatic principles
   b. Sense perceptions
2. Disproof through convention
   a. Accepted tradition
3. Logical disproof
   a. Indirect disproof
   b. Reductio ad absurdum
   c. Dilemma
C. Statements which remain doubtful
1. Proof rejected
   a. Proof irrelevant to statement
   b. Invalid syllogism
2. Disproof rejected
   a. Disproof irrelevant to statement
   b. Invalid syllogism
   c. Rebuttal
      1. According to your reasoning
      2. Just the opposite
      3. That proves my point, from there is a proof

252

D. Theory
E. Validity of deductions and proofs
    1. Relationship of subject to predicate
        a. What it is in itself
        b. What is unique to it
        c. Its attributes
        d. What it is in relation to something else
    2. Relationship of predicate to subject
        a. Potential
        b. Actual
F. Stylistic proofs and disproofs
    1. The statement as a whole
    2. The statement in terms of its parts

IX. CHAPTER NINE: Elements of debate in detail and their rules (pg. 162)

A. Statement
    1. First-hand knowledge
    2. Explanation
        a. Full explanation
        b. Forced explanation
            1. Forced explanation
            2. Presumption
    3. Inference
    4. Reported information
B. Question
    1. Query
    2. Question of principle
C. Answer
    1. Answer
    2. Determination
D. Proof
    1. Demonstration
    2. Validation
E. Contradiction
    1. Direct contradiction
    2. Opposition
F. Difficulty
    1. Objection
    2. Apparent contradiction
    3. Refutation
G. Resolution
    1. Settlement
    2. Alternative

X. CHAPTER TEN: Order of study (pg. 190)

   A. Be sensitive to the author's language
   B. Formulate a complete thought
   C. Determine purpose of statement
   D. Is the purpose actually served by the statement?
   E. Establish the truth of every premise
   F. Distinguish between the text and the elucidation
   G. Recognize whether terms are synonymous or not
   H. Recognize whether statements are synonymous or not
   I. Identify multiple purpose statements
      1. Proof by reported information
      2. Ascribed difficulty
   J. Review and reconsider the truth of each statement

XI. CHAPTER ELEVEN: Logical terminology and sequence (pg. 222)

   A. Logical terms
      1. Essence-Definition
      2. Parts
      3. Quality
      4. Quantity
      5. Material
      6. Form
         a. Abstract definitive form
         b. Concrete physical form
      7. Action
         a. Involuntary
         b. Voluntary
      8. Affection
      9. Kind, Species and Higher Kind
     10. Cause
         a. Generative cause
         b. Effective cause
     11. Means
     12. Motive
     13. Purpose
     14. Result
     15. Attribute
         a. Inherent, resting on, or associated
         b. Incidental
         c. Precedes or follows in time
     16. Position
     17. Situation
     18. Movement
     19. Time
     20. Relation
     21. Subject
     22. Comparison
     23. Difference
     24. Contrast
   B. Priority
      1. Temporal
      2. Conceptual
      3. Logical
   C. Logical Order
      1. Arrangement
         a. Theoretical knowledge
         b. Practical knowledge
      2. Definitions
      3. Analysis
         a. Primary
         b. Secondary
         c. Tertiary

# General Index

LEGEND:
–Italic numerals (*135*) indicate the page where a term is defined.
–An asterisk (*) indicates the page where an example is found.

| A |
| --- |

A fortiori, *see under* Syllogism
Absolute opposite, *see under* Opposite
Accepted tradition, *114*, 116*, 124, 124–126*
According to your reasoning, *136*
Action, *226*
   –Involuntary, *226*
   –Voluntary, *226*, 230
Actuality and Potentiality, *154*, 154–156*
Affection, *226*
Alternative, 184, *186*, 188
   –Rules of, 186–188
Analogism, *see under* Syllogism
Analysis, 238, *242*, 244, 246, 244–246*, *see also* Order
Answer, *14*, 18*, 132*, *172*, 172–174*, 194
   –Rules of, 172
Antecedent, *32*, 82, 84*, 86–88, 106, *see also* Consequent
Apparent contradiction, 38, 180, *182*, 182–184*, 186, *see also* Statement of discrepancy
Arrangement, *see under* Order
Ascribed difficulty, *214*, 216–218, 216–218*
Ascribed proof, *214*
Aspect, 2, 144, 146*, 148–156, 152*
   –Attributes, *150*
   –Potential and Actual, *154*, 154–156*
   –What is unique to it, *148*
   –What it is in itself, *148*
   –What it is in relation to something else, *150*
Attribute, *232*, 234, *see also* Aspect
   –Incidental, *232*
   –Inherent, resting, associated, 2, *232*
   –Precedes or follows in time, *232*
Axiomatic principles, *112*, 124

| C |
| --- |

Categorical statements, *22*, 56, 58, 62, 72
   –Inferences of, 72
Cause, *230*, 232, 236
   –Effective, 150, *230*
   –Generative, *230*
Certainty (Qualified statement), 26, 78
Classical syllogism, *see under* Syllogism
Comparative statement, *40*
   –Ultimate intention of, 88
Comparison, 40, 96–98, 126–128*, 140*, *234*
Complete converse, *see under* Converse
Compound statement, *32*, 34–38
   –Ultimate intention of, 86
Conceptual priority, *see under* Priority
Conclusion (of Syllogism), *94*, 98*, 108*, 122*, 126, 128*, 130*, 202–206*, 210*, *see also* Premise
Conditional statement, *30*, 144, 146*, 148–150
   –Ultimate intention of, 82

Consequent clause, *32*, 82–86, 106, *see also* Antecedent
Consequent statement, *40*, 44*, 126
   –Ultimate intention of, 88–90
Contradiction, *14*, 84*, 176–180
   –Direct contradiction, *178*
   –Opposition, *178*, 180, 186
   –Rules of 122–126, 142, 178
Contradictory statements, *see under* Opposite
Contrapositive, *see under* Converse
Contrast, *236*
Convention, *114*, 124
Converse, 48, *60*, 62–64
   –Complete, *62*, 74
   –Contrapositive *62*, 72
   –Limited, *62*, 72, 74
   –Limited Contrapositive, 74


D

Definition, *222*, 238, *252*
Definitive form, *226*
Demonstration, *174*, 176
   –Rules of, 112–118, 176
Determination, *172*, 174
   –Rules of, 174
Dialectics, 10, 156
Diametrically opposed statements (Absolute opposites), *see under* Contradictory
Difference, *236*
Difficulty, 12, *14*, 154*, 162*, 168*, *180*, 182–184
Dilemma, *132*
Direct contradiction, *see under* Contradiction
Discrepancy, Statement of, *38*
   –Ultimate intention, 88
Disjunction, *36*, 38, 108*, 110
Disjunctive syllogism, *see under* Syllogism
Disproof through convention, *124*
Disproofs of statements, *122*, 124–132
Distribution, 62, 68, 68*

Doubtful (Qualified statement), 28


E

Effective cause, *230*
Elucidation, *196*, 208–210*
Equivalent statements, *48*, 50*
Essence, *222*
Exception, Statement of, *30*
   –Ultimate intention, 80
Exclusion, Statement of, *28*, 44
   –Ultimate intention, 78–80
Explanation, *162*, 164–166
   –Forced, *164*
   –Full, *164*
   –Presumption, *164*, 166
   –Rules of, 164


F

Figurative statement, 42, 76
First-hand Knowledge, statement of, *162*
   –Rules of, 22–26, 42
Forced explanation, *see under* Explanation
Form, *226*
   –Definitive, *226*
   –Physical, *226*
"From there is a proof", *138*
Full explanation, *see under* Explanation


G

Generative cause, *230*

H

Higher kind, *see under* Kind
Hypothetical statement, *32*, 106*, 178*
   –Ultimate intention of, 82–86, 88
Hypothetical syllogism, *see under* Syllogism

**I**

Impossible (Qualified statement), *28*, 78
Incidental attribute, *232*
Incongruent statements, 48, *64*
Inference, 16, *66*, 68–74, 166, 174–176*
  –Logically necessary, 70, *72*, 74
  –Not logically necessary, *70*, 72
  –Rules of, 68–72
Inherent attribute, *232*
Involuntary action, *226*, *see also* Action

**J**

"Just the opposite", *138*, 140
Juxtaposition of statements, 48–64,
  72–74

**K**

Kind, *228*, 230
  –Higher kind, *228*
  –Species, *228*, 230

**L**

Limited contrapositive, *see under* Con-
  verse
Limited converse, *see under* Converse
Literal statement, 76
Logical disproof, 122, *126*, 128–132
Logical proof, 112, *116*, 118–122
Logical priority, *236*, *see also* Priority
Logical sequence, 238–246
Logically necessary inferences, *see
  under* Inference

**M**

Material, *226*
Means, *230*
Middle term, 60
  –Fallacy of, 144, 146*

**Motive**, *230*
Movement, *234*

**O**

Objection, *180*, 182, 184, 186
Obverse statements, 48, *64*
Opposite statements, *52*, 54–60, 116
  –Absolute opposites, *56*, 58, 74,
    178*
  –Contradictory statements, *56*, 58
Opposition, *see under* Contradiction
Order, 158, 182, *238*, 240–246
  –Analysis, 238, *242*, 244–246
  –Arrangement, 238, 240–242
  –Definitions, 222, 238, *242*

**P**

Particular statements, *24*, 58, 62
Partial statements, *24*, 56, 58, 74
Parts, 192, *222*, 240, 244, 244*
Physical form, *226*
Position, *234*
Possible (Qualified statement), *26*, 78
Postulated disproof, *124*
Postulated proof, *112*
Potential, *154*, 156
Practical knowledge, *238*, 240
Preclusive statement, *38*, 46*
  –Ultimate intention of, 88
Predicate, *22*, 24*, 68*, 144, 150, 192
  –Aspects of, 154
  –Categories of, 26–42
  –In Syllogisms, 92, 100, 104*
Premise, 92, *94*, 118*, 126, 130*, *see also*
  Antecedent
Priority, *236*
  –Conceptual, *236*
  –Logical, *236*
  –Temporal, *236*
Presumption, *164*, 166, *see also* Explana-
  tion
Proof, *14*, *112*, 114–122, 142, *174*, 176
Proof through convention, 112, *114*, 116

Purpose, *230*, 240

| Q |

Qualified statement, *26*
   —Ultimate intention of, 78
Quality, *224*
Quantity, *224*, 226
Query, *168*, 170, 172
Question, *14*, *168*, 170, 194
Question of principle, 168, *170*, 172

| R |

Reductio ad absurdum, 128
Relation, 150, *234*
Reported information, 162, *166*, 168,
   214–216
Resolution, *14*, 44*, 154*, 164*, *184*,
   186–188
Result, *232*
Rhetorical statements, 42, 44*

| S |

Sense perception, *114*, 124, 132, 134
Settlement, *184*
   —Rules of, 184
Simple compound, *32*, 34–36
Simple statement, *26*, 46
   —Ultimate intention of, 78
Situation, *234*
Species, *228*, 230, *see also* Kind
Statement 10, *14*, 42, 56, 150, *162*,
   192–194, 202*, 210*
   —Acceptance of, 112
   —Categories of, 22, 24, 26, 162–168
   —Inferences of, 66–74
   —Style, 156–158
Subject, *22*, 42, 68, 192, *234*
   —Aspects of, 144, 148–150, 152–154*
   —Categories of, 22–26
   —In syllogisms, 92–94
Syllogism, 20, 92, *94*, 96–110, 116

   —A fortiori, *98*, 100–104*, 136*, 152*
   —Analogism, *96*, 98, 100*, 128*
   —Classical, *94*, 96, 202
   —Disjunctive, *106*, 106–110*, 110,
   —Hypothetical, *106*, 118–122*, 130*,
     202–204*
Synonymous statements and terms, 56,
   64, 212

| T |

Temporal priority, *236*, *see also* Priority
Theoretical knowledge, *238*, 240
"That proves my point", *138*
The statement as a whole, 156d–158
The statement in terms of its parts,
   *158*
Theory, *142*, 144, 176, 180
Time, *234*
Truth and falsity, 76–90

| U |

Ultimate intention of statements, 76–90

| V |

Validation, 174, *176*
   —Rules of, 176
Variant statements, *52*
Voluntary action, *226*, *see also* Action

# Term Index

| א | ה | ח |
|---|---|---|

| ח | ה | א |
|---|---|---|
| חומר, 22 | הבדל, 235 | אבעיא, 169 |
| חילוק, 241 | הבחנות, 149 | אדרבא, 137 |
| חלוף, 59 | הגדה, 165 | אוקימתא, 163 |
| חלוף הפכי כולל, 71 | הוכחה, 173 | איכות, 223 |
| חלוף כולל, 71 | הוכחה והגדה, 213 | אמצעי, 229 |
| חלוף קצתי, 71, 73 | היא הנותנת, 137 | אפשרות, 25 |
| חלוף קצתי הפכי, 73 | הסכמה, 123 | |
| חלקים, 221 | הפך, 55 | |
| | הפכיים, 51 | |
| | הפכיים ממש, 55 | |

| ט | | ב |
|---|---|---|
| טבע, 123 | הפעל, 225 | באור המאמרים, 195 |
| | הקדמה, 93 | בחינות, 149 |
| | הקש, 93 | בכח, 153 |
| | הקש מחלק, 105 | בלתי מכרח, 69 |
| | הקש מופתי, 93 | בנין אב, 95 |
| | הקש תלוי, 105 | בפעל, 153 |
| | | בעצמו, 147 |

| י | | |
|---|---|---|
| יחס, 233 | | |
| ישוב, 183 | ו | ג |
| | ודאות, 25 | גדר, 221, 241 |
| | | גזרה, 61 |

| כ | ז | |
|---|---|---|
| כוללים, 21 | זמן, 233 | |
| כח ופועל, 153 | | ד |
| כל שכן, 97 | | דומים, 47 |
| כמות, 223 | | דחיה, 177 |
| | | דיוק, 165 |
| ל | | דמיון, 233 |
| לדידך, 135 | | |
| לטעמיך, 135 | | |

## מ

מדמה, 39
מה מצינו, 95
מה שביחסו אל זולתו, 149
מה שבמקריו, 149
מה שבסגלתו, 147
מה שבעצמו, 147
מהות, 221
מוגבל, 25
מוחשות, 111
מורגשת, 113
מוציא, 29
מושכלות הראשונים, 111
מימרא, 14, 161
מין, 228
מכיש, 37
מכרח, 71
ממה נפשך, 131
ממעט, 27
מניעה, 27
מסובב, 231
מעורר, 239
מעשיות, 237
מפרסמות, 113
מצב, 233
מקבלות, 113
מקום, 223
מרבה העניינים, 37
משם ראיה, 137
מתהפכים, 63
מתחבר, 231
מתחלפים, 51
מתנגדים, 55

## נ

נבדלים, 63
נגוד, 235
נושא, 21, 233
נמשך (מאמר), 39
נמשך (וקדם), 31
נשוא, 21

## ס

סבה, 229
סבה מולדת, 229
סבה פועלת, 229
סברא, 141
סדור, 237
סדר, 61
סוג, 227
סוג הסוג, 227
סוף גזרה, 79–90
סיעתא, 175
ספק, 27
סתירה, 13, 177
סתם, 25

## פ

פעולה, 225
פעולה טבעית, 225
פעולה רצונית, 225
פרוש, 161
פרוש דחוק, 163
פרוש מרוח, 163
פרטיים, 23
פרכא, 179
פשיטות, 171

## צ

צורה, 225
צורה המרגשת, 225
צורה העצמית, 225

## ק

קודם, 31
קודם ומאחר, 235
קושיא, 13, 179
קושיא מגדת, 213
קל וחומר, 97
קצתיים, 23

## ר

ראיה, 13, 173
ראיה מצד ההסכמה, 123
ראיה מצד ההקש, 115
ראיה מצד הטבע, 111
רומיא, 181
רצונית, 225

## ש

שאלה, 13, 167
שכליות, 237
שמועה, 81
שנוי, 185

## ת

תולדה, 93
תכלית, 229
תלוי, 31
תנועה, 233
תרוץ, 13, 183
תשובה, 13, 171

# Source Index

Italic numerals (*126*) indicate the page where the source is found.

## *TORAH*

Genesis 28:15, *184*
Genesis 32:7, *184*
Exodus 12:16, *28, 80*
Exodus 23:17, *124*
Exodus 35:3, *108*
Leviticus 5:13, *120*
Leviticus 11:2, *66*
Leviticus 22:11, *118*
Leviticus 24:17, *126*
Leviticus 24:20, *128*
Deuteronomy 17:15, *138*
Deuteronomy 25:11, *134*

## *PROPHETS*

II Samuel 23:1, *66*
I Kings 18:21, *84*
Isaiah 30:14, *142*
Isaiah 60:21, *116*

## *MIDRASH*

Bereshis Rabbah 51:3, *72*

## *MIDRASH HALACHAH*

Sifri, Naso 5:13, *152*
Toras Cohanim,
Sin Offerings, Section 5, *98, 104*

## *TALMUD BAVLI*

### *ZERA'IM*

Berachos 2a, *158, 234*
Berachos 4a, *184*
Berachos 10b, *234*
Berachos 15a, *16, 226*
Berachos 20b, *22, 26, 78, 162, 166*
Berachos 22a, *162*
Berachos 24b, *166*
Berachos 35a, *168*
Berachos 35b, *232*
Berachos 51b, *232*
Berachos 53a, *70*
Berachos 58b, *124, 134*
Pe'ah Chapter 7 Mishnah 4, *222*
Demai Chapter 1 Mishnah 2, *30, 82*
Demai Chapter 4 Mishnah 4, *32*
Demai Chapter 6 Mishnah 1, *34*
Demai Chapter 6 Mishnah 5, *40*
Kil'ayim Chapter 5 Mishnah 5, *224*
Kil'ayim Chapter 8 Mishnah 1, *32, 36*
Shevi'is Chapter 9 Mishnah 2, *222*
Terumos Chapter 1 Mishnah 7, *34*
Terumos Chapter 11 Mishnah 5, *38*
Ma'aseros Chapter 2 Mishnah 1, *40, 88*
Ma'aseros Chapter 5 Mishnah 8, *38*
Ma'aser Sheni Chapter 1 Mishnah 2, *34*

## MOED

Shabbos 2a, *246*
Shabbos 5b, *196*
Shabbos 19a, *168*
Shabbos 28b, *58*
Shabbos 40b, *228*
Shabbos 43b, *96*
Shabbos 57a, *54*
Shabbos 70a, *92*
Shabbos 76b, *58*
Shabbos 82a, *140*
Shabbos 101b, *234*
Shabbos 106a, *68*
Shabbos 124a, *56*
Eruvin 21b, *4*
Eruvin 75b, *234*
Eruvin 87b, *234*
Eruvin 102b, *56*
Pesachim 4a, *16*
Pesachim 5b, *108*
Pesachim 7b, *178*
Pesachim 9b, *26, 78*
Pesachim 14b, *234*
Pesachim 16a, *174*
Pesachim 17a, *212*
Pesachim 17b, *178*
Pesachim 19a, *106*
Pesachim 19b, *144*
Pesachim 22a, *236*
Pesachim 22b, *236*
Pesachim 50a, *234*
Pesachim 50b, *74*
Pesachim 74a, *228*
Pesachim 76b, *232*
Pesachim 82b, *50*
Pesachim 113a, *28*
Rosh Hashanah 29b, *56*
Yoma 76b, *239*
Sukkah 40a, *114*
Sukkah 53a, *32*
Megillah 21a, *234*
Mo'ed Katan 16b, *66*
Betzah 24a, *68*
Chagigah 4a, *124*
Chagigah 15b, *72*

## NASHIM

Yebamos 38a, *30*
Yebamos 40a, *116*
Yebamos 50a, *52*
Yebamos 58b, *170, 174*
Yebamos 66a, *62, 118*
Yebamos 84a, *24*
Yebamos 102a, *168, 172*
Yebamos 102b, *176*
Yebamos 104b, *186*
Yebamos 112b, *38, 86, 170, 172*
Yebamos 117b, *180*
Yebamos 118a, *182*
Yebamos 120b, *182*
Ketubos 36b, *48*
Ketubos 57a, *52*
Ketubos 60a, *236*
Ketubos 75a, *26, 28, 230*
Gittin 80b, *158*

## NEZIKIN

Babba Kamma 27a, *158*
Babba Kamma 29a, *132*
Babba Kamma 83b, *124, 126, 140, 168, 216*
Babba Kamma 84a, *130*
Babba Kamma 88a, *134, 136*
Babba Kamma 104a, *110*
Babba Kamma 117a, *76*
Babba Metzia 8b, *230, 232*
Sanhedrin 53a, *92*
Sanhedrin 90a, *24, 116*
Sanhedrin 91a, *84*
Horayos 9a, *120*
Horayos 10a, *100*

## KODASHIM

Zevachim 99a, *154*
Zevachim 116a, *230*
Menachos 94b, *226*
Chullin 2a, *16, 30, 80*
Chullin 17b, *234*
Chullin 19b, *144*
Chullin 43a, *222, 224*
Chullin 50a, *228*
Chullin 76a, *224*
Kerisos 26a, *100*

## TAHOROS

Kaylim Chapter 28 Mishnah 7, *226*
Nega'im Chapter 12 Mishnah 4, *24*
Parah Chapter 9 Mishnah 3, *148*

## These shall stand for a blessing.

Mr. Samuel Abramson
New York, New York

Mr. Yehoshua Ben Yehuda
Diaspora Yeshiva, Jerusalem

The Ingber Family
Jerusalem, Israel

Mr. Phillip Konvitz

Mr. Francis Mitterhoff
Newark, New Jersey

Mr. and Mrs. Leibel Lederman
Brooklyn, New York

## In memory of...

In memory of
**David Gold**
by his wife, Henrietta Gold,
and his son and daughter-in-law
Shalom and Yeshara Gold

In memory of
**Alta Chava Hentcha Green**
by her husband, family
and friends

In memory of
**Moshe Michael Harari**
by his loving parents
Neomi and Sami Harari

In memory of
**Eliahu Fisher**
by his daughter
Bat Sheva Mink

In memory of
**Tobias Sakowitz**
by his son and daughter-in-law
Alex and Ivria Sackton

In memory of
**Minna Shaftan**
by her daughter
Claire Ackerman

In memory of
**Reuven ben Yakov**
by his son
Menachem Mel Rosen

In memory of
**Eleazer Haim Mink**
by his son
Yechezkel Mink

# Other books by
# R. Moshe Chayim Luzzatto in
# Feldheim Publishers' Torah Classics Library series:

## מסלת ישרים
## The Path of the Just

*Mesillat Yesharim* has been treasured for centuries as the priceless legacy from R. Moshe Chayim Luzzato to the Jewish people, giving the key to complete spiritual development.

The framework for this book is taken from a luminous, intriguing passage by R. Pinchas ben Yair, in the Talmud: "Torah leads to watchfulness; watchfulness leads to zeal; zeal leads to cleanliness; cleanliness leads to separation; separation leads to purity; purity leads to saintliness; saintliness leads to humility; humility leads to fear of sin; fear of sin leads to holiness; holiness leads to the revival of the dead." From this, the author fashions a master-crafted ladder upon which a Jew can begin at the lowest rung and climb to the very heights of Divine worship.

Few could equal Luzzato in his mastery of Tanach, Talmud and *kabbala*; and none could match his ability to fuse these sources into a single stream of flowing, inspiring thought. Step by step, with poetic sensitivity, the author examines each segment of the Talmud that deals with human character, including its motives — known and unknown — and multiple facets that make up a person.

What emerges is a work of infinite wisdom derived from a masterful overview of the Torah, a work whose compassion and insight have given it a timeless place of honor in the wealth of our Jewish heritage.

Taken from the first edition (Amsterdam, 1740), the Hebrew text appears with full vowelization (*nikkud*), together with the careful, precise translation of Shraga Silverstein on facing pages.

*About the Translator*

An alumnus of Mesivta Rabbi Chaim Berlin, Shraga Silverstein also holds a B.A. and an M.A. from Brooklyn College, where he graduated *summa cum laude* and *Phi Beta Kappa*. In 1963, he settled with his family in Jerusalem, where he became an instructor in a foremost school of advanced Jewish education and a lecturer in English at Hebrew University.

In addition to this book, Shraga Silverstein has completed a sound translation of *Shaarei Teshuvah* (The Gates of Repentance) by Rabbeinu Yonah and *Daath Tevunoth* (The Knowing Heart) by R. Moshe Chayim Luzzatto, for publication in Feldheim Publishers' *Torah Classics Library* series. He is the author of *Hear My Son!*, a collection of original aphorisms, and *The Antidote: Human Sexuality in a Torah Perspective*, a Feldheim Publishers book.

# דרך ה׳
# The Way of God

Out of the probing, revealing world of *kabbala* came a wealth of teachings on the profoundest mysteries that confront the Jewish mind: the how and why of the world, the finite in the infinite, and the origin and purpose of human life on earth.

With the Torah, we grow aware of the Almighty as Creator and Regulator of the world. Yet how does His power operate? What forces, channels or modalities mediate between the human and the Divine?

In *Derech Hashem*, R. Moshe Chayim Luzzatto organizes the first clear, systematic outline of traditional Jewish thought concerning the interaction between the earthly and the heavenly, between man and Hashem. With his sensitive, luminous style, the author combines the light of *kabbala* with an in-depth study of the goals of Creation, man's primal sin, the ways of Divine justice, and the interdependent relationship between the *tzaddik* (the righteous) and the *rasha* (the wicked). He also elaborates on the World-to-Come, ultimate redemption in the Divine order, and the unique role of Torah and mitzvoth in man's interaction with the Divine.

R. Moshe Chayim Luzzatto, born in Padua, Italy in 1707, was regarded as a genius from childhood. After mastering Tanach and Talmud, Midrash and *halacha*, he studied *kabbala* with R. Isaiah Bassani until he had an unparalleled command of the entire field.

After moving to Amsterdam in 1731, Luzzato began writing a series of works, including *Derech Hashem*, while earning his living grinding optical lenses. In this edition, for the first time, the text is presented fully vowellized (*menukad*), with a careful English translation by Aryeh Kaplan on facing pages.

*About the Translator*

An alumnus of New York's Torah Vodaath and Mir yeshivas, Aryeh Kaplan ז"ל received *S'micha* from some of the foremost rabbinical authorities in Israel. He also earned an M.A. in physics.

Aryeh Kaplan was in the forefront of bringing Torah to the English-speaking Jewish masses, with his prolific writing and translations. Just a few of his published works are as follows: *Me'am Lo'ez, Waters of Eden, Sabbath — Day of Eternity, Tefillin, Light Beyond, Handbook of Jewish Thought,* and *Living Torah.*

# דעת תבונות
# The Knowing Heart

With the completion of this translation of *The Knowing Heart*, a trilogy of important works by R. Moshe Chayim Luzzatto, one of the great minds in religious Jewish thought, has joined Feldheim's *Torah Classics Library* series.

First came his *Mesillat Yesharim* (The Path of the Just), that guides the faithful Jew up a ladder of steady personal development to sublime levels of devotion and holiness.

Yet spiritual growth is not, by itself, the only goal for a Torah Jew. There must also be knowledge of the Creator's ways and the dynamics of interaction between the human and the Divine. Luzzatto's *Derech haShem* (The Way of God) is an enlightening exposition on the Divine regulation of the world and the integral role of Torah and *mitzvoth*.

Luzzatto explains that knowledge is gained by the intellect. Then it must influence the heart until it moves and exalts the soul, the very essence of a human being. *Da'ath Tevunoth* was written in 5494 (1734), as a dialogue between the intellect and the soul — hence its English title, *The Knowing Heart*.

Focusing on the profundity of meaning that lies in the unique oneness of God, the author brings the reader to a new awareness of the transcendental significance of the teaching that man was created in the Divine image. This is a work written, not to satisfy idle curiosity or empty philosophical speculation, but to give the earnest, searching student a vital foundation for a life imbued with the holiness and knowledge of Hashem. As always, the author draws widely on the Written and Oral Torah, and the sacred traditions of *kabbala*.

The Hebrew text, taken from the highly accurate edition of R. Chaim Friedlander (based on three early manuscripts), is printed with full vowelization (*nikkud*). On facing pages is the faithful, literate English translation by Shraga Silverstein, whose translations of *Mesillat Yesharim* and *Shaarei Teshuvah* have earned him a deserved reputation for quality.